Exchange Rate Volatility in Emerging Economies

TRANSNATIONAL PRESS LONDON

Books by TPL

Pricing – The New Frontier

Turkey's Syrians: Today and Tomorrow

A Defining Moment - Transnational Nursing Education

Civil Society Impact on the European Union Climate Change Policy

Economic Survival Strategies of Turkish Migrants in London

International Operations, Innovation and Sustainability

Overeducated and Over Here

Image of Istanbul: Impact of ECOC 2010 on the city image

Women from North Move to South: Turkey's Female Movers from the Former Soviet Union Countries

Turkish Migration Policy

Conflict, Insecurity, and Mobility

Little Turkey in Great Britain

Journals by TPL

Migration Letters

Remittances Review

Göç Dergisi

Border Crossing

Journal of Gypsy Studies

Kurdish Studies

Transnational Marketing Journal

Exchange Rate Volatility in Emerging Economies

Abdulkader M. Aljandali

TRANSNATIONAL PRESS LONDON
2018

Exchange Rate Volatility in Emerging Economies
by Abdulkader M. Aljandali

First Published in 2018 by TRANSNATIONAL PRESS LONDON in the United Kingdom, 12 Ridgeway Gardens, London, N6 5XR, UK.

www.tplondon.com

Paperback

ISBN: 978-1-910781-79-1

Cover Design: Gizem Çakır

www.tplondon.com

Contents

Acknowledgements

I would like to thank Professor John Trevor Coshall for his endless support throughout my research journey. John, as I have been used to address him, has been the source of much inspiration and a dedicated mentor who was determined to teach me how to become a professional researcher. I would like also to thank Dr Bode Akinwande and Richard Charlesworth for their support and supervision throughout the research on which this book draws upon.

This book and the research it is built on could never have been done without the financial and emotional support of Mohammad-Ayman Jandali, my beloved uncle. I would also like to acknowledge my sisters, Farah and Tijan, my dad and my mum for their continuous support and endless love.

About the Author

Dr Abdulkader Aljandali is a Senior Lecturer in Finance at Coventry University, London, UK. Previously, Dr Aljandali was a Senior Lecturer leading the Business Forecasting and the Quantitative Finance modules at Regents University London. Dr Aljandali is an established fellow of the UK Higher Education Academy and a current member of the British Accounting & Finance Association. Dr Aljandali has published textbooks in Quantitative Analysis and Multi-variate Methods for students/professionals in Business & Finance.

Symbols and Acronyms

ACF	Autocorrelations Functions
ADF t	Augmented Dickey-Fuller test
AEC	ASEAN Economic Community
AFC	Asian Financial Crisis
AR	Autoregressive Terms
ARCH	Autoregressive Conditional Heteroscedasticity
ARDL	Autoregressive Distributed Lag Method
ARIMA	Autoregressive Integrated Moving Averages
ASEAN	Association of Southeast Asian Nations
BIS	Bank of International Settlements
BOP	Balance of Payments
BRIC	Brazil, Russia, India and China
CACM	Central American Common Market
CAFTA-DR	Central American Dominican Republic Free Trade Agreement
CAN	Andean Community
CAPM	Capital Asset Pricing Model
CARICOM	Caribbean Community Common Market
CBI	Central Bank Intervention
CFA Franc	Central African Franc
CIA	Central Intelligence Agency
CMA	Common Monetary Area
DRC	Democratic Republic of Congo
CPI	Consumer Price Index
CUSUM	Cumulative Sum
CUSUM SQ	Cumulative Sum of Squares
DW-Statistic	Durbin-Watson Statistic
ECLAC	Economic Commission for Latin America and the Caribbean
ECM	Error Correction Model
EGARCH	Exponential GARCH
EMS	European Monetary System
ES/Exp	Exponential Smoothing

FDI	Foreign Direct Investment
FOREX	Foreign Exchange
FTA	Free Trade Agreement
GARCH	Generalised ARCH
GCC	Gulf Cooperation Council
GDP	Growth Domestic Product
GNP	Gross National Product
HIPC	Heavily Indebted Poor Countries
IFS	International Financial Statistics
IMF	International Monetary Fund
LDCs	Least Developed Countries
LL	Log-likelihood
Logs	Natural Logarithms
L-S test	Lee and Strazicich test
MA	Moving Average Terms
MAPE	Mean Absolute Percentage Error
MERCOSUR	Market of the South (Latin American Common Market)
NA	Non-Available
NAFTA	North American Free Trade Agreement
NEPAD	New Partnership for Africa's Development
ODA	Official Development Assistance
ODI	Overseas Development Institute
OECD	Organisation of Economic Development and Cooperation
OPEC	Organisation of the Petroleum Exporting Countries
PACF	Partial Autocorrelation Functions
PCA	Principal Component Analysis
PP t	Phillips-Perron test
PPP	Purchasing Power Parity
Q	The Ljung-Box Q statistic
QSQ	The Ljung-Box Q-squared statistic
RMSE	Root Mean Squared Error
SADC	Southern African Development Community
SADCC	Southern African Development Coordination Conference
SBC	Schwarz-Bayesian Criterion
SDR	Special Drawing Rights

SPSS	Statistical Package for Social Sciences
SQRT	Square root
SSE	Sum of the Squares of the Errors
TB	Trade Balance
TO	Trade Openness
TGARCH	Threshold GARCH
UNASUR	Union of South American Nations
US $	United States Dollars
WAEMU	West African Economic and Monetary Union

Preface

This book is a contribution to the knowledge concerning the volatility and forecasting of exchange rates in the emerging markets. It focuses on the exchange rates of the leading trading blocs in that part of the world and examines exchange rates of selected emerging countries across continents in order to explain local and regional variations in exchange rates and the determinants of fluctuations in selected countries in Africa, Asia, Central and Latin America. Exchange rates of countries from the four different regions are investigated separately, followed by an analysis within and across regions to identify common patterns of exchange rates fluctuations. Monthly forecasts are generated for a period of 24 months to test the performance of the times series, cointegration and combination techniques used in this book.

The results show that exchange rates of countries in the same region behave similarly following a shock to the system. Additionally, exchange rates of countries at the same stage of development albeit in different geographical location (Central America, Southern Africa, Latin America and Southeast Asia) share some similarities. In this book I argue that all exchange rates examined have been volatile. Furthermore, asymmetric volatility was particularly relevant in the modelling process mainly for countries that suffered from the aftermath of a financial or debt crisis, especially in Asia and Latin America. Exponential smoothing time series models provided the most accurate forecasts for the sampled exchange rates, while combination models outperformed single time series models in about 70% of the cases. ARDL cointegration models had limited success in the forecasting exercise but were particularly relevant as a composite method and were the best performing models when combined with time series techniques.

Chapter 1. Introduction

This book is about the exchange rates of selected emerging countries across continents. I offer an analysis of the determinants of their fluctuations within selected common markets in Africa, Asia, Central and Latin America. According to Molana and Osei-Assibey (2010), although exchange rate volatility is seen by many researchers to have the potential to impact upon the economic welfare of any nation, most studies of exchange rate volatility are focused mainly on developed countries, with studies of Least Developed Countries (LDCs) almost non-existent. In fact, numerous currencies featured in this book belong to the LDCs group with the rest being categorised as emerging markets currencies by the International Monetary Fund (IMF). In this book I explore the foundations that make those markets behave differently compared to developed markets and presents an in-depth investigation of exchange rate behaviour based on their regional settings.

Countries in the same region tend to respond to news (good or bad) in the same way. For example, the knock-on effect of the Asian Financial Crisis (AFC) that started in Thailand in mid-1997 or the debt crises that erupted in Latin America in 1982 and 2001 illustrate this. In both continents, the crisis spread to neighbours and across respective regions creating panic and making exchange rates more volatile. Currency speculators were held responsible for the crisis while government authorities were criticised for their lack of understanding of macroeconomic fundamentals. Aguiar and Broner (2006) proposed the study of the macroeconomic consequences of crises by assessing the behaviour of "effective" fundamentals through the study of the relative movements of stock prices. They found that effective fundamentals provide a different picture than those implied by observed fundamentals. Suffice to say, the statement by Aguiar and Broner (2006) cannot be verified in countries that do not have established stock markets where securities are traded.

However, this research borrows the concept of "effectiveness" from Aguiar and Broner (2006) to identify the macroeconomic fundamentals that affect exchange rates within selected regions. Different countries have different exchange rate drivers, especially in the emerging world. This book will shed light on those drivers/determinants. Another characteristic of exchange rates in the emerging world is the existence of "dual" rates in the foreign exchange (FOREX) market - one official and the other "unofficial" or black market rate - which is a common phenomenon in LDCs (Dornbusch, 1983; Phylaktis, 1991; Siddiki, 2000). Dual exchange rates emerge as a result of controls on access to the official market. Chronic and persistent balance of payments (BOP) problems, trade controls and financial repression lead to the emergence of a black market (Ghatak and Siddiqi, 2001). The study of exchange rates in LDCs and emerging countries is somewhat restrictive when compared with the confidence one can gain when examining currencies like the American dollar or the euro. This is due mainly to the existence of dual rates and the inability to examine effective fundamentals in the emerging world.

This book examines the effects that changes in macroeconomic fundamentals have on the exchange rates of forty currencies and in the process provides a customised analysis of exchange rate behaviour over time. Data are analysed using the IMF Special Drawing Rights (SDR) exchange rates to ensure research is based on credible sources which are internationally recognised. Developing countries are striving to improve the tarnished reputation they earned in past decades because of corruption, civil wars and scandals. There is a consensus that transparency is now thought of as a priority for nations that want to play an active role in the international scene.

The SDR exchange rates of countries from four different regions are investigated separately in this study, followed by an analysis within and across regions to identify common patterns in the way exchange rates fluctuate. The choice of regional analysis is in line with what Frankel (2002: ix) stated over 10 years ago: "Geography reappeared in international economics after a strangely long absence. The old question of exchange rate regimes was reinvigorated with theories of dynamically inconsistent monetary policy, credibility and target zone dynamics". This research explores the possibility of common exchange rate behaviour within regions by searching for common patterns in volatility responses (i.e. in the conditional variances) to shocks which is a neglected research theme, especially in LDCs. Originally, principal components analysis (PCA) was used to establish these common patterns. However, preliminary analyses suggest that the magnitude of the conditional standard deviations is so relatively low that Pearsonian correlation coefficients cannot be computed.

In the words of Servén (2002, 1), "Developing economies suffer from a high degree of macroeconomic uncertainty. Growth, inflation, real exchange rates and other macroeconomic variables are much more volatile than in industrial economies which have attracted attention in the recent empirical literature." This book investigates such uncertainties, especially the ones peculiar to exchange rates and to the FOREX market in the emerging world. Furthermore, this book seeks to improve the understanding of exchange rate volatility within the context of the regions that are making today's headlines because of their increasing economic prowess. This work is aimed at policy makers and researchers who wish to understand and forecast exchange rates in the emerging world. It is the belief of the author that this book will help equip those at the top of the decision-making process with the tools needed to better face the turbulence of the 21st century.

Section 1.2 of this chapter introduces the regional settings chosen as a framework for this research as well as a review of the financial crises that hit some of these regions. Section 1.3 describes the contribution of this book to modelling and forecasting knowledge and to the literature of the emerging world. The chapter concludes in Section 1.4 with an overview of the contribution of the thesis and the contents of the six other chapters.

1.1 Selected Regional Settings and Crises

Association of Southeast Asian Nations – ASEAN

ASEAN was launched in Bangkok by Indonesia, Malaysia, the Philippines, Singapore and Thailand. Brunei Darussalam then joined in 1984, Vietnam in 1995, Laos and Myanmar in 1997 and Cambodia in 1999, making up what is today the ten member states organisation (ASEAN, 2008). The association was established in August, 1967 to accelerate economic growth, social progress and cultural development in the region in order to promote peaceful prosperity. This book examines the exchange rates of the ten ASEAN countries over a period of 20 years starting from 1990 to 2009. Financial integration is high on the bloc's agenda as the members mooted the idea of a having a single currency by 2020 (Guerrero, 2009) and therefore, this book investigates the fluctuations of exchange rates in the region with that vision in mind.

The ASEAN Charter[1] came into force in 2008 and has among its purposes the enhancement of regional resilience by promoting greater political, security, economic and socio-cultural cooperation (ASEAN, 2008). The bloc aims to create a single market and a production base which is stable, prosperous, highly competitive and economically integrated with the effective facilitation of trade and investment in which there is free flow of goods, services and investment. The ASEAN region has a population of over 600 million and a combined nominal GDP of US $1.8 trillion (ASEAN, 2009). The association has already started implementing economic commitments and progressively reducing any barriers to regional economic integration in a market driven economy. This shows the willingness of ASEAN to emulate the European Union in creating an area where goods, people and capital can move freely between member countries. The fact that Southeast Asia has bounced back strongly from the crisis that hit the region in 1997 and that European and American economies are still struggling to fully overcome the effect of this recent financial crisis makes the ASEAN project a lot more relevant to the rest of the world than it would have otherwise been. Furthermore, it highlights the importance of research like that presented in this book to forecast the region's exchange rates, since the growth of the world economy seems to be driven by the ASEAN+3 countries (ASEAN + China, India and Japan). To put things into perspective, this area comprises around 40% of the inhabitants of the planet and contributes up to 50% of the world's GDP (ASEAN, 2012).

The ASEAN Vision 2020 (Guerrero, 2009) adopted by the association leaders agreed on the prospect of ASEAN as a concert of Southeast Asian nations. The Heads of States agreed to intensify community building through enhanced regional cooperation and integration; in particular by establishing the ASEAN economic community (AEC) which envisages the following key characteristics:

A single market and production base,

[1] The ASEAN Charter is a constitution for the Association of Southeast Asian Nations adopted at the 13th ASEAN summit In November 2007 (ASEAN, 2008)

A highly competitive economic region,

A region of equitable economic development, and

A region fully integrated into the global economy.

By 2015 a single market and a production base are to be established while the AEC addresses the development gaps and accelerates the integration of Cambodia, Laos, Myanmar and Vietnam. In fact, this increasing integration between ASEAN nations has created tremendous scope for Asian countries to boost intra-regional trade and investment. In respect of trade, it is already happening as intra-East Asian trade flows rose to 42% of total trade in 2008, up from 32% in 1990 (ASEAN, 2009). China is the source of much of this growth and remains a competitor to other developing Asian countries for rich world markets (one of the recommendations of this book is to assess the volatility of the exchange rate in the region against the Chinese yuan). ASEAN has also been busy signing Free Trade Agreements (FTAs) with regional powerhouses such as India. In addition, ASEAN continue to support the creation of 'ASEAN + 1' FTAs. ASEAN has ratified free trade agreements with Australia and New Zealand, China, India, Japan, and the Republic of Korea (Tumbarello, 2007).

A study of the exchange rates of the ASEAN nations is of particular relevance to countries which signed FTAs with the bloc and to international investors who might be attracted by demand growth and cheap labour in the region. This book is aimed at ASEAN policy makers, economic partners and investors alike. It contributes to knowledge through an examination of factors that affect exchange rate volatility in the ten ASEAN countries and by predicting the behaviour of exchange rates in the region using both established and innovative forecasting techniques. Figures 1-10 in Appendix 1 present plots of the exchange rates of ASEAN countries from 1990-2009. The following section addresses the impact that the Asian Financial Crisis (AFC) has had on the region and especially on ASEAN countries.

The Asian Financial Crisis - AFC

The AFC hit Southeast Asia in July, 1997 and had devastating effects on the economy of the region as high levels of growth rates turned sharply negative. The crisis will be a major feature in reporting the results of this book, especially in Chapters Four, Five and Six. Before the crisis, most Asian economies informally pegged their currencies to the US dollar (McKinnon and Schnabl, 2004). These soft dollar pegs (so called because they are not communicated as such to the IMF) made them vulnerable to the fluctuations of the yen against the dollar. The depreciation of the yen between 1995 and 1997 aggravated the crisis because it made Japanese exports more competitive in international markets. In addition, all intra-regional trade was invoiced in US dollar except when the trade was directly with Japan. The rationale for dollar pegging did not primarily arise because of strong ties with the US. In fact, there was a rapid increase in intra-East Asian trade from 1980 to 2001 and more than half of the overall trade of these countries is now with other Asian countries. China is becoming an important trading partner. According to Mishkin (1999), the US accounted for only 23.1% of overall exports from East Asian economies in 2001 – and for only 14.4% of their imports. Meanwhile, trade with the world outside Asia is in relative decline. Mishkin (1999) blamed the crisis on the breakdown of information in the financial markets which he called asymmetric information as financial markets were no longer able to channel funds efficiently to those with the most productive investment opportunities. He also blamed excessive risk taking in Asia on the lack of expertise in risk management and the lack of monitoring of lending activity. Bird and Rajan (2002) found that the pre-crisis soft peg to the US dollar was suboptimal and argued that Southeast Asian countries would have avoided the third currency phenomenon[2] - which may have contributed to the crisis - had they pegged their currencies to a basket of composite currencies (i.e. SDR). A Central Bank would be better off pegging the exchange rate to a basket of currencies as this will make it less volatile than if it was pegged to a single currency. McKinnon and Schnabl (2004) argued that the US dollar's role as the central anchor currency in East Asia could be replaced by the creation of an Asian 'euro', which could float freely against the dollar like its European counterpart. Figures 1 to 10 in Appendix 1 show that exchange rates in the ASEAN region have been extremely volatile, particularly in 1997-1998, the period when the crisis hit.

The crisis had a devastating effect on some ASEAN countries. In fact, more than half of Indonesia's banking assets were written off during the crisis and much of the system was put into receivership. The plot of the Indonesian rupiah overtime (Figure 3) shows the impact the crisis had as the currency lost almost 300% of its value in a period of less than 12 months. In the same graph, a spike in 2001 reflects the effects that the Argentinian default (which will be discussed later in this chapter) had on the exchange rate of the rupiah and outlines the prospect of a similar response to shocks of emerging markets at the same stage of development.

Thailand is another ASEAN country that was severely hit by the AFC. The Bank of Thailand introduced a series of measures to regulate transactions with foreign financial institutions and limit capital outflows by temporarily requiring that the baht proceeds from sales of stocks by non-residents be converted into foreign currency at the onshore exchange rate. In addition the authorities introduced a two-tier currency market creating separate exchange rates for investors who buy baht in domestic markets and those who buy it overseas. This latest measure had a devastating effect on the value of the currency as the baht lost about 90% of its value before the end of 1997 (see Figure 9).

In the Philippines, the Bankers' Association, which operates in the FOREX market, introduced a 4% volatility band during the 1997 crisis in an attempt to stabilise the market. In the first week of operation these limits were reached on several occasions and in both directions, which meant that trades could not be executed outside the 4% band for the remainder of the day. These imposed

[2] The third currency phenomenon is a situation whereby changes in the exchange rate of the anchor currency translate into changes in the local currency's exchange rate (Ngouana, 2012).

limits on trading activity which explain in part the relative performance of the Philippines peso (see Figure 6) compared to other currencies of the region. Similarly, Brunei did not suffer during the crisis in comparison to its neighbours (see Figure 1). It benefits from extensive petroleum and natural gas fields, the source of one of the highest per capita GDPs in Asia. Crude oil and natural gas production account for just over half of its GDP and more than 90% of its exports (CIA, 2012). Per capita GDP is among the highest in Asia. Substantial income from overseas investment supplements income from domestic production.

According to Duasa (2009), Malaysia was significantly affected by the terms of trade[3] during the AFC as Figure 5 in appendix 1 illustrates. There was an immediate impact of exchange rate shock on the volumes of exports and imports as the country heavily relied on international trade. Before the recession of 1997 Malaysia had a large trade surplus of US $4.0 billion which slumped to less than US $17.7 billion by 1998 (CIA, 2012). The Malaysian ringgit plot shows the severe drop in the value of the currency during the crisis. The impact of the crisis on the findings of this research is discussed in Chapters Four, Five and Six.

The paper by Mishkin (1999) provided an asymmetric information analysis of the AFC and outlined several lessons learned from it. He argued that the presence of an international lender of last resort can promote financial stability. Additionally, he stated that capital flows were a symptom rather than an underlying cause of the crisis; suggesting exchange rate controls are unlikely to be a useful strategy to avoid future crises. Finally, he argued against pegged exchange rate regimes since they are a dangerous strategy for emerging market countries and make financial crises more likely. Indeed, Muniandy and Uning (2006) found that de facto dollar pegging policy had vulnerable attributes during the period of 1995-1996 as the dollar strengthened against the yen, which led to an appreciation of the ASEAN currencies and thereby to a loss of export competitiveness and current account pressure.

Central American Common Market – CACM

The CACM was established by Guatemala, Honduras, El Salvador and Nicaragua (and later joined by Costa Rica) with the signing of the General Treaty of Central American Economic Integration in December 1960 (Bulmer-Thomas, 1998). During the 1960s and 70s, the CACM had a significant positive impact on trade flows in Central America. Intra-regional exports as a percentage of total exports grew dramatically from 7% to 25% in 1980 (Inter-American Development Bank, 2000). Of all goods traded within the region, 95% had attained duty-free status by 1967 and 90% of traded goods were covered by the common external tariff (Cline and Delgado, 1978), yet no single study has examined the exchange rates of countries in the region. This book

[3] This is the ratio of exports over imports, which measures the quantity of imports that can be purchased through the sale of a fixed quantity of exports and hence is used as a proxy to measure a country's relative social welfare (Duasa, 2009).

does that by examining the exchange rates of CACM (+Dominican Republic) countries and by generating related forecasts using various statistical and econometric techniques.

As with ASEAN, CACM countries are signatories of various FTAs. Central American integration was given a boost with the signing of the North American Free Trade Agreement (NAFTA) between Canada, Mexico and the United States (Hornbeck, 2012). Central American countries actively lobbied for incorporation into NAFTA and were expanding ties with the G-3 (Mexico, Colombia, and Venezuela) and the Caribbean Community Common Market (CARICOM). In the late 2000's, CACM economies grew slowly and performed poorly compared to countries in neighbouring Latin America. This relative underperformance can be explained by the fact that Central America was hurt by the rise in the international prices of raw materials as a net importer of petroleum, which worsened the terms of trade and generated inflationary pressures. Furthermore, Central American light manufacturing exports lost momentum in the face of competition from China, other Asian countries in their major market and the United States (Jeffrey and Kotschwar, 2002). The crises in Central America erupted because of a sharp deterioration in the region's terms of trade which induced a decline in demand for its primary exports. The rise in international interest rates made matters worse as it raised the debt burden and increased the pressure on the region's economies. In the last decade, Central America has made significant efforts to complete its FTA, expand its customs union and launch the Central America-Dominican Republic-United States Free Trade Agreement (Morley and Piñeiro, 2007)

The CACM is fundamentally different from other trading blocs examined in this book in that the remittances from citizens overseas are particularly important as a source of financing the trade deficit in the region, which impacts on exchange rates. Fajnzylber and Lopez (2008) argued that transfers from migrants in El Salvador, Guatemala, Honduras and Nicaragua are associated with a drop in poverty. These authors suggest that remittances increase access to education for children and improve access to health services. A study by the United Nations Economic Commission for Latin America and the Caribbean (ECLAC, 2007) found that an increase in remittances is the main factor behind the real appreciation recorded by the exchange rates of Guatemala and Honduras between the early 1990's and mid-2006 (24% and 18% respectively). Conflicts in both El Salvador and Nicaragua and political unrest elsewhere left the region in confusion and disarray and both currencies are perceived as being particularly volatile over the period that this book examines (1990-2009). In fact, the countries of Central America's northern triangle (Guatemala, Honduras and El Salvador) are now among the most violent places on earth. Guatemala's rate of 46 murders per 100 000 people is more than twice as high as Mexico's and nearly ten times greater than that of the United States. Costa Rica is much better off and better governed than its neighbours (The Economist, 2011).

This book examines the exchange rates of CACM countries to fill gaps in the literature pertaining to the region. Trade seems to be of particular relevance to Central America, therefore the relationship between trade and exchange rates will be examined thoroughly in Chapter Five to identify any type of relationship (long or short-term) between both variables. Ideally, the relationship between remittances and exchange rates has to be examined, but this has not been possible because of the absence of remittances data in the International Financial Statistics (IFS) database used in this research. The expansion of intra-regional trade made the CACM's overall trade pattern more diverse and therefore particular attention is given to the relationship between trade and exchange rates. Figures 11-16 in Appendix I present plots of CACM countries (+ Dominican Republic) exchange rates from 1990-2009.

This book attempts to compare the behaviour of exchange rates in the region with those of countries in neighbouring Latin America and the other trading blocs covered by this study. Central America has been ignored by researchers for many years because of the unstable political situation in the region and one of the main contributions of this book is an assessment of the performance of exchange rates in CACM countries during a period of 20 years followed by an analysis of the factors that affect their volatility and an attempt to generate empirical forecasts over a period of 24 months.

The Market of the South – MERCOSUR

This book also examines the exchange rates of one of the fastest growing regions in the world - Latin America. In the five years to 2008, the region's economies grew at an average rate of 5.5% (The Economist, 2010) and by an average of 6% in 2010 according to an estimate from the United Nations Economic Commission for Latin America and the Caribbean (ECLAC, 2011). This strong performance is linked in large part to the global commodity boom which has attracted large inflows of foreign cash. With this has come a familiar problem: the region's currencies have soared in value against the dollar making life uncomfortable for Latin American manufacturers. After the cataclysmic debt crisis of 1982 (discussed in the next section), the region's policymakers abandoned the protectionism and fiscal profligacy that had brought hyperinflation and bankruptcy. Instead, they adopted market reforms and opened up their economies to trade, foreign investment, privatisation and deregulation which increased the need for studies that examine exchange rate behavior as it became more volatile.

The framework used for the study of exchange rates in Latin America is the "Common Market of the South, MERCOSUR", an economic and political agreement between Argentina, Brazil, Paraguay, Uruguay and Venezuela that seeks to promote the free movement of goods, services and people among member states (Lorenzo and Vaillant, 2004). MERCOSUR was created in 1991 and encompasses Bolivia, Chile, Colombia, Ecuador and Peru as associate members. Brazil and Argentina are MERCOSUR's economic giants. MERCOSUR is South America's leading trading bloc (Cordoba, 2012). It aims to bring about the free movement of goods, capital, services and people among its member states. With an area of 12 million square kilometres, it is four times as big as the EU; the bloc's combined market encompasses more than 250m people and accounts for more than three-quarters of the economic activity on the continent (Malamud, 2005). It is the world's fourth-largest trading bloc after the European Union (EU), North American Free Trade Agreement (NAFTA) and the Association of Southeast Asian Nations (ASEAN). So in ASEAN and MERCOSUR, this research is investigating the leading trading blocs of the emerging world.

MERCOSUR's primary interest has been to eliminate obstacles to regional trade, such as high tariffs and income inequalities, with the ultimate goal of full South American economic integration. In the longer term, MERCOSUR aims to create a continent-wide free-trade area while the creation of a MERCOSUR development bank has been mooted. The European Union has favoured the strengthening of MERCOSUR and supported its initiatives, notably through an inter-institutional agreement to provide technical and institutional support for its newly created structures. China, the bloc's second-largest buyer, has proposed the creation of a free trade zone with MERCOSUR. The possibility of a single currency was raised by the Argentinian president in 1997 and Eichengreen (1999) stated that if the MERCOSUR countries intend to press ahead with deeper integration they may have to contemplate a European-style monetary integration. Deeper integration means that the economies of the region will have to unify their exchange rate policy in the future. It's on this point that this book makes its main contribution to knowledge about this region by providing the foundations to understand the behaviour of exchange rates in Latin America's MERCOSUR ahead of the single currency project.

Argentina, one of the biggest economies in the bloc, is one of only a handful of countries that refuse all dealings with the IMF (Bértola and Ocampo, 2012). It is one of the richest countries in Latin America as it benefits from abundant natural resources and a diversified industrial base. The peso was pegged to the US dollar from the early 1990's until early 2002 (CIA, 2012). A severe economic depression hit the country following growing public and external indebtedness as well as a bank run which culminated in the most serious economic, social, and political crisis in the country's turbulent history in 2001. Interim President Rodriguez declared a default on the government's foreign debt and abruptly resigned only a few days after taking office. A new currency with a new parity was introduced in 2002, which is the reason the Argentinian peso was dropped from the sample of currencies examined in this book. Exchange rates are examined from 1990 to 2009 and it was during this period that Argentina had a regime switch, which is not a topic that this book aims to cover.

Similarly, Ecuador suffered a severe economic crisis towards the end of 1999, with GDP contracting by 5.3% (CIA, 2012). Poverty increased significantly, the banking system collapsed and Ecuador defaulted on its external debt. In March 2000, its Congress approved a series of structural reforms that also provided for the adoption of the US dollar as its currency. Dollarization stabilised the economy and positive growth returned in the years that followed, helped by high oil prices, remittances, and increased non-traditional exports. From 2002-06 the economy grew by an average of 5.2% per year (CIA, 2012), the highest five-year average in 25 years. Ecuador's currency has also been left off the analysis because it adopted the US dollar as legal tender which means that the Central Bank has lost authority over monetary policy. Currency fluctuations are now dependent on the performance of the US dollar rather than the local factors such as macroeconomic policy and trade terms which this book intends to cover. Figures 17-25 in Appendix 1 present plots of other MERCOSUR countries exchange rates from 1990-2009.

Debt Crisis in Latin America

What in August 1982 seemed to be an isolated case of temporary illiquidity soon spread out to most of the developing world, placing the stability of the international financial system in serious jeopardy (Edwards, 1989). The debt crisis of the 1980s, which began in Mexico in August 1982, was a major economic crisis that had the potential to destabilise the international financial system. The crisis lasted for almost a decade, haunting in the process the financial world and policy makers. When Mexico defaulted on its portfolio in 1982 and others soon followed, the debt crisis was officially proclaimed (Stensnes, 2006).

The debt crisis of the 1980s is the most traumatic economic event in Latin America's economic history. During the "lost decade" that it generated, the region's per capita GDP fell from 112% to 98% of the world average and from 34 to 26% of that of developed countries (Bértola and Ocampo, 2012). In terms of its strong adverse effects, the only comparable case is the "lost half-decade" of 1998-2003 induced by the series of crises in emerging countries that started in Southeast Asia in 1997. It involved all 18 countries. The most disturbing feature of the exchange-rate regimes in place during this period was their high degree of volatility around the long-term trend of the (basic) real exchange rate, especially in economies that were prone to inflation. Starting in the mid-1960s, crawling exchange-rate peg systems[4] were introduced in an effort to manage this problem (Frenkel and Rapetti, 2011).

The crisis began on the 12th of August, 1982, when Mexico's minister of finance informed the Federal Reserve chairman, the secretary of the treasury and the IMF that Mexico would be unable to meet its obligation to service an US $80 billion debt on the 16th of August, 1982. The situation continued to worsen and by October 1983 twenty seven countries, owing US $239 billion, had rescheduled their bank debts or were in the process of doing so. Others soon followed. Sixteen of the nations were from Latin America, and the four largest - Mexico, Brazil, Venezuela, and Argentina - owed various commercial banks US $176 billion, or approximately 74 percent of the total LDCs outstanding debt (Wellons, 1987). In 1984-87 there was a moderate recovery but the situation deteriorated in the closing years of the decade. Few countries were able to put their economies back onto a stable growth path in the second half of the 1980s. Those that did were generally countries with moderate external

[4] See Appendix 3: IMF (2011) Classification of Exchange Rate Arrangements

debt coefficients (Colombia) or ones that received large amounts of official external financing (Chile and Costa Rica).

The social costs of the crisis were huge. The poverty rate climbed sharply between 1980 and 1990 from 40.5% to 48.3% of the population (Bértola and Ocampo, 2012). It only returned to 1980 levels in 2004, indicating that in relation to poverty there was not a lost decade but a lost quarter century. Bouts of hyperinflation overtook Argentina, Bolivia, Brazil, Nicaragua and Peru in the mid-1980s and early 1990s and triple-digit inflation hit Mexico, Uruguay and Venezuela. Panama (the only dollarized economy at the time) was the only country in which inflation did not climb above 20%. The median rate of inflation soared to nearly 40% in 1990 and the mean inflation to over 1,000% before beginning to subside in the years that followed (Laeven and Valencia, 2012). In fact, the depreciation of the real exchange rate, which was necessary in order to support external-sector adjustment, was inevitably accompanied by a surge in inflation which reached proportions never experienced before in Latin America, even taking into account the poor inflationary histories of some of the region's countries. The decline in commodity prices also proved to be a long-term break from earlier trends and would last until the early 2000s. At their lowest point between 1992 and 2001, real commodity prices were 37% (and at times as much as 40%) below their average for the 1970s (Ocampo and Parra, 2010).

Southern African Development Community – SADC

Africa has a long tradition of regional cooperation, its trade and monetary integration schemes being the oldest in the developing world. Since the beginning of the 1990's, African regional cooperation has been revitalised due to two main developments. Firstly, the abolition of the apartheid regime in South Africa began a process of normalisation of economic relationships and led to a deepening of already existing regional integration. Secondly, the transformation of the Organisation of African Unity into the African Union and the launching of the New Partnership for Africa's Development (NEPAD) initiative in 2001 revitalised the old idea of a common African currency. NEPAD considers regional economic communities as building blocks for pan-African cooperation and integration; a process which would enlarge the already existing sub-regional groups and finally result in a pan-African political and economic area with an African Parliament, an African Central Bank, an African Monetary Fund and a common African currency.

With regard to Southern Africa, attention was given to the unusually long-standing monetary coordination efforts of the Common Monetary Area (CMA) agreement which provides for fixed exchange rates among its members as well as intra-regional capital account liberalisation and intra-regional financial transfers. Figures 29, 34, 36 and 37 in Appendix I show that exchange rates in South Africa, Namibia, Lesotho and Swaziland are identical, reflecting the perfect financial integration between them as Namibia, Lesotho and Swaziland have adopted a peg of their currencies on a par with the rand. This is the reason all three exchange rates have been left off the analysis section. Although each of the four members has its own Central Bank issuing its currency and is formally responsible for monetary policy within its respective country, the rand functions as the regional anchor currency. The South African Reserve Bank determines monetary policy for the CMA member countries via its interest rate policy. Another important element of the arrangement is that the South African Reserve Bank acts as a lender of last resort for Lesotho and Namibia with a view to ensuring financial stability in the CMA (Metzger, 2008).

As mentioned at the start of this section, the African continent is known for its long-standing integration projects. In fact, "the most successful and promising attempt in Africa to achieve regional integration so far has been the Southern African Development Community (SADC) - whose currencies are examined in this book. Regional integration appealed as a concept to many economists, politicians and business people for one simple reason: it promised to increase the wealth and well-being not just of one but a number of countries at a rate greater than the sums of the separate development of the economies of the participating countries" Peters (2010, 22-23). SADC has been labelled by other experts as currently the most successful and promising attempt at regional integration in Africa (see for example ECA, 2008a; Mair and Christian, 2001; Brandt et al., 2000). SADC started in 1992 with ten members (the original members of the former SADCC) but quickly incorporated South Africa and Mauritius in 1994. Three years later, the Democratic Republic of Congo (DRC) and the Seychelles joined SADC. When the Seychelles left SADC again in 2005, Madagascar joined to keep the membership at fourteen. Seychelles applied to re-join SADC in 2007 and this was approved in 2008. SADC's mission is to promote sustainable and equitable economic growth and socio-economic development through efficient production systems, deeper co-operation and integration, good governance and durable peace and security, so that the region emerges as a competitive and effective player in international relations and the world economy.

Currently SADC has a membership of 15 Member States, namely Angola, Botswana, the Democratic Republic of Congo (DRC), Lesotho, Madagascar, Malawi, Mauritius, Mozambique, Namibia, the Seychelles, South Africa, Swaziland, the United Republic of Tanzania, Zambia and Zimbabwe. SADC's vision is of a common future with a regional community that will ensure better standards of living and quality of life, freedom and social justice and peace and security for the people of Southern Africa. This shared vision is anchored in the common values and principles and the historical and cultural affinities that exist between the peoples of Southern Africa. This book examines exchange rate fluctuations in the SADC region from 1990 to 2009. Exchange rates are first analysed on an individual basis followed by a regional comparison to assess the degree of financial integration in the trading bloc. Forecasts are generated using time series, econometric and combination approaches. The performance of the forecasting techniques is then compared across regions.

1.2 Contribution of the Book

Because of the apparent risk that emerging markets have faced as a consequence of their pegging policies, there is an urgent need for studies that improve the understanding of the peculiarities of the FOREX market in these regions to allow policy makers to manage their exchange rates more effectively. This book contributes to providing decision-makers in the emerging world with tools to enable them to face the challenges of the 21st century with a better insight into the factors that were behind past crises and knowledge to face the opportunities that they are presented with as part of a globalised and changing world. When account is taken of the shocks to the world's financial markets during the last two decades it becomes clear that no straightforward comparison of the fixed and floating exchange rate periods can reasonably be made. The FOREX market is far more turbulent in a number of respects compared to the Breton-Woods [5]period and this is still a reality in the second decade of the 21st century.

This book uses time series techniques including volatility analysis, cointegration and combination techniques to forecast the exchange rates of ASEAN, CACM, MERCOSUR and SADC countries. This is the first time such a study is conducted for many of the currencies examined. Autoregressive Moving Averages (ARIMA) volatility, exponential smoothing and Naïve 1 are the three time series techniques used. Cointegration methods originally introduced by Engle and Granger (1987) are used in this book to identify any long or short-run relationships between selected macroeconomic fundamentals and respective exchange rates. The Autoregressive Distributed Lag (ARDL) method of cointegration was adopted because it does not require data to be pre-tested for unit roots and can integrate variables with different optimal lags. This method is rarely applied to FOREX series, although it has been proven to be popular elsewhere. Equally, combination forecasting has had minimal application in the FOREX market especially in LDCs and had been suggested as a research priority in this field by Granger and Poon (2003). In this book the various time series and ARDL forecasts are combined using equal weights and variance-covariance methods.

1.3 Organisation of the Book

Chapter Two reviews the literature on exchange rate theories and introduces the explanatory variables selected as a precursor to the macroeconomic analysis presented in later chapters. Chapter Three examines the literature on volatility, cointegration and combination techniques. In addition it introduces the FOREX market and discusses the main trends of the last two decades. Chapter Four provides an application of time series methods to the study of exchange rates. The forecasts of volatility, exponential smoothing and Naïve1 models are computed and compared against each other for model adequacy, thus laying the foundations for the combination exercise carried out in Chapter Six. Chapter Five employs the ARDL cointegration method to forecast

[5] Discussed in Chapter three

exchange rates in the selected regional settings using the explanatory variables introduced in Chapter Two while Chapter Six presents an analysis of the forecasts computed based on the combination of time series and cointegration techniques using equal weights and variance-covariance methods of combination. This research represents the first attempt in the literature to forecast exchange rates in the ASEAN, CACM, MERCOSUR and SADC countries using combination methods. Chapter Seven concludes with a summary of the findings and recommendations for policy-makers.

Chapter II. Foreign Exchange Forecasting using Macroeconomic Variables

This chapter reviews the theories of exchange rate determination as well as various exchange rate regimes adopted by Central Banks across the globe. The chapter provides empirical evidence of exchange rate studies conducted and sheds the light on the various macroeconomic variables used by researchers to explain exchange rate fluctuations. The prime objective of this chapter is to discuss these macroeconomic variables and to support the choice of the set of exchange rate determinants used in the selected regional settings in this book.

Ever since the breakdown of the Bretton-Woods system in 1973, the exchange rates of many countries have been fluctuating considerably overtime and there has been more interest in predicting exchange rates. Research related to exchange rate management still remains an area of interest to economists and finance experts, especially in developing countries, despite a relatively enormous body of literature in this area. This is largely because the exchange rate is not only an important relative price of one currency in term of other that connects domestic and world markets for goods and assets, but it also signals the competitiveness of a country's exchange power with the rest of the world in a global market. Besides, it also serves as an anchor which supports sustainable macroeconomic balances in the long-run. There is, therefore, no simple answer to what determine the equilibrium real exchange rate and estimating the degree of exchange rate volatility and misalignment remains one of the most challenging empirical problems in macroeconomics (Adedayo, 2012).

The effect of real exchange rate misalignment on economic decisions has received considerable attention in the literature, not only because of its significant impact on other macroeconomics variables, but also because there has been a number of significant developments in recent time, with substantial contributions being made to both the theory and empirical understanding of exchange rate determination. Important developments in econometrics, together with the increasing availability of high quality data, have also stimulated a large output of empirical work on exchange rate (Botha and Pretorius, 2009). The importance of studies such as the present one come over ten years after the first text on 'Emerging Financial Markets' was published by Beim and Calomiris (2001). They classified ninety six financial crises in the period of 1976-99 and found that twenty one episodes were caused by currency crises. This latter list included Argentina (1980, 1989, 1995), Brazil (1990), Chile (1976, 1981), Indonesia (1997), Korea (1997), Malaysia (1997), Mexico (1982, 1995), Nigeria (1992), Philippines (1998), Russia (1998), Thailand (1986, 1997) and Uruguay (1981). Most of these crises had international ramifications and nine were combinations of banking and currency crises. The text by Beim and Calomiris (2001) reflects the tremendous research in the years following financial crises in the emerging world. It sought to explain their causes, related issues such as currency regimes and the functions and structure of financial systems. The text explored the foundations that explain why emerging markets behave differently compared to developed markets with a particular emphasis on inflation and currency stability. This book builds on the research findings of Beim and Calomiris (2001) and brings a new insight to the study of exchange rates in emerging financial markets. The crises in both Southeast Asia and Latin America, discussed in Chapter One, are particularly relevant to the understanding of the reasons behind the current economic prowess of these regions.

Section 2.2 of this chapter reviews various exchange rate regimes. Section 2.3 discusses exchange rate determination theories while section 2.4 provides empirical evidence on the relationship between exchange rates and macroeconomic fundamentals laying the ground for section 2.5 which introduces the explanatory variables chosen as exchange rate determinants in this book. Section 2.6 concludes.

2.1 Exchange Rate Regimes

Klein and Shambaugh (2010, 3) defined the exchange rate regime as the "overarching policy toward the exchange rate" – to allow it to float or instead to fix or peg its value to another currency. They argued that different regimes lead to different economic and political implications for their nations. Similarly, Flood and Rose (1995, 1999) found that the choice of an exchange rate arrangement affects the pricing of the currency - higher flexibility is linked with increasing volatility and vice-versa. The choice of exchange rate regime is one of the most important factors that explain the changes on exchange rates, since different countries enter different currency arrangements to manage their currency which consequently affects its pricing (Flood and Rose1995, 1999). Empirical findings by Payasliogiu (2008) showed that the responses to currency shocks under different regimes differ in terms of size and persistence. He studied East Asian currencies following the AFC and found that Indonesia Rupiah was most sensitive to regime shifts with other currencies in the region showing similar patterns that varied in size.

Emerging economies are seeing freer flow of capital, thanks to globalisation as much as the removal of restrictions. On paper, their currency regimes are also becoming more flexible. When foreign capital pours in, Central Banks buy FOREX to stem the rise in the values of their currencies. Many emerging economies are reluctant to risk their competitiveness by letting their currencies rise by much. It is within this framework that the present study has evolved illustrating the increasing importance of the forecasting of exchange rates to emerging nations in a new changing environment. This exercise can never be underestimated if one recalls the devastating effects the currency crises in Southeast Asia and the debt crisis in Latin America had on the economies of respective regions. A review of fixed and floating exchange rate regimes can hardly be ignored if one wishes to understand how the choice of either regime might affect economic output and the welfare of nations. Rogoff et al. (2003) showed that countries which adopt a flexible exchange rate regime outperformed those that opt for a peg. The annual real per capita growth rate averaged 3.9% in the former category and only 2% in the latter over the same sample period. Although this is a considerable difference, the statement by these authors should be measured against the fact that many countries examined in this book still have their currency pegged informally (*de facto*[6]) although they report floating exchange rate regime to the IMF (*de jure*[7]). Klein and Shambaugh (2010, 7) noticed that the pattern of exchange rate regimes during the past four decades is marked by pervasive "flipping", that is, going off a peg for a short period of time and then re-establishing a new peg. In other words, the effects of manipulation of exchange rates on global economic output are most likely to be underestimated. This might be particularly true in the developing world where transparency is in the process of becoming a priority. Table 2.1 lists exchange rate arrangements for ASEAN, CACM, MERCOSUR and SADC countries while Appendix 3 reports IMF classifications and definitions of various exchange rate regimes used in this book.

Financial literature reports four exchange rate regimes: fixed exchange rate, freely floating, managed floating and hybrid system (Rogoff et al., 2003). Under the fixed exchange system, the government is committed to maintain a target exchange rate. In fact, a pegged or fixed exchange rate is where the country sets the value of its national currency according to the value of a foreign currency like the US dollar or to a basket of currencies. Central Banks intervene to keep the rate between narrow bands through international reserves. A pegged exchange rate may help establish the credibility of a program to reduce inflation as the expectations of inflation are reduced through the knowledge that government policy must be subordinated to the needs of maintaining the peg, the threat of chronic inflation is reduced. A pegged exchange rate is not sustainable in the long-run (Cappiello and Ferrucci, 2008). Crawling pegs is another example of fixed exchange rate regime. With crawling pegs the country sets its exchange rate according to a criterion such as the relative change in inflation. Countries with higher inflation rates than their trading partners often depreciate their currencies to prevent a loss of competitiveness (Caramazza and Aziz, 1998). Under the freely floating exchange system, exchange rates are determined by the interaction of demand and supply of FOREX. A floating exchange rate system is where the exchange rate is free to adjust to respond to changes in relative macroeconomic systems. Floating exchange rates reflect the speculative dynamics of the market. Levich (2001) argued that economic shocks such as a steep rise in international interest rates, a slowdown of growth in the industrial world, and the debt crisis often require currency depreciations and the adoption of more flexible

---

[6] The de facto exchange rate arrangement are classified into 10 categories: (1) hard pegs comprising (a) exchange rate arrangements with no separate legal tender and (b) currency board arrangements; (2) soft pegs consisting of (a) conventional pegged arrangements, (b) pegged exchange rates within horizontal bands, (c) crawling pegs, (d) stabilised arrangements, and (e) crawl like arrangements; floating regimes, under which the exchange rate is market determined and characterised as (a) floating or (b) free floating; and (4) the residual category, other managed arrangements (IMF, 2011).

[7] The de jure arrangements are reported as described by the countries (IMF, 2011)

exchange rate regimes. The increased capital mobility and waves of capital inflows and outflows have heightened the potential for shocks and the pressure for flexibility. In general a floating exchange rate is preferred if real changes such as technology changes or shifts in consumer preferences affect the relative prices of domestic goods. Examples of floating exchange rate regimes are managed floating or independent floating. Under the managed floating system, exchange rates are rekindled through a Central Bank intervention which Friedman and Schwartz (1963) advocated as a tool to keep the supply and demand for money at equilibrium, as measured by growth in productivity and demand. Syrichas (2010) argued that Central Banks play an eminent role in maintaining the exchange rate in a desirable range depending on the monetary and fiscal policy followed by governments. Many developing countries have thin financial markets where a few large transactions can cause extreme volatility. The hybrid exchange system combines free float, managed float, and fixed exchange system. Exchange rate regime and arrangements for selected regional settings are discussed in Section 2.5 as well as in Chapter Five of this book.

Table 2.1 Exchange Rate Arrangements in ASEAN, CACM, MERCOSUR and SADC

Currencies	Codes	Regimes
Brunei Dollar	BND	Currency board
Cambodia riel	KHR	Stabilised arrangement
Indonesia rupiah	IDR	Floating
Laos kip	LAK	Stabilised arrangement
Malaysia ringgit	MYR	Other managed arrangement
Myanmar kyat	MMK	Other managed arrangement
Philippines Peso	PHP	Floating
Singapore dollar	SGD	Other managed arrangement
Thailand baht	THB	Floating
Vietnam dong	VND	Stabilised arrangement
Belize dollar	BZD	Conventional peg
Costa Rica colon	CRC	Other managed arrangement
El Salvador Colon	SVC	No separate legal tender
Guatemala Quetzal	GTQ	Floating
Honduras lempira	HNL	Stabilised arrangement
Nicaragua cordoba	NIO	Crawling peg
Domincan peso	DOP	Crawl-like arrangement
Argentina pesp	ARS	Crawl-like arrangement
Bolivia boliviano	BOB	Stabilised arrangement
Brazil real	BRL	Floating

Chile peso	CLP	Free floating
Colombia peso	COP	Floating
Ecuador sucre	USD	No separate legal tender
Paraguay guarani	PYG	Other managed floating
Peru nuevo sol	PEN	Floating
Uruguay peso	UYU	Floating
Venezuela bolivar	VEF	Conventional peg
Angola kwanza	AOA	Other managed arrangement
Botswana pula	BWP	Crawling peg
Congo franc	CDF	Crawl-like arrangement
Lesotho loti	LSL	Conventional peg
Madagscar ariary	MGA	Floating
Malawi kwacha	MWK	Stabilised arrangement
Mauritius rupee	MUR	Floating
Mozambique metical	MZN	Floating
Namibia dollar	NAD	Conventional peg
Seychelles rupee	SCR	Floating
Swaziland lilangeni	SZL	Conventional peg
South African rand	ZAR	Floating
Tanzania shilling	TZS	Floating
Zambia kwacha	ZMW	Floating

Source: IMF (2011) "Annual Report on Exchange Arrangements and Exchange Restrictions"

2.2 Theories of Exchange Rate Determination

There is no general theory of exchange rate determination (Levich, 2001). In fact, exchange rates between currencies have long baffled academicians (MacDonald, 1990) and traders alike (Simons, 2004). MacDonald (2007) argued in his book that macro-fundamentals are important for explaining exchange rate behaviour at various points and can explain the main puzzles in the exchange rate literature. The following sections review exchange rate determination theories in the literature which are presented in this book as complementary rather than competing theories. This section is organised by three major schools of thought (Balance of Payment Approach, Monetary Approach and Parity conditions) and secondly by the individual drivers within those approaches.

2.2.1 Purchasing Power Parity

The starting point of exchange rate theory is purchasing power parity (PPP), which is also called the inflation theory of exchange rates – one of the main reasons why exchange rates in this book have been measured against consumer price index (CPI) values. PPP can be traced back to sixteen-century Spain and early seventeen century England, but Swedish economist Cassel (1918) was the first to name the theory PPP. Cassel once argued that without it, there would be no meaningful way to discuss over-or-under valuation of a currency. Since then, PPP was been widely used by Central Banks as a guide to establishing new par values for their currencies when the old ones were clearly in disequilibrium. In fact, PPP is often used to forecast exchange rates (Shapiro, 2010). Absolute PPP theory was first presented to deal with the price relationship of goods with the value of different currencies. The theory requires very strong preconditions. Absolute PPP holds in an integrated, competitive product market with the implicit assumption of a risk-neutral world, in which the goods can be traded freely without transportation costs, tariffs, export quotas, and so on. However, it is unrealistic in a real society to assume that no costs are needed to transport goods from one place to another. The theory is based on the 'law of one price', which argues that should a euro price of a good be multiplied by the exchange rate then it will result in an equal price of the good in US dollars. Absolute PPP states that since the prices should be the same across countries, the exchange rate between two countries should be the ratio of the prices in each country:

$$E = \frac{P}{P*} \qquad (2.1)$$

where E is the nominal exchange rate, defined as domestic currency value of a unit of foreign currency; and the foreign price level. This equation implies that an equivalent change in P requires a change in P^* to keep the exchange rate stable (Wilson, 2009). Inflation differentials between countries will also be eliminated in terms of their effect on the prices of the goods because the PPP will adjust to equal the ratio of their price levels. More specifically, *the currency of the country with the higher rate of inflation will depreciate against the other country's currency by approximately the inflation differential.* In accordance with the PPP concept, the inflation differentials between countries affect the exchange rate, and consequently the PPP could be thought of as a major determinant in the forecast exchange rates. This leads to the consideration of CPI as a potential predictor of FOREX movement in this book. Cochran and Defina (1995), show that the exchange rates, although they deviate from the PPP, finally return to their PPP levels. The relative version of PPP, which is used more commonly now, states that the exchange rate between the home currency and any foreign currency will adjust to reflect changes in the price level of two countries. Feridun (2005) presents this relationship as follows:

$$e_u = q_u \left(\frac{P_t^*}{P_u}\right) \qquad (2.2)$$

Where

e_u	is the real exchange rate,
q_u	is the nominal exchange rate,
P_t^*	is the US consumer price index
P_u	is the CPI for country i

2.2.2 The Balance of Payments Flow Approach

Traditionally, it was common to emphasise international trade flows as primary determinants of exchange rates. This was due, in part, to the fact that governments maintained tight restrictions on international flows of financial capital. The role of exchange rate changes in eliminating international trade imbalances suggests that we should expect countries with current trade surpluses to have an appreciating currency, whereas countries with trade deficits should have depreciating currencies. Such exchange rate changes would lead to changes in international relative prices that would work to eliminate the trade imbalance. As it is known from macroeconomics, the balance of payments is a method of recording all the international monetary transactions of a country during a specific period of time. The theory argues that the equilibrium exchange rate is found when currency flows match up current account and capital account activities. Under the Balance of Payments Flow approach, the domestic price of a foreign currency is determined by the intersection of the market demand and supply curves for that foreign currency (Copeland, 2008). According to Feridun (2005), the Balance of Payment Flow approach to exchange rate determination can be illustrated as follows:

$$e = b_1\,(y - y^*) - b_2\,(i - i^*) + b_3\,(x - x^*) \tag{2.3}$$

where b_1 >0, b_2 >0, b_3 >0,

e is the real exchange rate at equilibrium,

y is the national income,

i is the interest rate,

x is the the market's expectation of the future exchange rate,

* are the foreign country variables

According to the traditional view of the balance of payment flow approach, the equilibrium value of the exchange rate maintains the equilibrium of the Balance of Payments, i.e. it balances the flows of imports and exports. This is particularly true in most countries examined in this book because of the importance of trade in the economies of the regions selected in this research. Consequently, this book examines the relationship between exports, imports, trade balance and exchange rate fluctuations in the belief that trade variables are particularly important in the selected regional settings. A surplus in the

BOP implies that the demand for the country's currency exceeded the supply and that the government should allow the currency value to increase – in value – or intervene and accumulate additional foreign currency reserves in the Official Reserves Account. A deficit in the BOP implies that an excess supply of the country's currency on world markets and the government should then either devalue the currency or expand its official reserves to support its value. A nation's balance of payments interacts with nearly all of its key macroeconomic variables. A country's BOP can have a significant impact on the level of its exchange rate. In fact, the balance of payments theory of exchange rate is also named as 'General equilibrium theory of exchange rate' (Otuori, 2013). When the exchange rate of a country falls below the equilibrium exchange rate, it is a case of adverse balance of payments. The exports increase and eventually the adverse balance of payment is eliminated. The equilibrium rate is restored. When the balance of payments of a country is favourable, the exchange rate rises above the equilibrium exchange rate resulting in the decline of exports (Kanamori and Zhao, 2006). This leads to the consideration of exports and trade balance as potential predictors of FOREX movements in this book.

2.2.3 Monetary Approach

Modern exchange rate models emphasise financial-asset markets. Rather than the traditional view of exchange rates adjusting to equilibrate international trade in goods, the exchange rate is viewed as adjusting to equilibrate international trade in financial assets. Because goods prices adjust slowly relative to financial asset prices and financial assets are traded continuously each business day, the shift in emphasis from goods markets to asset markets has important implications. Exchange rates will change every day or even every minute as supplies of and demands for financial assets of different nations change. An implication of the monetary approach is that exchange rates should be much more variable than goods prices.

According to the monetary theory of exchange rate determination, exchange rates adjust to ensure that the quantity of money in each currency supplied is equal to the quantity demanded. The monetary model of the exchange rate seeks to explain exchange rate changes with relative rates of growth of the domestic and foreign money supplies and output. Neely and Sarno (2002) argued that the monetary approach to exchange rate determination emerged as the dominant exchange rate model at the outset of the recent float in the early 1970s and remains an important exchange rate paradigm. An expansionary monetary policy will lead to a depreciation of the domestic currency, because lower interest rates will generate an outflow of capital. According to Feridun (2005), the exchange rate should equal the ratio of the relative money stocks of two countries to relative money demands from these two countries and he suggested that the monetary model to exchange rate determination could be presented as follows:

$$e = (\frac{M}{M^*})/(\frac{k_y}{k^*y^*}) \tag{2.4}$$

where

M is the money stock,

K a positive parameter where * denotes inputs from foreign countries (Copeland, 2008). Examining the relationship between monetary variables and exchange rate changes in the present study was made almost impossible due to the lack of appropriate data (i.e. money supply) as illustrated in Table 2.2.

2.2.4 The Real Interest Rate Differentials Model

As early as the period of the gold standard, monetary policymakers found that exchange rates were influenced by changes in monetary policy. The rise of the home interest rate is usually followed by the appreciation of the home currency and a fall in the home interest rate is followed by a depreciation of the home currency. The interest rate parity condition was developed by Keynes (1924), to link the exchange rate, interest rate and inflation. Interest rate parity connects the forward rate to the spot rate and interest rates in the domestic economy to those abroad (Sercu-Uppal, 1995). According to Feridun (2005), the relationship between the real exchange rate and the real long-term interest rate differential can be represented as:

$$e = e' + (i^* - i) + \emptyset \tag{2.5}$$

where

e' is the real long-run equilibrium exchange rate,

$(i^* - i)$ the real long-run interest rate differential between two countries

$\emptyset$ the level of risk premium on domestic securities

$*$ the foreign country variables

Table 2.2 Exchange Rate Determinants used in ASEAN, CACM, MERCOSUR and SADC countries

Currency	Trade variables	Monetary variables	Commodities	Others
Angola kwanza	Exports	Capital Account	Oil price	Interest rate, CPI
Bolivia boliviano	TO	NA	Gold	Interest rate, CPI
Botswana pula	Exports, TB, TO	NA	NA	Interest rate, GDP
Brazil real	Exports, imports, TB	NA	Gold	GDP
Brunei dollar	Exports, imports, TB, TO	NA	NA	GDP
Chile peso	TB, TO	NA	Copper price	Interest rate, GDP
Colombia peso	Exports, imports, TB, TO	NA	NA	GDP

Table 2.2 *(Cont'd)* Exchange Rate Determinants

CDR franc	Exports, imports	NA	NA	CPI
Costa Rica colon	Exports, imports, TB, TO	NA	NA	GDP
Dominican peso	Exports, imports, TB, TO	NA	NA	GDP
El Salvador colon	Exports, imports, TB	NA	NA	Interest rate
Guatemala quetzal	Exports, imports, TB	NA	NA	Interest rate, CPI
Honduras lempira	Exports, imports, TB	NA	NA	Interest rate, CPI
Indonesia rupiah	Exports, TO	NA	NA	GDP, GDP change
Madagascar ariary	Exports, imports	Capital Account	NA	CPI
Malawi kwacha	Exports, imports, TB	Capital Account	NA	CPI
Malaysia ringgit	Exports, imports, TB, TO	NA	NA	Interest rate
Mauritius rupee	Exports, Imports, TB	NA	NA	CPI
Mozambique metical	NA	Capital Reserves	NA	Interest, CPI
Nicaragua cordoba	Exports, imports, TB	NA	NA	Interest rate
Paraguay guarani	Exports, imports, TB	NA	NA	NA
Peru new sol	Exports, imports, TB, TO	Capital Account	NA	Interest rate, GDP
Philippines peso	Exports, imports, TB, TO	NA	NA	GDP
Seychelles rupee	Exports, imports, TB	Money supply	NA	Interest rate
Singapore dollar	Exports, imports, TB, TO	NA	NA	Interest rate, GDP
Tanzania shilling	Exports, imports, TB	NA	NA	Interest rate
Thailand baht	Exports, imports, TB	NA	Gold	NA
Uruguay peso	Exports, imports, TB	NA	NA	Interest rate
Venezuela bolivar	Exports, imports, TB	NA	NA	Interest rate

The real value of the home currency would rise if there occurred a rise in relative real long-term interest rates. This leads to the consideration of interest rate as a potential predictor of FOREX movements. In fact, this book examines the relationship between exchange rates and interest rates in ASEAN, CACM,

MERCOSUR and SADC countries. There is little evidence to suggest that exchange rates changes are dictated by changes in the level of interest rates. Chapter Five discusses the results.

2.3 Empirical Evidence on the relationship between FOREX and Macroeconomic Variables

As discussed in previous sections in this chapter, there are many factors contributing to real exchange rate fluctuations. Among these factors are the level of national output, inflation, the openness of an economy, interest rates, domestic and foreign money supply, the exchange rate regime and Central Bank independence (Stancik, 2007). The degree of the impact of each of these factors varies and depends on a particular country's economic condition. For any country in general and a developing country in particular, a thorough understanding of the sources of fluctuations of the real exchange rate is essential to design a more effective macroeconomic policy (Adom et al. 2012). Exchange rate fluctuations have been largely explained by macroeconomic variables (Yin and Li, 2014). In fact, identifying key empirical determinants of the real exchange rate remains an active research area. As discussed in Chapter Three, one line of research has focused on establishing significant relationships between the long-run real exchange rate and economic fundamentals using cointegration tests. The following sections examine the work of researchers who attempted to explain exchange rate fluctuations using macroeconomic determinants.

2.3.1 Empirical Evidence on the relationship between Exchange Rates and Inflation

In many countries the exchange rate is used as a tool to bring down inflation; in general, a country with a consistently lower inflation rate exhibits a rising currency value, as its purchasing power increases relative to other currencies. Both Inflation and exchange rates determine if a nation is likely to be economically stable or not. A high inflation rate increase foreign exchange rates and hence weakens the local currency. According to IMF (2005) 18 emerging countries have changed their exchange rate regime from fixed to floating and their nominal anchor from exchange rate to inflation. Some economists state that one of the costs of inflation targeting is precisely the higher volatility of exchange rate which can entail negative effects of particular relevance to emerging economies given their greater financial and real vulnerabilities (Cavoli, 2009). In fact, this is the basis of the "fear of floating" (Calvo and Reinhart, 2002), which is a phenomenon associated with emerging countries as discussed earlier in this book. Broto and Berganza (2011) found that lower inflation rates led to lower exchange rate volatility in Latin America while Pincheira (2013) concluded that there is no significant relationship in the long term between exchange rate and inflation rates although there exists a significant short term relationship.

2.3.2 Empirical Evidence on the relationship between Exchange Rates and Monetary Variables

Many researchers presented supportive literature relating monetary models to exchange rate determination such as that of Dutt and Ghosh (2000), Miyakoshi (2000), Taylor and Peel (2000), Kilian and Taylor (2001), Rapach and Wohar (2002), Rogoff (2002), Jimoh (2004) and West (2004). Using a variety of currencies, they all tend to support a short-run dynamic or long-run equilibrium relationship between exchange rate and those macro fundamentals. Other studies include those of MacDonald and Taylor (1994), Strauss (1996) and Clark and MacDonald (1999). Frömmel and Menkhoff (2003) additionally identified changes in monetary policy settings as a determinant of volatility switches. They suggest that changes in monetary policy may lead to structural breaks on exchange rate volatility. Structural break theory is discussed in Chapter Four.

In his most recent study, Frömmel (2010) investigated the exchange rate volatility of six emerging countries between 1994 and 2004. He argued that the credibility of the exchange rate system cannot be separated from the credibility of the monetary policy and that an increase in the flexibility of the exchange rate regime leads to an increase in exchange rate volatility. Saeed et al. (2012) discussed the issue of exchange rate regime choice and examined the period of managed floating in Pakistan using monthly time series data from January 1982 to April 2010. In particular, they investigated the relationship between exchange rates and monetary variables (stock of money, foreign exchange reserves and total debt of Pakistan) and found that stock of money, debt and FOREX reserve balance all in relative terms are significant determinants of exchange rate between Pakistani Rupee and US Dollar. Dara and Samreth (2008) examined the validity of both short-and long-run equilibrium among variables of the monetary models exchange rate determination for the case of the Philippines. Their results indicated that all variables in the estimated model have significant short-run effects on the exchange rate with coefficient signs consistent with conventional economic theory. The results of a study by Bissoondeeal et al. (2009) suggest that the monetary models of exchange rates contain information about future movements of exchange rates, but the success of such models depends on the stability of money demand functions and the specifications of the models. Since monetary models of exchange rates depend on underlying money demand functions, it is therefore not surprising that monetary models which performed well in the early 1970s broke down in the early 1980s (Bissoondeeal et al. 2009). The present research looks at monetary aggregates to assess the importance of such factors as determinants of exchange rate changes. Chapter Five provide results of conducting cointegration tests to assess relationships between those macro fundamentals and exchange rates.

2.3.3 Empirical Evidence on the Relationship between Exchange Rates and Trade Openness

A recent strand of the literature, the so-called 'new open economy macroeconomics', argues that non-monetary factors have gained importance in explaining the real exchange rate variability (Zakaria and Ghauri, 2011). That is, in addition to monetary variables, variables like productivity shocks, terms of trade shocks, government spending, capital flows should be taken into account while explaining real exchange rate variability. The literature explaining the effect of trade openness on real exchange rate remains mixed. Some studies show that openness has a positive influence on real exchange rate and that it depreciates after trade liberalisation (Edwards, 1993; Elbadawi, 1994; Connolly and Devereux, 1995; Hau, 2002). In turn, some studies find statistically insignificant effects of openness on real exchange rate (Edwards, 1987). More recently, Li (2004) has shown that credible trade liberalisation leads to real exchange rate depreciation but non-credible ones could lead to short-run real exchange rate appreciation.

More than two decades ago, McCarthy and Dhareshwar (1992) sought to explain why external shocks affect some economies more severely than others. A key finding of their study is that the size and various components of the shock depend on such factors as (a country's) degree of openness, export/import composition. Economies with an export concentration in commodities may be particularly susceptible to external shocks. The World Bank (2002) emphasised the advantages of trade openness for developing economies in a global context. It classifies developing countries into the more globalised and the less globalised and found that some 24 developing countries – with 3 billion people – have doubled their ratio of trade to income over the past two decades. The rest of the developing world trades less today than it did 20 years ago. The more globalised developing countries have increased their per capita growth rate from 1 per cent in the 1960's to 3 percent in the 1970's, 4 percent in the 1980's and 5 percent in the 1990's. Much of the rest of the developing world – with about 2 billion people – is becoming marginalised. Their aggregate growth rate was actually negative in the 1990's (World Bank, 2002).

Empirical evidence tends to show that in the long-run more outward oriented countries register higher economic growth performances (e. g., among others, Sachs and Warner, 1995; Edwards, 1998a; Frankel and Romer, 1999; Dollar and Kraay, 2004; Lee etal., 2004). Using broader databases and cross-section or panel-data estimations, Chang et al. (2009) and Freund and Bolaky (2008) also showed that trade openness has a positive effect on income and that this positive relationship is enhanced by complementary policies. Ulaşan's (2012) findings indicated that many openness variables are positively and significantly correlated with long-run economic growth. However, in some cases, this result is driven by the presence of a few outlying countries. Adding to the fragility of the openness-growth association, the significance of openness variables disappears once other growth determinants, such as institutions, population heterogeneity, geography and macroeconomic stability are accounted for. This book investigates long-run relationships between exchange rates and trade openness where the latter is conventionally expressed as the ratio of exports plus imports to GDP.

2.3.4 Empirical Evidence on Relationship between Exchange Rates and Trade Balance

Researchers have also looked at the relationship between exchange rates and trade balance and there are studies which argue that there is statistical evidence connecting the two (for example Himarios 1989, Bahmani-Oskooee, 2001). A study by Arize (1994) used cointegration to examine the relationship between real effective exchange rates and the trade balances in nine Asian economies. The results indicate that there exists a positive relationship between the trade balance and the real effective exchange rates in Asia. Baharumshah (2001) found a positive long term relationship between exchange rates and trade balances in Thailand and Malaysia with one of their major trading partners - Japan. More recently, Duasa (2007) analysed the relationship between real exchange rates and trade balance and imports and exports demand in Malaysia. He found evidence that there exists an asymmetric relationship between balance of trade and real exchange rate. The study also found asymmetric relationship between export volumes and real exchange rates. Adeneyi et al. (2011) established that a relationship exists between the trade balance, foreign income, the real effective exchange rate and domestic income in Ghana, Gambia, Nigeria and Sierra Leone based on quarterly data from 1970 to 2007. An investigation involving ASEAN-5 countries by Liew et al. (2003) showed that trade balance in these countries are affected by real money rather than nominal exchange rates and therefore concluded that the role of exchange rate changes on trade balance has been exaggerated. A study involving Malaysia and other ASEAN countries also found a weak relationship between exchange rates and trade. This research assesses the relationship between exchange rates and trade balance for ASEAN, CACM, MERCOSUR and SADC countries, results are reported in Chapter Five.

2.3.5 Empirical Evidence between Exchange Rates and Economic Growth

In the short run if the economy is growing stronger relative to other economies the increases in economic activity that create attractive investment opportunities will strengthen the currency. Adeneyi et al. (2011) established that a relationship exists between effective exchange rate and domestic income in Ghana, Gambia, Nigeria and Sierra Leone based on quarterly data from 1970 to 2007 while Tehranchian and Behravesh (2011) provided evidence of a long-run relationship between exchange rates, money demand, GDP, inflation rates and interest rates in Iran. He found that GDP has the greatest effect on the country's money demand so that depending on the intensity and stability of other factors, an increase of 1 percent in GDP will averagely increase the money demand by 3.26 percent. Dollar and Kraay (2004) used the Frankel-Romer measure of constructed openness to analyse decadal growth of per-capita GDP, reporting that a doubling of trade integration raises the annual growth rate by 2.5 percentage points. The ARDL approach which will be discussed in the next chapter validates the existence of cointegration between the GDP and the exchange rate, both the long and short term interest rates and credit for Malaysia and Indonesia. In Thailand, application of the ARDL method revealed evidence of cointegration between the real GDP and interest rates, exchange rates and share prices plus a cointegration between interest rates, the exchange rates and the asset prices in the Philippines. Specifically, Indonesia currency is affected by the long term interest rate and changes in asset prices. Malaysia ringgit and Singapore dollar are significantly influenced by interest rates and exchange rate changes. The Thai baht is influenced by the interest rate, exchange rate and the asset price channels; while the Philippines is affected by the interest rate, exchange rate, credit, and asset price channels. In very few countries examined in this book the author had access to GDP data, hence the relationship between exchanges rate and GDP have only been investigated in countries where such data was available.

2.3.6 Empirical Evidence between Exchange Rates and Commodity Prices

Commodity exporting countries face large terms of trade fluctuations which render their real exchange rate volatile. Increased volatility in the real exchange rate hurts the economy through its adverse consequences on private agents' consumption and investment decisions. The literature provides robust empirical evidence of the relationship between the level of the exchange rate and the level of commodity prices as the latter seems to drive the former (Arezki et al. 2012). Rapid, unexpected and often large movements in commodity prices are an important feature of the behavior of commodity prices. Such movements can have serious consequences for the terms of trade, real income and fiscal position of commodity-dependent countries. They also have profound implications for the achievement of macroeconomic stabilisation in developing countries, many of which depend on one or two commodities for their main export earnings (Cashin and McDermott, 2001). Chen and Rogoff (2003) provided early evidence of the relationship between commodity prices and exchange rates for a selected number of resource-rich developed economies such as Australia, Canada and New Zealand. They found that the real exchange rates of Australia and New Zealand are driven by world commodity prices. The result is consistent with the analysis of Cashin et al. (2004) who provided additional evidence for a larger set of developing countries and commodities while Frankel (2007) showed that an index of mineral prices is one, but not the only, important determinant of the real value of the South Africa Rand. These results were confirmed by Ngandu (2005) who surveyed the literature on the relation between commodity prices and the real exchange rate of commodity exporting developing countries. Chen and Rogoff (2003) also examined the fluctuations in commodity prices and their impacts on the real exchange rate in developed countries and suggested that for primary product exporting countries, commodity prices are very important determinants of the real exchange rate. Chen (2004) argued that the heavy reliance on primary products for export earnings implies that price fluctuations in the world commodity markets would exert pressure on the relative demand for the home currencies, which, in principle, may lead to fluctuations in the values of their exchange rates. This book examines the relationship between commodity prices and exchange rates; there is little evidence to suggest that commodity prices play an eminent role in the exchange rate determination except for few countries. Findings in Chapter Five will shed light on that.

2.3.7 Empirical Evidence between Exchange Rates, Central Bank Policy and Currency Arrangements

The argument most often used to justify Central Bank intervention in FOREX markets is that the exchange rate is "simply too important a price to be left to the market" (Rosenberg, 2003, 205). The assumption is that Central Bank authorities can do a better job in the market in terms of driving exchange rates toward their long-term equilibrium values. Unlike the major developed countries, which generally stopped intervening after the mid-1990s, the developing and emerging market economies continue frequent operations in their FOREX markets. In fact, these small, open economies show a striking aversion to exchange rate volatility (Calvo and Reinhart, 2002). As discussed in Chapter Three, exchange rate volatility can often have serious macroeconomic consequences in these economies because they frequently lack hedging facilities that protect domestic firms from that volatility. Ironically, the frequent interventions that developing and emerging market countries undertake, together with other policies that they pursue to increase the effectiveness of those interventions, can limit the very financial development that they so badly need.

In many developing and emerging market economies, the FOREX market is a key asset market, and the local Central Bank is often the dominant player in that market. Almost by definition, FOREX markets in these developing and emerging market countries are underdeveloped, particularly at the interbank level (Canales-Kriljenko 2004). In a survey of FOREX activity in developing and emerging market economies Canales-Kriljenko (2003, 2004) found that most Central Banks in these countries participate in the market irrespective of the underlying exchange rate regime. They often intervene heavily in markets characterised as flexible or floating. Surprisingly, however, less FOREX intervention occurs under credible fixed exchange-rate regimes. If an exchange-rate peg is credible, FOREX intermediaries tend to act as stabilising speculators, minimising the need for official intervention (Canales-Kriljenko, 2003). As the literature clearly suggests, the relative success that developing and emerging market economies may have in conducting effective FOREX market operations can intensify the very problem that they seek to avoid. In their desire to foster stability through intervention, regulation and control, monetary authorities in these countries often discourage private-sector financial innovation and maintain the market's backwardness. When such operations hamper financial-market development, they can actually intensify the macroeconomic consequences of exchange-rate volatility. The effects of currency arrangement and Central Bank intervention on the selected regional settings of this book are discussed in Chapter Five.

2.4 Exchange rate determinants - Explanatory variables

As the above sections clearly show, the statement made by Mussa (1983) more than 30 years ago is still valid today; he indicated that there exists no simple model of exchange rate determination which provides an adequate explanation of most of the observed movements in nominal and real exchange rates under a floating regime. Exchange rates share many of the general behavioural characteristics of the prices of assets such as stocks and bonds. An exchange rate is a financial asset price and therefore it would seem straightforward to examine exchange rate changes in respect of the changes in the demand and supply of money (Melvin, 2004). The current price of such an asset is linked to economic conditions that are expected to affect the ultimate demand and supply of that asset in the future.

In the monetary model of exchange rate determination, there is a consensus that an exchange rate is priced at a level where the wealth holders with internationally diversified portfolios are willing to hold the outstanding stocks of monies. The asset approach to exchange rate determination emphasises the importance of financial asset prices as explanatory variables for the movements in the FOREX market. The monetary approach theory of exchange rate determination argues that financial assets are traded continuously each business day which means that exchange rates will change every day or even every minute as supply and demand of financial assets fluctuate continuously on trading platforms. In other terms, this theory suggests that exchange rate changes cannot be explained by changes in trade but rather by financial drivers. This theory was given more impetus when Melvin (2004) found that volatility of exchange rates averaged four to seven times the volatility of prices of goods. He argued that such figures are consistent with the fact that exchange rates respond to changing conditions in financial asset markets and not simply to changes in international goods trade. Obviously, for this assumption to hold, a stock exchange needs to exist in the country under study since this is where financial transactions take place. As far as the present research is concerned, most countries in Central America and sub-Saharan Africa do not have established stock exchanges and consequently no securities are traded on daily basis which justifies the limited evidence of cointegration between exchange rates and monetary aggregates in this part of the world (please refer to the findings section in Chapter Five).

The traditional view of exchange rate determination remains relevant today because some economies in Africa still attract little by way of private international capital flows and the trade account continues to dominate the balance of payments. The traditional view of exchange rate determination promotes the idea that exchange rates will adjust to changes in the trade balance of the country under study regardless of changes in monetary aggregates (Hallwood and Macdonald, 2000). Hence this book reviews this statement and investigates potential relationships between exchange rates and various trade aggregates such as volume of exports, volume of imports, trade balance and trade openness. Countries with current trade surpluses would be expected to have appreciating currencies, while countries with trade deficits will have depreciating currencies. Chapter Five discusses the results of applying the ARDL method to exchange rates of more than 30 countries and assesses the relationship between trade aggregates and exchange rates.

It is now recognised that a comprehensive theory of the exchange rate must include the trade account. The trade variables used in this book are not uniform over the panel of countries examined because of data unavailability. Nonetheless, in the context of the present research, the data collected reflect the importance of particular economic variables in the exchange rate determination for some countries. For example, copper prices are of particular importance to countries like Chile and Zambia as leading world exporters of that commodity. The CPI is thought of as a particularly important variable for countries in Africa and Central America especially those that have been struggling with high rates of inflation for the last two decades. Gold reserves and prices are particularly important for Peru, the world's sixth-biggest producer and Colombia which has an output of around 50 tons per year (CIA, 2012). The relationships between GDP, capital account and exchange rates have been investigated thoroughly for all countries. Data were collected from the IMF- IFS database facility. One of the contributions of this book is therefore to investigate trade and non-trade variables (Central Bank intervention and the choice of exchange rate regime) that can be identified as drivers of exchange rates volatility in selected common markets. As the reader will notice throughout the review provided in Chapter Three, exchange rate studies on emerging markets tend to focus a lot on East Asian economies, while the rest of the emerging world gains little attention in comparison. This research aims to fill this gap in the literature, since there is no evidence of any work that compares exchange rate movements in major trading blocs in the developing world neither there is a single study of exchange rate determination in Central America and some parts of sub-Saharan Africa. This section is dedicated mainly to justify the choice of variables used as determinants of exchange rate movements and shed the light on other non-quantitative factors which need to be taken into consideration in the analysis of exchange rates. Exchange rates are not only dependent on trade and/or money supply but also on policies and currency arrangements. The magnitude of the latter varies from country to country but is evident in developing as much as it is in developed economies.

The exchange rate policy that Central Banks adopt vis-a-vis exchange rate management seems to be the starting point for a thorough understanding of the peculiarities of exchange rate determination. Various currency arrangements are adopted by countries examined in this book. Bolivia, Costa Rica and Nicaragua, for example, have crawling pegs where the exchange rate is adjusted periodically by the Central Bank in small amounts at a fixed, preannounced rate or in response to certain indicators. In Honduras, Uruguay and Venezuela, exchange rates are maintained within certain fluctuation margins around a central rate that is periodically adjusted (crawling bands).

Angola, Cambodia, Dominican Republic, Guatemala, Indonesia, Laos, Mauritius, Myanmar, Paraguay, Singapore, Thailand, Vietnam and Zambia manage the floating of their respective exchange rates and therefore allow the Central Bank to influence the exchange rate through active FOREX market intervention. Exchange rates are independently floating (market determined) and any intervention is aimed at moderating fluctuations rather than determining the level of exchange rate in Argentina, Brazil, Chile, Colombia, DRC, Madagascar, Peru, Philippines, South Africa and Tanzania. In Brunei, a fixed exchange rate is established by a legislative commitment to exchange domestic currency for a specified foreign currency at a fixed exchange rate. New issues of domestic currency are typically backed in some fixed ratio by additional holdings of the key foreign currency. Exchange rates were fixed in Seychelles until 1996.

2.5 Conclusion

This chapter was devoted to the review of the theoretical models of exchange rate determination. Existing models were reviewed and discussed and the selection of explanatory variables used in this book was justified by the existing theories as well as the existing literature. Throughout the developing world, the choice of exchange rate regime stands as perhaps the most contentious aspect of macroeconomic policy. Despite the perceived centrality of the exchange rate regime to long-run growth and economic stability, the existing theoretical and empirical literatures on exchange rates seem to offer little guidance on this subject. The theoretical exchange rate literature seems to be mainly tailored to richer countries with highly developed institutions and markets (e.g., Garber and Svensson, 1995; Obstfeld and Rogoff, 1996). Due to its widespread economic implication, evaluating causes and determinants of exchange rate volatilities remains one of the key research agenda for both academics and policy makers.

This chapter reviewed various models of exchange rate determination and provided the reader with empirical evidence that supports the choice of each explanatory variable selected in this book. Several attempts have been made to particularly examine the role of external debt/borrowing in explaining the fluctuations of the local currency. For instance, Corsetti et al. (1999) argued that external borrowing, particularly by private commercial banks and firms is among the key factors responsible for the severity of the East Asian financial and currency crises during the late 1990s. Ideally, external borrowing would have been used as explanatory variable to examine the fluctuations in the exchange rates in various highly indebted countries but this endeavour could not be pursued in this book because of the unavailability of such data on the IMF-IFS database.

Chapter III. Empirical Methods and Applications

The aim of this chapter is to provide the reader with the context in which the present research is to be examined. It outlines gaps in the study of exchange rates that the present research aims to fill. The chapter introduces the FOREX market and its characteristics. It then go on to list the events that shaped the volatile nature of the FOREX scene during the period ranging from the early 1980's till the start of the 21st century with a particular focus on the regions that make up the sample chosen for this book. Section 3.2 reviews exchange rate volatility applications while Section 3.3 lists empirical evidence of using cointegration and ARDL methods in the study of financial series in general and exchange rate in particular; cointegration and ARDL studies are reviewed so as to gain a better understanding of the various determinants of exchange rate introduced in Chapter Two and their importance in dictating changes overtime. Section 3.4 highlights the fact that combination methods have been under-used in Finance having performed particularly well in other disciplines. The same section provides a listing of combination papers that relate to the study and the forecast of exchange rates using composite methods.

Each country examined in this book is a stand-alone case and will need to be considered separately - the analyses in Chapters Four, Five and Six do that. However, the links between global markets require a holistic-led approach to understand how an event in a nearby country can affect the local currency. The high integration of financial markets is thought of as the reason behind crisis spill-over in the emerging world particularly those that struck Southeast Asia and Latin America. The acuteness of these crises varied between regions and was dependent on the speed and efficiency of Central Bank interventions and the extent to which the IMF was willing to bail out hit countries; a solution which proved to provide too little too late considering the scale of some of these crises.

3.1.1 The FOREX Market

The FOREX market is an over the counter market[8] which involves the exchange of one currency for another and which handles a daily volume of more than 4 trillion US $ (Valdez and Molyneux, 2013). The major participants

[8] There are two basic ways to organize financial markets—exchange and over the counter (OTC). Unlike exchanges, OTC markets have never been a "place." They are less formal, although often well-organized, networks of trading relationships centred around one or more dealers. Dealers act as market makers by quoting prices at which they will sell (ask or offer) or buy (bid) to other dealers and to their clients or customers (IMF, 2012)

in the FOREX market are banks, brokers, commercial firms and central banks. The FOREX market is international and operates 24/7 on a global scale; it is composed of two main elements: spot[9] and term[10] (McInish, 2000). It is a highly speculative market which experiences many imbalances and growing volatility – particularly in downturn periods. As participants tend to exploit opportunities and immunise themselves against risk, there is constant development of new instruments which contributes to further growth of the market in the longer perspective (Howells and Bain, 2007). It is an electronic market that is active 24 hours a day without any particular geographical location. However, it is common thinking that the trading process operates according to time zones. Indeed, the vast majority of trading is concentrated in the three major markets of London, New York and Tokyo. Of these three markets, the New York and London markets are by far the largest in terms of total volume traded (McInish, 2000); the US dollar, the Euro, the British Pound, the Swiss Franc and the Yen are the most actively traded currencies in these markets although emerging world currencies like the Chinese Yuan and the Brazilian Peso have been gaining ground during the last couple of years.

Trading in FOREX markets averaged US $5.3 trillion per day in April 2013. This is up from US $4.0 trillion in April 2010 and US $3.3 trillion in April 2007 (BIS, 2013). One of the most popular theories explaining the fluctuations of exchange rates is Purchasing Power Parity (Valdez, 2007; Pilbeam, 2005; Mishkin, 2004; Copeland, 2008) which was discussed in Chapter Two. It relates the purchasing power of a national currency to a given basket of goods that can be bought for a given amount of money. This involves the appreciation/depreciation mechanism and also takes into account inflation levels in different countries. In the FOREX market, the standard practice is to quote all exchange rates against the US dollar. If the quote is in the form of one US dollar against an amount of another currency, the quote is in European terms. If the quote is in the form of the number of US dollars for one unit of another currency, the quote is in American terms (Valdez and Molyneux, 2013). European terms are used in the interbank market for most currencies (McInish 2000). According to the IMF (2003), the major market participants in the FOREX market are the commercial and investment banks that make up the interbank market. They are considered as the core of the exchange currency system since they account for the largest share of market turnover and perform a vital economic function of mediating currency flows. Second are the Central Banks which are charged with the broader responsibility to maintain reasonable market order and sometimes as a lender of last resort in crisis time. They tend to absorb market pressures when they are judged to be excessive and stand as a supplier of the local currency to make sure that the FOREX market clears at a given exchange rate. Third are large companies, including multinational corporations. Derivative traders are the fourth category operating in the FOREX market and can cause major, if short term, currency unrest when

[9] The rate of a foreign exchange contract for immediate delivery (McInish, 2000)

[10] The exchange rate at which the currency can be exchanged at a pre-determined time in the future (McInish, 2000)

hedging positions. This assumption is given more impetus since 80% of exchange rate transactions last for less than two days and 95% of the transactions last no more than a week (Valdez and Molyneux, 2013). The last category of agents involves the nonbank financial institutions. They usually invest in longer-term analysis and forecasting and maybe among the first to see the upcoming currency pressures and realignments. The findings of this book are likely to be relevant for those who operate in this last category and for policy makers at Central Bank level.

Since its institution in 1944, the IMF has overseen the international monetary system to ensure exchange rate stability. This was possible through a set of conventions, rules, procedures and institutions that govern the conduct of financial relations between nations which have been established right after the World War II. The proposal of Breton-Woods system in 1944 was to peg the currencies of countries members of the IMF to the US dollar which was convertible to gold ($35 per one ounce of gold) in the belief that this would be enough to guarantee the stability of the international monetary system (Shapiro, 2010). In August 1971, President Nixon officially announced that the dollar was no longer convertible to gold which meant that currencies became free floating. Since that date, exchange rates have become more volatile and governments have allocated their resources to try to forecast values of their currencies by looking at various economic variables, macroeconomic fundamentals and past movements of exchange rate series.

As the strains between America's budget deficit and the dollar's peg emerged, an artificial reserve asset run by the IMF was created – SDR, whose value is based on a basket that contains the US dollar, Euro, British Pound and Japanese Yen. The IMF's members agree on periodic allocations of SDR which countries can convert into other currencies if need be. They make up less than 5% of global reserves (The Economist, 2011). The Governor of China's Central Bank argued in 2009 that the SDR should become a true global reserve asset to replace the dollar. Moghadam (2011) suggested that the SDR can play a major role amid the current problems in the international monetary system and can be used as a tool to reduce volatility in financial markets. This belief is shared by the author of this book which explains why exchange rates of sample countries are examined against SDR rates.

3.1.2 Features of the FOREX Market in the 1980's and 1990's

The beginning of 1973 has been characterised by a number of attempts to reinstate fixed exchange rates, all of which have failed for one reason or another. The floating exchange rate era has certainly not delivered anything approaching the degree of stability its advocates had hoped to see. In the mid-1970's, currency values have been subject both to wild day to day fluctuations and to long-run swings into apparent over or under-valuation. The breakdown of the Breton-Woods system of pegged exchange rates made currencies volatile both on the short and medium term. Additionally, following the first oil price shock of 1973, when the oil price was quadrupled by Organisation of the

Petroleum Exporting Countries (OPEC) many countries - that make the sample examined in this book - suffered high and volatile inflation rates.

Huge sums of money were lent to developing countries in the 1980's; the source of these funds was mainly the surplus OPEC have accumulated after the soaring prices of oil during the 1974 crisis. In fact, OPEC doubled the price of oil between 1978 and 1980 (Mabro, 1984). The latter led to an increase in interest rates and pushed industrial countries into recession whilst contributing heavily to the "third world" debt crisis of the 1980's and 1990's. These crises hit Africa, Central and Latin America and Southeast Asia indiscriminately. According to the World Bank (1992), 15 countries had debts equivalent or greater than their GNP including Mozambique (399.7%), Nicaragua (112.1%), Bolivia (93.3%) and the DRC (98%) in 1988. These debt crises have desperate human costs in places like Central America and sub-Saharan Africa.

The 1990's period was marked by the unprecedented increase in the use of new technology and especially the widespread use of computers in the financial services industry. The new technology has brought with it new issues of security and reliability which are associated with its use; in fact, cases of 'hacking' and people gaining access to confidential client information have been big worries since. Another characteristic of the 1990's period was general trend towards deregulation of national financial systems although there were clear exceptions to this trend in the Basle Accords (1988, 2004 and 2010) to ensure greater consistency of capital adequacy ratios between banks in various countries. Globalisation has also brought with it increased hardship for financial markets in the shape of the AFC which was discussed in Chapter One.

Later on, deregulation and financial liberalisation have led to the creation and spread of new financial assets (options, derivatives) and the appearance of new agents (hedge funds, pension funds and so on). That said, the operations of international capital markets have proved to be very unstable, with high volatility in capital flows and the permanent threat of systemic risks. These problems are not distributed symmetrically, with the developing countries being affected the most although developed countries are also affected. The importance of the trends of the 1980's and 1990's did not fade away and still manage to make the headline in the FOREX market on the second decade of the 21st century as Kevin Rodgers, global head of FX spot, e-trading and derivatives at Deutsche Bank, FT recently stated that "The mega-trends in FX are globalisation and, to some extent, technology", (Financial Times, 2011).

2.6 3.2 Exchange Rate Volatility Applications

Researchers and practitioners have investigated volatility in the FOREX market extensively in the belief that a good knowledge of the topic's underlying causes will lead to better predictions. Changes in exchange rate volatility may have different reasons. For example, the choice of exchange rate regime – discussed in Chapter Two – is known to strongly impact upon exchange rate volatility (Flood and Rose, 1999). Bissondeeal (2008) studied different exchange rates for the post-Breton Woods period and concluded that there is a relationship between nominal exchange rates and prices. Krugman (1991) argued that widening the fluctuation band will make a currency more credible, because it gets less likely that the fluctuation margins are reached and consequently volatility decreases.

Ruiz (2009) examined whether there are common factors or a mechanism driving volatility across Latin American markets. Her results display evidence that volatility movements in FOREX markets are mainly country specific and concluded that common volatility processes seem to be present only for a few South American markets. This research examines the findings by Ruiz (2009), which pertain to the MERCOSUR region and discuss them in Chapters Four and Five. Findings from Berger et al. (2008) indicated that not only does the type of exchange rate regime affects volatility, but even a "wrong" choice of a peg induces higher exchange rate volatility than a peg which is in line with the macroeconomic condition. Chang and Tabak (2007) tested the assumption that volatilities extracted from option prices give superior forecasts compared to other models. They presented evidence that implied volatilities contain information not present in past returns for the Brazilian exchange rates and confirmed the findings of Andrade and Tabak (2001) who reached the same conclusion.

Furthermore, Liu (2007) examined the effects of derivative trading on the pricing efficiency of the underlying currency market. He gathered thirty derivative listings on sixteen different currencies at the end of 2004 and found that since the commencement of derivatives trading on two exchanges (Chicago and Philadelphia), returns of the underlying currencies have become significantly random, on average, and thus less predictable. He concluded that the trading of currency derivatives has enhanced pricing efficiency in the underlying currency market and made exchange rates harder to predict for market participants. The author of the present book chose not to assess the impact of derivatives on exchange rate volatility for two reasons: the first one is that many countries examined in this book do not have established stock exchanges where derivative products are traded. In addition, derivatives are exchanged on a daily basis while the present study examines the monthly changes on exchange rates as mentioned in Chapter One.

Gokcan (2000) suggested that volatility is related to the stage of market development. Risk and uncertainty of returns in emerging markets are typically higher than in developed markets. As such, volatility in emerging markets is generally larger and more persistent than volatility in developed markets. One explanation to this is the difference in the speed and reliability of information available to investors, which is associated with modes of telecommunication and possibly the accounting system in place. As such, a small and relatively under-developed FOREX market exhibit relatively larger volatility clustering (when positive changes in the market are likely to be followed by changes with the same sign and vice-versa). The general presumption is that an increase in exchange rate uncertainty will have an adverse effect on trade flows and consequently, the overall health of the world economy. The next section looks at this relationship more closely and reviews the effects of exchange rate volatility on trade. Trade is of particular relevance to the countries examined in this book if we recall the fact that each trading bloc is in the process of signing FTAs with regional and international partners. Trade is therefore is a big focus of this research.

3.2.1 Exchange Rate Volatility and Trade

The primary reason why exchange rate volatility is of interest to economists is the notional premise that volatility may act as an impediment to international trade. This section presents a detailed assessment of this hypothesis by examining the impact of good and bad news in volatility modelling. Throughout much of the last century, governments pursued a mixed system of exchange rate determination. However, the collapse of the Breton Woods exchange rate system in 1971 changed this as many of the major participants in the global trade arena made the transition to a floating regime. This meant that the rate at which currencies were traded was now subject to the forces of supply and demand in the FOREX market. The growing trend towards floating exchange rates drew attention to the welfare effects of exchange rate policy. The focus of this debate has largely centred on the issue of exchange rate volatility and its possible impact on the economy during the last two decades.

Accepting the fact that obstacles to international trade lead to the reduction of global welfare, volatility is of potentially great concern. More specifically, it is argued that volatility equals confusion in trading terms and thereby adds risk to the trading process. The standard argument that exchange rate volatility acts to impede trade flows has been well documented in the works of Broll (1994), Ethier (1973), Hooper and Kohlhagen (1978) and Wolf (1995). Yet, models such as those of Giovannini (1988) and Baron (1976) show how an increase in exchange rate volatility may not necessarily have an adverse effect on the trade levels. Furthermore, some authors have been able to show how an increase in exchange rate volatility may prove to be beneficial for trade. One view maintains that the capacity to export is tantamount to holding an option and that an increase in exchange rate volatility, also leads to a rise in the value of that option. Sercu and Vanhulle (1992) developed models in which companies on average enter a market sooner and exit it later where exchange rate volatility increases.

De Grauwe (1988) constructed a simple model analysing choices when faced with risk of exchange rate volatility. He maintains that an increase in exchange rate risk raises the expected marginal utility of export revenue and therefore increases export activity if producers are sufficiently risk averse. Longmore and Robinson (2005) argued that volatility in emerging markets is larger and more persistent than developed markets. There is no consensus as to whether exchange rate volatility influences trade volumes and the sign of the relation has also been a matter of dispute. According to McKenzie (1999), the empirical evidence most commonly fails to identify a statistically significant relationship between exchange rate uncertainty and the volume of trade and that is an assumption that the present book will examine thoroughly in Chapter Five.

The negative relationship between exchange rate volatility and trading volume can be found in numerous papers such as Cushman (1983), De Grauwe and

Verfaille (1988), Giovannini (1988), Broll and Eckwert (1999), Chou (2000), Sukar and Hassan (2001) and Nieh (2002). Negative effects of exchange rate uncertainty on trade flows are also reported by Arize et al. (2000) for developing countries while Baum, Caglayan and Ozkan (2003) reported that the impact of exchange rate volatility on export flows differs in sign and magnitude across the countries studied. In an emerging country context, the negative relationship between exchange rates and trade is not clear cut if local traders import inputs to be included in the production process since this will offset the declining exports revenues in the form of lower input costs. This can be very true especially for ASEAN countries since various countries in the region provide the components used to produce one item. For example, given the very cheap labour costs in Cambodia compared with the rest of the region, items tend to be channelled to this country for assembly purposes. In some cases, whole production channels are transferred there while important parts that are not available locally are shipped from elsewhere. Some other companies and governments choose to hedge out their positions or engage in a multi-currency environment in which the effect of exchange rate fluctuations in one or another direction, on total profitability, cancels each other out.

More recently, Shehu and Youtang (2012), examined the causal relationship between exchange rate volatility, trade flows and economic growth of the sub-Saharan African countries from 1970-2009 with specific reference to Nigeria. They found that exchange rate volatility has significant effects on trade flows and economic growth. Huchet-Bourdon and Korinek (2012) examined the impact of exchange rate and their volatility on trade flows in two small, open economies - Chile and New Zealand - with three major trading partners namely China, the Euro area and the US. The study looked at two broadly defined sectors - agriculture and manufacturing/mining on the other. They found that exchange rate volatility impacts on trade flows in the smaller, open economies more so than was found for larger economies, although findings do not clearly indicate the direction of the impact (effects vary across countries and sectors). They concluded that depreciation in the exchange rates in Chile and New Zealand would not lead to a strong change in their trade balances with three main trading partners across the board.

3.2.2 Exchange Rate Volatility and Foreign Direct Investment

As discussed earlier in this chapter as well as in Chapter One, developing countries struggled with huge amounts of debts during the 1980's and 1990's. Many countries investigated in the present research are receivers of increasing amounts of international aid and FDI particularly in Africa. The literature suggests that the heavy reliance of sub-Saharan African countries on external development finance is not without some inherent disadvantages. In general, the level of Official Development Assistance (ODA) - as measured by and introduced by the Organisation of Economic Development and Cooperation (OECD) - and per capita economic growth of recipient countries have shown no systematic relationship.

Ogunleye (2009) analysed the relationships between volatility of exchange rates and FDI in Nigeria and South Africa and found that the risk of exchange rate volatility weakens FDI flows. Coleman and Tettey (2008) studied exchange rate volatility and FDI link in Ghana. Results showed a negative impact of volatility of exchange rates on inward flows of FDI. Chowdhry and Wheeler (2008) examined the relationship between volatility of exchange rates in Canada, Japan, the United States and the United Kingdom. They found that shocks to exchange rate volatility have positive and significant impact on flows of FDI. Kiyota and Urata (2004) analysed the link between exchange rates, volatility of exchange rates and FDI for the industrial sector in Japan. It specifically analysed the impact of volatility of exchanges rate on trends of FDI. Findings suggested that currency depreciation of the host country attract FDI flows, while on the other hand uncertainty and volatility of exchange rates affects negatively these flows.

3.2.3 Exchange Rate Volatility, Crises and the Risk of Contagion

Forbes and Rigobon (2002) defined contagion as a significant increase in the cross market correlation during the period of crisis. If two markets are moderately integrated during periods of stability and a shock to one market leads to a significant increase in market co-movement, this would generate contagion. They argued that contagion is the transmission of a crisis to a particular country due to its real and financial inter-dependence with countries that are already experiencing a crisis. In other words, contagion happens when cross market correlation increases significantly in crisis period. Naoui et al. (2010) found evidence of contagion from US market to Brazil, Korea, Malaysia, Mexico and Singapore. Sahoo (2012) analysed volatility spill-overs from exchange rates of the Indian Rupee against those of the Brazilian Real, the Russian Rouble, the South Korean Won, the Singapore Dollar, the Japanese Yen, the Swiss Franc and the British Pound from 2005 to 2011. He employed multiple volatility models to examine the dynamics of exchange rate volatility and found that all currencies included in the study exhibited presence of conditional autocorrelation and volatility persistence. These findings support the view that volatilities observed in the exchange rate of the leading currencies cause volatility in the daily exchange rate of the Indian Rupee. Exchange rate volatility, as suggested by Calvo and Reinhart (2002), has often been associated with economic crisis and may be a signal of lack of policy credibility, which gives rise to the fear of floating. Fratzcher (2003) for instance stressed the role of contagion in currency crises and argued that the poor performance of standard empirical models of currency crises such as logit-based prediction methods (Berg and Pattilo, 1999) lies in their neglect of the role of contagion. Both methodologies focus exclusively on the country-specific factors and macroeconomic fundamentals as the sole sources of crises while omitting the effects of contagion. He stated that economists still lack the answer as to why many currency crises of the 1990s were clustered within regions and affected a broad range of countries almost simultaneously with the conclusion that no open emerging market, even one with relatively sound fundamentals and policies, is capable of totally insulating itself from events in the rest of the world.

In fact, Fratzcher (2003) found strong evidence in support of financial contagion in East Asia and concluded that this might be among key factors contributing to the spread of the crisis. After controlling for own-country news and other fundamentals, Baig and Goldfajn (1999) provided similar evidence of cross-border contagion in the region's financial markets. Hurley and Santos (2003) studied the volatility aspect of the East Asian currencies and concluded that the Thai baht was the main channel through which currency linkages were transmitted and all five ASEAN countries experienced volatility after the breakdown of the Breton Woods system in spite of the adoption of the crawling peg exchange rate regime. This latest conclusion reiterates the assumption that the author made at the beginning of this book – countries in the same region are likely to respond to shocks in an almost similar way.

3.2.4 Exchange Rate Volatility and Interventions

In sharp contrast to the studies about developed countries, there are few attempts to investigate the effectiveness of Central Bank intervention in emerging countries. In this book, Chapter Two reviewed empirical work on the effect Central Bank interventions might have on exchange rates while Chapter Five discusses the same for selected regional settings. The main reason for paucity of such studies for developing countries is the unavailability of high frequency data which are required to investigate this phenomenon. Unlike in the case of developed countries, the evidence is more clear-cut with respect to the volatility than the exchange rate level (Simwaka and Mkandawire, 2008). These studies indicate that although intervention reduces volatility contemporaneously, persistent operations actually increase volatility due to greater market uncertainty. There are several reasons for these overwhelming results: (i) FOREX markets in developing and emerging economies are shallow with a low turnover and many countries intervene in amounts that are largely relative to market turnover and (ii) besides FOREX intervention, Central Banks supplement these interventions through FOREX controls, monetary instruments and banking regulations that increase the efficacy of their interventions.

Baillie and Osterberg (1997) found evidence that interventions are associated with slight increases in the volatility of exchange rates in the US and Germany. Dominguez (1998) examined the effects of US, German and Japanese monetary and intervention policies on dollar-mark and dollar-yen exchange rate volatility from 1977 to 1994. Their results indicate that interventions generally increase exchange rate volatility. Beine et al. (2006) investigated the effects of Central Bank interventions on exchange rates. They estimated the effects of Central Bank interventions on both the variance and covariance between the Yen and the Deutsche Mark in terms of US Dollar. Their results suggest that coordinated CBIs not only tend to increase the volatility of exchange rates but also explain a significant amount of the covariance between the major currencies (a useful result for short-run currency portfolio management).

Suardi (2008) used volatility models on the Japanese yen-US dollar exchange rates and found that interventions of the Bank of Japan and Federal Reserve are more effective in changing the direction of the exchange rate movements and reducing its volatility level in a regime where the exchange rate is severely misaligned. They argued that the presence of asymmetric volatility in exchange rate returns may be a result of active Central Bank intervention while Pontines and Rajan (2011) confirmed the existence of asymmetry in Central Bank intervention responses to currency movements in China, Hong Kong, India, Japan, Singapore and South Korea. They also argued that the response of Central Banks to specific basket of currencies is stronger than others which imply that intervention is not a standard process. Nikkinen and Vähämaa (2009) showed that Japan's Central Bank interventions significantly affect the market expectations about future exchange rate co-movements for the Yen, the Euro and the Pound against US Dollar. Beine et al. (2006) provided evidence of a temporary increase in exchange rate volatility after a coordinated Central Bank intervention. Going a step further, Popper and Montgomery (2001) assumed that Central Banks do not produce their own information, but rather pick up pieces of information from some specific informed traders. Morana and Beltratti (2000) confirmed the view that interventions are not particularly effective. They found that the Mark-Dollar exchange rate moved in the desired direction for only about 50% of the time and often with a substantial increase in volatility.

Emerging market countries intervene in the currency market very often to manipulate their respective exchange rates. The reasons behind this practice are multiple. One of them is the need to preserve their economies in time of transition towards a free market economy. Additionally, they aim to prevent possible adverse impact of speculative operations. There are also important goals of monetary policy like inflation targeting, maximising employment, maintaining sustainable balance sheet etc. Bank officials find it very important to limit volatility and/or to maintain the exchange rate within accepted margins. Measures undertaken by governments and Central Banks are focused on absorbing and managing shocks and "guiding" expansion of their developing countries. In particular, interventions on FOREX markets are usually spectacular and exciting for market participants. This comes as no surprise, since exchange rates have a proven impact on financial institutions in particular and on the economy as whole.

3.3 Cointegration and ARDL Applications in Finance and Exchange Rates

3.3.1 Cointegration in Finance

Several studies have used cointegration techniques to understand the behaviour of financial series. Cointegration is extremely popular in financial markets where asset prices and capital market series are thought to be cointegrated with each other either on the short or the long term. The popularity of cointegration techniques is motivated by the fact that forecasters are looking for methods to capture the fluctuations of series overtime. A simple analysis of historical data might not be enough to account for changes that dictate future behaviour. Rather, the use of historical data (only) had disastrous consequences where the seemingly linear data had jumped to unexpected highs and/or lows following fluctuations in a particular macroeconomic variable or a sudden change in a distant stock market. According to Alexander (1999), investment management strategies that are based only on volatility and correlation of returns cannot guarantee long term performance. She argued that hedging methodologies based on cointegrated financial assets maybe more effective in the long term since cointegration measures long-run co-movements, which may occur even when static correlations appear low. She also mentioned that an advantage of cointegration lies in the fact that it overcomes the problem of non-stationary data, since general cointegration requires the series to be integrated of the same order whereas most other methods need data to be stationary as a prerequisite.

Two decades ago, Koutmos and Booth (1995) found evidence that stock markets in France, Germany and the UK were cointegrated because they were affected not only by local news, but also by international news especially unfavourable 'bad news' emanating from other markets. This brings the old argument to the surface - that market shocks following bad news have a greater impact than market shocks following good news - a pattern otherwise known as asymmetric information effect. Recent cointegration studies in Finance include Ivanov (2010) who documented that the US, Canada and Mexico stock markets are cointegrated as a result of the North America Free Trade Agreement (NAFTA). The assumption was that the US market would dictate price changes in other NAFTA stock markets considering the large variety of instruments and the speed of innovation; instead, it was the Canadian stock market that assumed the role of leadership among other regional hubs. Erdinc and Milla (2009) tested the hypothesis of positive cointegration between stock markets studied by Koutmos and Booth (1995) - France, Germany and the UK - from 1991 to 2006. They argued that cointegration between capital markets might be attributed to the liberalisation of the financial sector which makes changes in one stock market systematically felt elsewhere. They concluded that capital markets all over the world have become increasingly integrated and co-movements among major financial markets have been rising which means that investing at the same time on a set of cointegrated markets, will not hedge the risk of investing for stakeholders. Both the studies by Erdinc and Milla (2009) and Koutmos and Booth (1995) came to the same conclusion, whilst studying different data frequency for the same panel of countries. Koutmos and Booth (1995) used monthly rather than daily series in his study. He argued that cointegration is a long-run property and hence large spans of data, rather than high data frequency, is essential to appropriately test for the existence of cointegration. That is, the high number of observations as a result of long time series grasps better the cointegration relation among capital market returns. The author of the of this manuscript agrees with this assumption and hence both exchange rates and macroeconomic data series are collected and analysed on a monthly basis over a period of 20 years. Other well-known cointegration studies include the study of bubbles in asset prices (Campbell and Shiller, 1987), the predictability of stock prices (Lettau and Ludvigson, 2001), the consumption-income relationship (Campbell, 1987), the role of productivity shocks in the post-war US economy (King et al. 1991), the demand for money (Johansen and Juselius, 1990), the term structure of interest rates (Hall et al. 1992) and the Purchasing Power Parity (Froot and Rogoff, 1995; Sarno and Taylor, 2002)

3.3.2 Applications of the ARDL model in Finance

The literature abounds with recent studies that examine various aspects of Finance using the ARDL method although few researchers have applied the method to examine exchange rates. This research aims to address the balance. In particular, researchers have investigated the assumption that there exists a relationship between the demand for money and macroeconomic variables via the ARDL method. Most of these papers are less than five years old which suggests that the potential to use the ARDL approach in international Finance forecasting is huge. The economic balance of power is shifting from west to east and research seems to follow suit in that an increasing number of studies are looking to investigate aspects of Finance in emerging markets. Recent ARDL studies in international Finance cover the BRIC's, Pakistan, the Gulf countries and a score of Southeast Asian and emerging economies. For example, Shahrestani and Sharifi-Renani (2008) estimated the demand for money in Iran using ARDL model. Their empirical results show that there is a unique cointegrated and stable long-run relationship between money supply (M1)[11], income, inflation and exchange rate. Tang (2007) investigated the presence of a long-run relationship of money demand function for five Southeast Asian countries. The results demonstrated that a long-run relationship exists between volume of money demanded and real income, exchange rates and inflation rates in Malaysia, Thailand, Singapore, the Philippines and Indonesia. More recently, AbuDalu and Almasaeid (2011) examined the demand for money in the same countries using an ARDL method. Their results confirmed those of Tang (2007) and showed that there is a stable long-run relationship between monetary aggregates, income, interest rates, exchange rates and inflation in the ASEAN-5 countries. Hassan and Al Refai (2012) tested for the long-run relationship between some key macroeconomic indicators and equity returns in Jordan. They used ARDL approach to cointegration and found that the trade surplus, FOREX reserves, the money supply and oil prices are important macroeconomic variables which have long-run effects on the Jordanian stock market. Their results were consistent with similar studies carried out for other emerging economies.

---

[11] Money currently in circulation and the money most likely to come into circulation in the shortest possible amount of time (Shahrestani and Sharifi-Renani, 2008)

Achsani (2010) demonstrated that the demand for real money aggregate (M2)[12] is also cointegrated with real income and interest rate in Indonesia. Real income has positive relationship with real money demand, both in the long-run and short-run. On the other hand, interest rates have a negative influence on money supply (M2) in the short-run, but have no statistically significant relationships in the long-run. The relationship between exchange rates and macroeconomic fundamentals in ASEAN countries are investigated in Chapter Five. A specific section on ASEAN findings is dedicated to the discussion of the results in which the author draws parallel with previous studies, particularly those of Tang (2007) and AbuDalu and Almasaeid (2011). Other studies have used ARDL cointegration techniques to examine long-run relationships between the demand for money and its determinants, for example, Halicioglu and Ugur (2005) for Turkey, Bahmani-Oskooee and Rehman (2005) for seven Asian countries, Akinlo (2006) for Nigeria, Samreth (2008) for Cambodia, Dara and Samreth (2008) for the Philippines, Baharumshah, et al. (2009) for China. A paper by Sbeiti and Al Shammari (2010) examined integration among the GCC (Golf Cooperation Council has six members namely, Bahrain, Oman, Saudi Arabia, Kuwait, Qatar and UAE) stock markets using the ARDL approach. Their results evidenced the existence of a long-run relationship among the six GCC stock indices. The study conducted by Dritsakis (2011) examined the demand for money in Hungary using the ARDL cointegration framework. The results confirm that a stable, long-run relationship exists between demand for money and its determinants: real income, inflation rate and nominal exchange rate.

ARDL models were also used by Konstantakopoulou and Tsionas (2001) who investigated the business cycles of Eurozone economies. Long-run estimated coefficients confirm the positive relationships between the business cycles of countries such as Germany with those of the Netherlands, Austria, Belgium, Greece and Ireland. Liow (2006) investigated the long-run and short term relationships between stock and property markets using ARDL cointegration procedure. A long-run contemporaneous relationship was found between the stock and property prices; the stock market prices were largely influenced by the office property prices in the long-run while the residential property prices impact is stronger on the stock market prices in the short term. Jalil et al. (2010) examined the finance-growth nexus in China using principal components analysis and ARDL bounds testing approach to cointegration. Their results suggest that financial development indeed fosters economic growth in China. They found that growth of the Chinese economy is, among other factors, driven by financial development. They argued that although China has been phenomenally successful in transitioning from a centrally-planned economy into a more market-oriented, trillion dollar economy, the country still faces some challenges such as rising urban unemployment, the inefficient state sector, large-scale rural-urban migration in reaction to a growing urban-rural income

---

[12] The European Central Bank defines M2 as the aggregation currency in circulation, overnight deposits, and deposits with maturities of up to two years and deposits redeemable with notice of up to three months (European Central Bank, 2010)

inequality and significant amounts of non-performing loans held by state-owned banks, to name a few.

The article by Jalil and Feridun (2011) investigated the impact of financial development, economic growth and energy consumption on environmental pollution in China from 1953 to 2006 using ARDL bounds testing procedure. The results of the analysis reveal a negative sign for the coefficient of financial development, suggesting that financial development in China has not taken place at the expense of environmental pollution. On the contrary, they found that financial development led to a decrease in environmental pollution. They concluded that carbon emissions are mainly determined by income, energy consumption and trade openness in the long run. Kollias et al. (2008) addressed the saving-investment (SI) correlation for the EU 15 member countries using the ARDL procedure and found no evidence to point to any particular direction in terms of country size, or level of development, or economic and capital market structure. They attributed their finding to higher capital mobility, lower transaction costs in the international capital markets, and the declining status of long-run current account targeting as a primary government objective. Enisan and Olufisayo (2009) examined the long-run and causal relationship between stock market development and economic growth for seven countries in sub-Saharan Africa. Using the ARDL bounds test, the study found that the stock market development is cointegrated with economic growth in Egypt and South Africa. They suggested that stock market development has a significant positive long-run impact on economic growth. Their paper argued that stock markets could help promote growth in Africa. However, to achieve this goal, African stock markets need to be further developed through appropriate regulatory and macroeconomic policies. Kontonikas (2010) tested the inflation-real marginal cost relationship using data for the United States over the period 1965–2009 using ARDL bounds approach. He found that higher marginal costs increase inflation. Their results support the existence of a long-run relationship between the two variables with higher marginal costs increasing inflation.

Hoque and Yusop (2010) examined the impact of trade liberalisation on the aggregate import in Bangladesh, using the ARDL bounds Test approach with annual time series data from 1972-1973 to 2004-2005. Empirical results suggested that trade liberalisation through reduction of the import duty rate increases the aggregate import substantially in the short-run, but insignificantly in the long-run. Higher income elasticity compared to price elasticity indicates that an effort to maintain imports at the desired level by increasing import duty could be counter balanced and ineffective. Rushdi et al. (2012) conducted an empirical investigation into the long-run relationship between real stock returns and inflation in Australia by employing the ARDL bounds tests. Their empirical results showed that the expected inflation had no significant effect on real stock returns, while the observed inflation had a significant and negative effect. Furthermore, the data generating process of the returns–inflation relationship was not affected by the change in monetary policy regime in the early 1990s. Their findings imply that Australian stocks have been very effective instruments for hedging against expected inflation. Because of the resilience of

Australian economy to the current global financial and economic crisis, their finding has implications for long term domestic and foreign investors in Australia. The next section reviews applications of ARDL models to FOREX studies.

3.3.3 Applications of ARDL to FOREX Studies

Since the seminal work of Meese and Rogoff (1983), who found that a range of exchange rate models was unable to outperform a random walk model, the role of economic fundamentals in real exchange rate determination has come under scrutiny. Fundamentals are believed to exert a more significant impact at longer horizons (greater than six months) although the identification of fundamentals remains problematic. Most studies that use ARDL models for exchange rate determination in developing countries are quite recent. The reason is simple. Emerging world countries adopted fixed exchange rate regimes in the past which meant that quantitative studies of their currencies would have yielded results of little relevance. Exchange rates did not respond to the traditional forces of the market but were rather manipulated by respective Central Banks. This trend had lost momentum during the last couple of years and a number of researchers have already used the ARDL cointegration method to investigate various areas that are of interest to learners and traders in the FOREX market. Chaudhary et al. (2012) investigated the effect of volatility of fourteen exchange rates on the FDI in Asian economies. Their sample was selected from south, southeast, east and west Asia. Their results show the existence of both long and short term relationships between exchange rate volatility and FDI in Pakistan, India, Sri Lanka, South Korea, Turkey and Israel. No relationship was found between these variables for Bangladesh, China, Malaysia, Indonesia, Thailand, Singapore and Iran. In almost half of the sampled countries, there is no relationship between these variables. They suggested that their study could be extended by adding more variables such as interest rate differentials, GDP growth, taxes and other macroeconomic variables, in addition to the volatility of exchange rates. This is something the current book aims to achieve specifically what Chapter Five is about – looking at an array of explanatory variables that account for exchange rate changes not only in Africa, but also in Asia, Central and Latin America. Variables such as GDP growth, gold reserves and capital account are tested under the assumption that they dictate changes to exchange rates in either the short-or-long-run or both.

Bahmani-Oskooee and Nasir (2004) examined the productivity bias hypothesis which states that a relatively more productive country should experience a real appreciation of its currency. They tested the hypothesis by using time-series data over the 1960-90 period for a sample of 44 countries using the ARDL approach and found that for most countries there is strong evidence supporting the hypothesis. Égert and Morales-Zumaquero (2008) analysed the direct impact of exchange rate volatility on the export performance of ten Central and Eastern European transition economies, as well as its indirect impact via changes in exchange rate regimes. The results suggested that the size and the direction of the impact of FOREX volatility and of regime changes on exports vary considerably across sectors and countries and those may be related to specific periods. Baharumshah et al. (2008) investigated the behaviour of real exchange rates of six East-Asian countries in relation to their two major trading partners – the United States and Japan. These countries, except Singapore, were affected by the financial crisis of 1997. Using monthly frequency data from 1976 to 2002 and the ARDL cointegration procedure they tested for the long-run PPP hypothesis, they found no evidence for the weak form of PPP in the pre-crisis period, but strong evidence in the post-crisis period. For the post-crisis period, we also find very small persistence of PPP deviations as indicated by very small half-lives (<7 months) and narrow confidence intervals with an upper bound of 1 year or less in most countries. Our findings reveal that the East Asian countries are returning to some form of PPP-oriented rule as a basis for their exchange rate policies. Tian and Ma (2010) employed the ARDL cointegration approach in order to examine the impact of financial liberalisation on the relationships between the exchange rate and share market performance in China. They discovered that cointegration has existed between the Shanghai Share Index and the exchange rate of the renminbi against the US dollar and Hong Kong dollar since 2005, when the Chinese exchange rate regime became a flexible, managed, floating system. They found that both the exchange rate and the money supply influenced stock price, with a positive correlation. They further showed that the money supply increase was largely caused by a huge 'hot money' inflow from other countries in recent years. After local currency appreciation, hot money, followed by the money supply increase, pushed the market into a high level, based on expectations regarding the local currency's further appreciation. Sekantsi (2011) empirically examined the impact of real exchange rate volatility on trade in the context of South Africa's exports to the U.S. for the South Africa's floating period January 1995-February 2007. In measuring real exchange rate volatility, his study utilised GARCH – same measure used in this book. After establishing the existence of cointegration among the variables involved in two-country export model, they estimated long-run coefficients by means of ARDL bounds testing procedure proposed by Pesaran, et al. (2001). His results indicate that real exchange rate volatility exerts a significant and negative impact on South Africa's exports to the U.S. He concluded that stable and competitive exchange rate and sound macroeconomic fundamentals were required in order to improve international competitiveness and greater penetration of South African exports to international markets. Saeed et al. (2012) examined the period of managed floating in Pakistan using monthly time series data from January 1982 to April 2010. They investigated the relationship between exchange rates and monetary variables (stock of money, FOREX reserves and total debt of Pakistan). Empirical results confirm that stock of money, debt and FOREX reserve balance are significant determinants of exchange rate between Pakistani Rupee and US Dollar. Furthermore, political instability negatively affects the value of the currency.

Lin (2011) investigated the co-movements between exchange rates and stock prices in six Asian emerging markets namely India, Indonesia, Korea, Philippines, Taiwan and Thailand via the ARDL method. Empirical results suggest that co-movements between exchange rates and stock prices are stronger during crisis periods, consistent with contagion or spillover between asset prices, when compared with quiet periods. Furthermore, most of the spillovers during crisis periods may act as shocks to the exchange rate, suggesting that governments should stimulate economic growth and stock markets to attract capital inflow, thereby preventing a currency crisis. However, analysis shows that the co-movements are not stronger for export-oriented industries for all periods thus implying that co-movements between exchange rates and stock prices in the Asian markets are generally driven by capital account balance rather than that of trade. The relationships between exchange rates and its determinants in this book were identified following a process during which the author had looked and tested various macroeconomic and monetary variables.

AbuDalu and Almasaied (2011) investigated the long-run and short-run variables that affect PPP for ASEAN-5 real exchange rates against the Euro. They used ARDL over the period 1991-2006. Their results suggested that the domestic money supply (M1) is the significant long and short-run forcing variable of PPP for ASEAN-5 exchange rates. The findings could have policy implications for the monetary authorities in Malaysia, Indonesia, Philippines, Thailand, and Singapore. They argued that the AFC caused the ASEAN-5 economies to become more sensitive to changes and fluctuations in the world economy - particularly the economy of Europe and the euro. Poon (2010) used quarterly data from 1980 to 2004 to assess the impact of monetary policy in ASEAN-5 founder countries economic performance. He used the ARDL method to estimate the relationship between real GDP and interest rates, exchange rates, corrected exchange rates and other macroeconomic variables namely real GDP and asset prices. The ARDL approach validates the existence of cointegration between the GDP and the exchange rate, both the long and short term interest rates and credit for Malaysia and Indonesia. In Thailand, application of the ARDL method revealed evidence of cointegration between the real GDP and interest rates, exchange rates and share prices plus a cointegration between interest rates, the exchange rates and the asset prices in the Philippines. Specifically, Indonesia currency is affected by the long term interest rate, exchange rates and asset prices. Malaysia and Singapore are significantly influenced by interest rates and exchange rates. The Thai baht is influenced by the interest rate, exchange rate and the asset price channels; while the Philippines is affected by the interest rate, exchange rate, credit, and asset price channels.

Adeneyi et al. (2011) established that a cointegration relationship exists between trade balance, real effective exchange rate and domestic income in Ghana, Gambia, Nigeria and Sierra Leone based on quarterly data from 1970 to 2007 using ARDL approach while Tehranchian and Behravesh (2011) provided evidence of a long-run relationship between exchange rates, money demand, GDP, inflation rates and interest rates in Iran. He found that GDP has the greatest effect on the country's money demand so that depending on the intensity and stability of other factors, any increase of one percent in GDP will averagely increase the money demand by 3.26 percent. Umar (2010) argued that there is evidence of long-run relationship between demand for FOREX and marginal rate of the Nigerian naira. Tian and Ma (2009) employed the ARDL approach to examine the impact of financial liberalisation on the relationships between three Chinese main bilateral exchange rates and its share market performance. They discovered that a long term relationship established by cointegration has emerged between the exchange rate of the Rembini against the Japanese Yen and, to a lesser extent, the exchange rate against both the US dollar, Hong Kong dollar and the Shanghai Composite Index since 2005. They documented that after local currency appreciation, 'hot money' flowing from foreign funds into the local markets followed by local investors' speculations on markets pushed the market into a high level based on the expectation of the local currency's further appreciation. Dara (2008) examined the validity of both the short-run and long-run PPP hypotheses in Japan using ARDL test. Quarterly data from 1970 to 2006 was extracted from the IFS database and used for the analysis. Results showed a strongly robust long-run PPP relationship but no significant short-run relationship. Overall, the results suggest that PPP hypothesis in Japan strongly holds for the long-run.

Adebeyi (2007) investigated the impact of FOREX intervention by the Central Bank of Nigeria on the exchange market using an ARDL modelling approach. The variables used include cumulative net foreign assets, cumulative aid, broad money supply and GDP. Quarterly time series data spanning from 1986 to 2003 were used and the overall finding was that there is a relationship between FOREX intervention in Nigeria and the cumulative aid, which constitute part of FOREX inflows and net foreign assets. Azali et al. (2007) investigated the long-run real convergence in GDP per capita growth involving Malaysia, Thailand, Singapore, Indonesia, and the Philippines, over the period from 1978 to 2004. The results indicated that the exchange rate and surplus ratio show a positive relationship with the GDP per capita. The authors concluded from the findings that the ASEAN-5 countries have fulfilled the Maastricht Criteria except for Singapore's exchange rate and Indonesia's debt ratio. Hence, those ASEAN-5 countries have potential to form a single currency.

Morley (2007) examined the relationship between the stock market index and exchange rates. The dynamic results suggest that in the short-run stock prices significantly affect the exchange rate for the UK sterling against the US dollar. These results support those of other studies that indicate that in the short and long-run equities are an important determinant of the exchange rate in developed countries. Aguirre et al. (2007) investigated the possible existence of a long term relationship between Brazilian manufactured exports, on the one hand and the real effective exchange rate and its volatility, the rate of capacity utilisation in the domestic industry and the level of world imports, on the other hand. They found that, in addition to the other explanatory variables in the model, exchange rate volatility significantly affected Brazilian manufactured exports in the period from 1986 to 2002.

Bahmani-Oskooee and Goswami (2004) investigated the impact of exchange rates movement on Japan's bilateral trade flows with its nine major trading partners that include Australia, Canada, France, Germany, Italy, the Netherlands, Switzerland, the UK and the US. Their results revealed that when trade flows are measured in terms of foreign or reserve currency, Japan's exports are not sensitive to real exchange rates. This indicates that the impact of exchange rate changes on trade balance is either vague or ambiguous in advanced economies. Over the 1987-2001 period, De Vita and Abbott's (2004) examined the impact of exchange rate volatility on US exports in relation to its five major trading partners (Canada, Mexico, Japan, the UK and Germany) by means of ARDL. They used real export volume as the dependent variable in respect of relative price, foreign income and of volatility. The ARDL method pointed to the existence of a unique cointegrating relationship among export volume, relative price, foreign income and real exchange rate volatility. They found that in most cases, export volume is significantly affected by volatility, although the sign and magnitude of this effect varies across markets. A study by Coakley and Fuertes (2001) addressed real exchange rate adjustment for 18 OECD economies 1973-1998. They tested for real exchange rate mean reversion by allowing for nonlinearities in the data generating process. They found significant nonlinearities in real exchange rate adjustment to PPP. Bahmani-Oskooee and Alse (1994) employed the Engle and Granger (1987) cointegration method on data from 41 countries and found that the effect of currency depreciation on the trade balance was positive for Brazil, Costa Rica and Turkey with a negative effect in the case of Ireland. For the remaining 37 countries, this effect was found to be nil.

3.4 Combination Forecasting Applications in Finance and FOREX Studies

3.4.1 Overview of Combination Forecasting

More than twenty years have passed since Clemen (1989, 567) wrote his seminal paper on combining forecasts. He reviewed 207 references and wrote in conclusion: "Combining forecasts has been shown to be practical, economical and useful. Underlying theory has been developed and many empirical tests have demonstrated the value of composite forecasting. We no longer need to justify this methodology; we need to find ways to make the implementation of the technique easy and efficient". He added that combining forecasts should become part of the mainstream of forecasting practice and that practitioners should be encouraged to combine forecasts and that software designed to produce combined forecasts could easily be developed. According to Clemen (1989), there is a consensus among researchers that combining forecasts produces more accurate results than single model forecasts. The forecast method matters less since it has been proved that even just averaging out single forecasts enabled researchers to reduce the sum of squared errors. Armstrong (1989) described Clemen's work on combining forecasts as a milestone in the topic. He stated that combined forecasts produce consistent but modest gains in accuracy. He argued that existing research does not well define the conditions under neither which combining is most effective nor how methods should be combined in each situation. He suggested that future research should attempt to answer the following questions:

- Under what conditions is combining most useful?
- What methods should be used to select the component forecasts?
- Is the simple average the best way to combine forecasts in all situations?
- To what extent can accuracy be increased by combining forecasts?

Several studies have found that both human judgment and statistical methods have been valuable and complementary to the forecasting process. A study by Lim and O'Connor (1995) found that forecasters tend to under-weigh statistical forecasts in favour of their own judgments. Maines (1996) examined how individuals subjectively form combined models using forecasts obtained from experts. His results suggest that subjectively combined forecasts are likely to differ from those based on theoretical forecast combination models. Hibon and Evgeniou (2005) conducted the M3-competition where they compared the performance of combination and single models. Their results indicated that it is less risky to combine forecasts than to select an individual forecasting model. Their work puts into perspective the fact that combination can be a solution for researchers who have little or no knowledge of the best single method to use. This statement is perfectly applicable to the present research giving the fact that it examines exchange rates in regions that have never been investigated before due to various factors, which means that there is little or no information of the best model to use as a benchmark for exchange rate forecasts. This is particularly true in Central America and many parts of sub-Saharan Africa although it is applicable to most under-developed countries. The work is still embryonic in respect of emerging markets where research is yet to disentangle its novel character. Combination forecasting has been used in various disciplines and proved to be accurate in many occasions. Shen et al. (2011) examined the performance of combination forecasts in the context of international tourism demand. Their results suggest that combination forecasts, in general, outperform the best individual forecasts. They argued that combined forecasts improve accuracy when compared with single models and the former are particularly useful when the forecaster is uncertain about which approach/method to use. Assenmacher-Wesche and Pesaran (2008) combined results from different long-run structural models to forecast Switzerland's real GDP, real money stock, inflation, three-month interest rate and the ratio of domestic to foreign prices. They found that forecast averaging tends to improve forecasting performance and provides a hedge against poor forecast outcomes. Fullerton's (1989) paper examined the effectiveness of composite forecasting of sales tax revenues in Idaho. Projections were provided by an econometric model and a univariate time series model. The composite forecasts were found to outperform both base line forecasts. Combined forecasts were also found to be more accurate than the executive branch forecasts actually utilised from

1982 through 1985. A combination of projections provided by an econometric model and a univariate time series model was superior to a single model Autoregressive Integrated Moving Averages (ARIMA) forecast in predicting tax revenues. Hibon and Evgeniou (2005) conducted empirical research which concluded that managers and researchers should treat statements of the type "combined forecasts are better" with some caution. The best combinations are, on average across series, no better than the best individual forecasts. This is to say that if the researcher has a previous knowledge of the exchange rate he intends to forecast, it belongs to him to decide whether to combine or not based on his past experience. In fact, Hibon and Evgeniou (2005) and Larrick and Soll (2006) showed that under some conditions, it is better not to combine forecasts of experts. Diebold and Lopez (1996) argued that the attractiveness of combined forecasts breeds from the fact that various types of forecasts, such as probability forecasts and volatility forecasts, are becoming more integrated into economic and financial decision making, leading to a derived demand for new types of forecast evaluation procedures. Dunis et al. (2001) showed that a non-parametric model outperforms others in forecasting volatilities, while the performance of a combination of these models gives superior results. Fang (2003) found that combined forecasts often lead to increased forecast accuracy, defined as a smaller root mean squared error (RMSE) than any of the individual model forecasts.

3.4.2 Combination Forecasting in Finance

Combination forecasting in Finance is set to become popular because of the need for new methods which incorporate various market elements that influence financial time series. Andrawis et al. (2011, 686) used combination methods to forecast 111 time series representing daily cash withdrawal amounts at ATM machines in various cities in the UK (known as the NN5 competition). They found that the combination aspect was "one of the most significant" because of the careful and principled selection of the individual forecasting models in their research. Bjørnland et al. (2010) developed a system that provided model-based forecasts for inflation in Norway. Using a weighting average method, they combined various time series and econometric models and established that combination forecasts improve upon the point forecasts derived from individual models. Furthermore, combination forecasts outperformed Norges Bank's own point forecast for inflation. They showed that there are clear advantages to averaging forecasts from several individual models when predicting inflation in the short term (up to a year). Rapach et al. (2010) recommended combining individual forecasts to predict equity premiums. They argued that the strength of combination methods stems from the fact that they incorporate information from numerous economic variables while reducing forecast volatility. Guidolin and Timmermann (2009) developed a flexible approach to combining forecasts of future spot interest rates with forecasts from time series models or macroeconomic variables. They found empirical evidence that accounting for both regimes in interest rate dynamics and combining forecasts from different models help improve the out-of-sample forecasting performance for US short term interest rates. Becker and Clements

(2008) considered whether combination forecasts of S&P 500 volatility are statistically superior to a wide range of individual model-based forecasts and implied volatility. They found that a combination of model-based forecasts is the dominant approach.

Kapetanios et al. (2008) evaluated the Bank of England suite of statistical forecasting models - a combination of a small number of forecasts generated using different sources of information and methodologies - which provides judgment-free statistical forecasts of inflation and output growth in Britain. The forecasts were evaluated over the period of Bank independence (1997 Q2 to 2005 Q1) by the mean square error criterion. Forecast combinations generally led to a reduction in forecast errors, although over this period, some of the benchmarks models were hard to beat. Terregrossa (1999) found that combining financial analysts' consensus forecasts with capital asset pricing model simulated ex-ante forecasts consistently leads to superior forecasts of five-year earnings-per-share growth rates. The reader can sense that applications of combination forecasting in Finance are relatively recent and focus mainly on advanced countries. One cannot deny that combination is yet to be the first choice of forecasters in Economics and Finance. The author of this book believes that the current turmoil and uncertainty in financial markets makes the need for an alternative to existing methods more of a priority.

3.4.3 Combination Forecasting Applications in FOREX Studies

Combination forecasting is a relatively new area in FOREX studies. The first paper to discuss the topic was written by MacDonald and Marsh (1994) who examined whether individual forecasts produce efficient exchange rate predictions when they are combined. They used a database of disaggregate exchange rate forecasts, gathered from over one hundred institutions in the leading financial centres around the world. They combined nineteen forecasts for the Deutsche Mark, Pound sterling and Japanese Yen and found that the average forecast is frequently as accurate as the optimal combinations. Furthermore, they argued that combining large numbers of forecasts tends to give poor results and that updating weights as new information becomes available generally reduces errors whereas using only the most recent observations in calculations appears to be detrimental. Finally, they found that combining the forecasts produced very accurate results for the yen but the method was outperformed by the random walk model in the forecast of the sterling and the Deutsche Mark. More recently, Shahriari (2011) examined the performance of Regression, Naïve1 and an ARIMA model in forecasting the exchange rate of the Iranian Rial against the British Pound. He compared single models with two-way combination models and concluded that the forecasts generated from the latter fared better than any single model forecast. Altavilla and De Grauwe (2010) investigated the out-of-sample forecasting performance of a set of competing models of exchange rate determination. They found that combining competing models of exchange rate forecasts reflecting the relative ability that each model has over different sub-samples leads to more accurate forecasts. They argued that combining individual forecasts typically achieves the best performance among all the competing forecasts. Overall, their empirical results suggest that the relative success of competing models of exchange rate forecasting mostly depends on how quickly changes in macroeconomic fundamentals affect exchange rates.

Maté (2011) suggested that combining forecasts is an adequate methodology to optimise the use of the various popular forecasting methods in a multivariate analysis. He argued that every forecasting method has its own advantages and bringing the methods together will provide more accurate forecasts. Fernandez-Rodriguez and Sosvilla-Rivero (1997) proposed a model that combines information from different sources in order to forecast exchange rates in selected European countries. They apply their model to nine European Monetary System (EMS) currencies, using daily data for the January 1973-December 1994 period. Their results suggest that the local predictors perform marginally better than a random walk model in forecasting the nominal exchange rate. They suggested that the forecasting accuracy of local predictors can be improved by using its multivariate version that considers further relevant information contained in other related exchange rates series.

Benavides and Capistran (2009) provided empirical evidence that combinations of option-implied and time series volatility forecasts are statistically superior to individual models. They applied combination methods to volatility forecasts of the Mexican Peso-US Dollar daily spot exchange rates. They used a sample period of 2499 observations from January 2nd, 1998 to December 31st, 2007 and found that the best forecast overall is obtained when one volatility-type forecast and one forecast from the implied options are combined using time-varying weights. Corte et al. (2007) implemented Bayesian methods for estimation and ranking of a set of empirical exchange rate models and constructed combined forecasts based on Bayesian model averaging. They found that strategies based on combined forecasts yield large economic gains over the random walk benchmark.

3.5 Conclusion

This chapter reviewed the applications related to Volatility, ARDL-cointegration and Combination methods. The rationale behind it was to provide the reader with the background against which this book is to be assessed. In addition, it lays out the empirical basis on which the coming chapters build on. In fact, Chapter Four examines exchange rate volatility in the regional settings selected for this book while Chapter Five uses macroeconomic determinants of exchange rates to forecast its value in the future. Chapter Six combines the findings of both Chapter Four and Five to generate a new set of forecasts based on two, three and four-way models. Before moving on to discussing the findings in the coming chapters, there is an important aspect that this chapter has covered. The reader can sense that there is paucity in both ARDL and Combination studies peculiar to exchange rates in the emerging markets and in particular in sub-Saharan Africa, Central and Latin

America. This book aims to fill this gap in the literature and the author deeply believes that the findings of this research will be extensively used in the future as an exploratory work that will guide those interested in learning more about the exchange rate dynamics of a rather forgotten regions of the world.

Chapter IV. Times Series Forecasting

Although volatility has been a recurrent theme in the FOREX market for the past decade, studies examining exchange rates in the emerging world tend to examine single countries rather than regional markets. This chapter aims to fill this gap in the literature – exchange rate volatilities of more than 30 emerging nations are examined from a regional perspective namely in Asia, Africa, Central and Latin America. Chapter three discussed various reasons for researching exchange rate volatility especially in developing countries. In this chapter, formal statistical tests and computation that led to the generation of volatility models are presented. Sections 4.1, 4.2 and 4.3 review the theory that underpins time series models (Volatility, exponential smoothing and Naïve) used in this research followed by a discussion of the results of applying these techniques to the forecasting of exchange rates in selected common markets. Parameter stability test are reported in Section 4.4. Section 4.5 summarises the findings from a regional perspective while Section 4.6 concludes.

4.1 Volatility Models

Since the international stock market crash in 1987 and until the latest financial crisis (2007-2008) which underpins many summits in Europe and around the globe, the focus of regulators, practitioners and researchers has been increasingly upon volatility. Volatility forecasts have many practical applications such as in the analysis of market timing decisions and portfolio selection as well as the pricing of primary and derivative assets. The major issue of any study about the effect of exchange rate volatility is to specify an appropriate measure for it. While most researchers agree that volatility is predictable in many asset markets (see survey by Bollerslev et al. (1992)), they differ as to how the prediction of volatility should be modelled. Previous research has in general tended to use measures of volatility which quantified either the range of observations or the degree of dispersion of the observations around a mean. This is to say that the simplest model for volatility was an historical estimate which involves calculating the variance (or standard deviation) of returns over some historical period and this then becomes the volatility forecast for all future periods. The variance or standard deviation of the observations was used in studies by Akhtar and Spence-Hilton (1984), Gotur (1985), Kenen and Rodrick (1986), Koray and Lastrapes (1989), Bini-Smaghi (1991) and Cushman (1983, 1988). Hooper and Kohlhagen (1978) used both a variance measure and the average absolute difference between the previous forward exchange rate and the spot exchange rate. Recent volatility models are based on influential papers by Engle (1982) and Bollerslev (1986) which were motivated by the observation that volatility in financial markets tends to occur in clusters; large returns (of either sign) are expected to follow large returns and small returns (of either sign) tend to follow small returns. Engle (1982) introduced a volatility model that explicitly recognises the difference between the unconditional and the conditional variance allowing the latter to change over time as a function of past errors. Bollerslev et al. (1992) indicated that financial time series are typically heteroscedastic[13], leptokurtic[14] and exhibit volatility clustering. They suggested that these features may be handled by modelling the volatility in financial time series as conditional on past behaviour.

An important feature in the study of volatility is the "asymmetric" or "leverage" volatility model, in which good and bad news have different impacts on the degree of volatility present. The model is motivated by the empirical works of Christie (1982), French et al. (1987), Nelson (1990), Schwert (1990) and Kim and Kon (1994)). When applied to the FOREX market, a shock, which increases the volatility of the market, increases the risk of holding the currency. This induces a portfolio shift out of the currency, leading to a depreciation of the exchange rate. While asymmetry has been found in stock returns, there is very little evidence that it exists in FOREX returns. This could be due to the fact that such studies generally focus on highly developed markets. In the case of emerging markets, adverse shocks can have more persistent effects than positive shocks, an assumption that is to be examined in this chapter.

4.1.1 The Mean Equation: Theory and Results

The derivation of mean equation is the precursor to developing volatility models. Brooks (2008) describes univariate time series models as formal tools for modelling and predicting financial data sets which utilise only their historical values and error terms. Univariate models are designed to capture realised empirical features of the data, without reference to explanatory variables, although they need data to be transformed before application as data must be stationary. Stationarity of data set is defined as a statistical equilibrium, where the distribution of the variable does not differ or differ insignificantly over time and is characterised by the following properties:

1. **No trend** - a trend is any general tendency of data to move up or down. There are several formal tests for the trend in variables. This study used the Augmented Dickey-Fuller (ADF t) test and the Phillips-Perron test (PP t); both were used to examine whether data is trend stationary. Test statistics results are reported in Tables 4.1, 4.2, 4.3 and 4.4 of this Section.

[13] Heteroscedastic is an adjective describing a data sample or data-generating process in which the errors are drawn from different distributions for different values of the independent variables; In statistics, it is as measure that refers to the variance of the errors in the sample. Most financial instruments, such as stocks, follow a heteroscedastic error pattern [www.investopedia.com, accessed on May 1st, 2010]

[14] Leptokurtic distributions have higher peaks around the mean compared to normal distributions, which leads to thick tails on both sides. These peaks result from the data being highly concentrated around the mean, due to lower variations within observations [www.investopedia.com, accessed on May 1st, 2010]

2. **No seasonality** - Seasonality occurs when systematic peaks and troughs are observed during the year. There is very little evidence to suggest that the exchange rates examined in this book show a seasonal pattern.
3. **Homoscedasticity** - means that data should possess a relatively constant spread over time. In this research, all data sets were examined graphically and natural logarithms (logs) were calculated when needed to reduce the spread. In sum, a stationary process has a constant mean, a constant variance and a constant auto-covariance.

The Auto Regressive Integrated Moving Average (ARIMA) model is used in this research to generate mean equations that model exchange rate behaviour. The model was introduced by Box and Jenkins (1976). It consists of extracting predictable movements from the observed data through a series of iterations. An ARIMA model can be represented as follows:

$$Z_t = \mu + \emptyset_1 Z_{t-1} + \emptyset_2 Z_{t-2} + \cdots - \theta_1 e_{t-1} - \theta_2 e_{t-2} - \ldots + e_t \quad (4.1)$$

Where Z_t, Z_{t-1} are stationary data points; e_t, e_{t-1} are present and past forecast errors and $\mu, \emptyset_1, \emptyset_2 \ldots, \theta_1, \theta_2 \ldots$ are parameters of the model to be estimated. When differencing has been used to achieve stationarity the model is said to be integrated and is written as ARIMA (p,d,q). The values of p and q represent the orders of the autoregressive (AR) and moving average (MA) terms respectively. The d parameter is the number of times that the series had to be differenced before stationarity was achieved. Autocorrelation Function (ACF) and Partial Autocorrelation Function (PACF) plots were generated to identify which order of MA and AR processes should be considered respectively in an initial ARIMA model. The ACF measures the relationship between an observation and its lags in a time series while the PACF presents a measure of correlation between the value of variable observed k periods earlier and the most recent observation, when the impact of the observations lying in between (for lags< k, i.e.: $(y_{t-k+1}, y_{t-k+2}, \ldots, y_{t-1})$) is controlled (Brooks, 2008). Tables 4.1, 4.2, 4.3 and 4.4 provide fitted ARIMA models of exchange rates from 1990 to 2007 (forecasts are generated from January 2008 to December 2009) for the four regions namely ASEAN, CACM, MERCOSUR and SADC. The parentheses in the (p,d,q)(P,D,Q) notation represent the respective orders of non-seasonal and seasonal parameters respectively. One would expect the exchange rate usually not to follow a seasonal pattern since 98% of the transactions in the FOREX market are purely speculative (Valdez and Molyneux, 2013). Overall, this is true in this study although seasonal parameters were required to model the data in Malaysia, Guatemala, Nicaragua and Mauritius. These currencies are affected by seasonal patterns, probably because of the importance of their tourism sector (Mauritius and Malaysia) and the reliance on remittances from citizens' overseas (Guatemala and Nicaragua) both of which are naturally seasonal. As indicated, data for some exchange rates required natural logarithms (logs) to be taken in order to reduce the variation. The choice of an ARIMA model for the data is based on it being parsimonious, having significant parameters, errors that are white noise and minimum Schwarz Bayesian Criterion (Schwarz, 1978). Brooks (2008) described the white noise process of variable as one with the stochastic structure. A white noise process is characterised by constant mean and variance, with auto-covariance equivalent to zero. This property - that each model residual is not correlated with any other one over time in the data set - is crucial for the linear time series analysis.

Table 4.1 ASEAN exchange rates: mean equations

Brunei Dollar	**AR(5)**	**MA(5)**		
ARIMA (5,1,5)(0,0,0)	0.892	0.857		
t-statistic	4.220	3.536		
Significance	0.000	0.000		
	PP t =	ADF t=		
	-17.275(0.000)	-15.755(0.000)		
Cambodia Riel	**Constant**	**AR(1)**	**AR(2)**	
ARIMA (2,1,0)(0,0,0)	27.727	0.276	-0.290	
t-statistic	2.293	4.200	-4.421	
Significance	0.023	0.000	0.000	
	PP t =	ADF t=		
	-12.098(0.000)	-12.278(0.000)		
Indonesia Rupiah (logs)	**AR(8)**	**MA(5)**	**MA(9)**	
ARIMA (8,1,9)(0,0,0)	0.208	-0.408	0.241	
t-statistic	3.096	-6.662	3.933	
Significance	0.002	0.000	0.000	
	PP t =	ADF t=		
	-15.319(0.000)	-12.291(0.000)		
Laos Kip (logs)	**AR(2)**	**MA(2)**		
ARIMA (2,1,2)(0,0,0)	0.905	0.766		
t-statistic	15.190	8.384		
Significance	0.000	0.000		
	PP t =	ADF t=		
	-14.823(0.000)	-8.462(0.000)		
Malaysia Ringgit (logs)	**AR(1)**	**MA(1)**	**SAR(1)**	**SMA(1)**
ARIMA (1,1,1)(1,0,1)	-0.837	-0.952	0.984	0.964
t-statistic	-11.887	-22.779	3.736	2.577
Significance	0.000	0.000	0.000	0.011
	PP t =	ADF t=		
	-16.465(0.000)	-15.460(0.000)		

Table 4.1 (Cont'd) ASEAN exchange rates

Philippine Peso	AR(4)	MA(4)
ARIMA (4,1,4)(0,0,0)	-0.781	-0.857
t-statistic	-8.640	-11.610
Significance	0.000	0.000
	PP t =	ADF t=
	-14.396(0.000)	-13.415(0.000)
Singapore Dollar	**AR(7)**	**MA(7)**
ARIMA (7,1,7)(0,0,0)	-0.296	-0.547
t-statistic	-3.052	-5.844
Significance	0.003	0.000
	PP t =	ADF t=
	-2.040(0.000)	-15.664(0.000)
Thailand Baht	**MA(2)**	
ARIMA (0,1,2)(0,0,0)	0.196	
t-statistic	2.919	
Significance	0.004	
	PP t =	ADF t=
	-14.097(0.000)	-11.688(0.000)
Vietnam Dong	**Constant**	**MA(11)**
ARIMA	93.397	-0.311
(0,1,11)(0,0,0)	2.805	-4.673
t-statistic	0.005	0.000
Significance	PP t =	ADF t=
	-12.639(0.000)	-12.639(0.000)

According to Table 4.1, the exchange rates of Brunei, Indonesia, Philippines, Singapore and Vietnam require ARIMA equations with high number of lags. A common characteristic of these countries is that they were impacted by the AFC in 1997 which affected their economies and exchange rates alike. It shows also the importance of past data (up to a year) in dictating the nature of changes of the exchange rate behaviour. It also outlines the importance of the regional aspect in that countries located in the same geographical area have reacted in an almost concerted (and fatal) way to the shocks that hit the exchange rate market following speculators' attacks on their currencies. The story is slightly different in the CACM region (Table 4.2), since ARIMA with small lags was deemed enough to model exchange rate behaviour (except in Nicaragua).

For countries like Costa Rica, Dominican Republic, Guatemala and Honduras an ARIMA mean equation with up to two lags was deemed enough to model the exchange rates overtime. Other countries in Central America include

Belize, El Salvador which have their currencies pegged to the US $ while Panama use the US $ as its official currency. Nonetheless, what has been said about ASEAN currencies might be valid for MERCOSUR's Brazil, Chile and Venezuela for which their exchange rates were optimally modelled by particularly high lagged ARIMA's (see Table 4.3).

Table 4.2 CACM exchange rates: mean equations

Costa Rica Colon (logs)	**Constant**	**MA(1)**	
ARIMA (0,1,1)(0,0,0)	0.009	-0.191	
t-statistic	7.222	-2.818	
Significance	0.000	0.005	
	PP t = -11.939(0.000)	ADF t= -11.827(0.000)	
Dominican Peso (logs)	**AR(1)**	**AR(2)**	**MA(1)**
ARIMA (2,1,1)(0,0,0)	0.676	-0.178	0.707
t-statistic	4.987	2.464	5.496
Significance	0.000	0.140	0.000
	PP t = -15.674(0.000)	ADF t= -15.573(0.000)	
Guatemala Quetzal	**SAR(1)**	**SMA(1)**	
ARIMA (0,1,0)(1,0,1)	0.977	0.922	
t-statistic	19.114	8.781	
Significance	0.000	0.000	
	PP t = -12.777(0.000)	ADF t= -12.777(0.000)	
Honduras Lempira (logs)	**Constant**	**MA(1)**	
ARIMA (0,1,1)(0,0,0)	0.012	0.406	
t-statistic	2.835	6.377	
Significance	0.005	0.000	
	PP t = -15.239(0.000)	ADF t=-15.277	
Nicaragua Cordoba (logs)	**MA(1)**	**MA(9)**	**SMA(1)**
ARIMA (0,2,9)(0,0,1)	0.735	-0.177	0.373
t-statistic	16.392	-3.826	5.521
Significance	0.000	0.000	0.000
	PP t = -13.623(0.000)	ADF t= -13.619(0.000)	

Latin America was shaken in 2001 following the failure of Argentina to honour its US $80 billion debts it owed to the IMF – discussed in Chapter One. The default of Argentina spread panic not only in neighbouring countries but also in the rest of the emerging world as the confidence of international investors was shaken which made them decide to pull out indiscriminately from various regions as they feared a repetition of the Argentinean scenario. The latest remark brings to the fore the debate about countries at the same stages of development sharing similarities in the way their exchange rates behave following a shock to the system. Table 4.4 reports mean equations for Africa's SADC. ARIMA's with small number of lags typified historical patterns of exchange rates in the majority of the SADC countries. Needless to say that this presents a stark difference in comparison with ASEAN and MERCOSUR since many of the African countries examined in this chapter seem to be at a different stage of development; this is to say that although Africa's SADC suffered no financial crisis of its own, the region was plagued with bloody conflicts for many years. Violent conflict in sub-Saharan Africa led to the deaths of millions of civilians and contributed significantly to the low levels of human security in the region. The countries of sub-Saharan Africa that were embroiled in violent conflict are characterised by abject poverty, political instability, retarded economic growth and other challenges to overall development (Bowd and Chikwanha, 2010).

Table 4.3 MERCOSUR exchange rates: mean equations

Bolivia Boliviano (logs)	**Constant**	**MA(1)**
ARIMA (0,1,1)(0,0,0)	0.005	-0.440
t-statistic	4.417	-2.121
Significance	0.000	0.035
	PP t = -12.888(0.000)	ADF t= -12.869(0.000)
Brazil Real	**AR(7)**	
ARIMA (7,1,0)(0,0,0)	-0.174	
t-statistic	-2.100	
Significance	0.038	
	PP t = -15.431(0.000)	ADF t=-13.413
Chile Peso	**AR(11)**	
ARIMA (11,1,0)(0,0,0)	0.228	
t-statistic	3.378	
Significance	0.001	
	PP t = -12.865(0.000)	ADF t= -12.923(0.000)

Table 4.3 *(Cont'd)* MERCOSUR exchange rates

Colombia Peso (logs)	**Constant**	**MA(1)**	
ARIMA (0,1,1)(0,0,0)	0.008	-0.206	
t-statistic	3.200	-3.034	
Significance	0.002	0.003	
	PP t = -13.344(0.000)	ADF t= -12.339(0.000)	
Paraguay Guarani (logs)	**Constant**	**AR(1)**	
ARIMA (1,1,0)(0,0,0)	0.007	0.253	
t-statistic	2.920	3.816	
Significance	0.004	0.000	
	PP t = -10.989(0.000)	ADF t= -10.838(0.000)	
Peru New Sol (logs)	**AR (2)**	**MA (2)**	
ARIMA (2,1,2)(0,0,0)	0.862	-0.156	
t-statistic	68.058	-2.390	
Significance	0.000	0.018	
	PP t = -4.839(0.000)	ADF t= -4.407(0.000)	
Uruguay Peso (logs)	**AR(1)**	**AR(2)**	**MA(1)**
ARIMA (2,1,1)(0,0,0)	1.277	-0.285	0.909
t-statistic	15.370	-3.588	21.403
Significance	0.000	0.000	0.000
	PP t = -11.131(0.000)	ADF t= -10.092(0.000)	
Venezuela Bolivar (logs)	**Constant**	**AR(4)**	**MA(1)**
ARIMA (4,1,1)(0,0,0)	0.017	0.205	0.139
t-statistic	3.302	3.207	2.145
Significance	0.001	0.002	0.033
	PP t = -16.868(0.000)	ADF t= -13.166(0.000)	

4.1.2 The Volatility Equations

Volatility modelling employs a variance equation which is based on the residuals derived from the mean equations. In his seminal work, Engle (1982) introduced the term 'conditional' variance of the error term, denoted by σ_t^2. Conditional variance means that σ_t^2 is estimated given information about the errors in previous time periods. Engle (1982) characterised the changing variance using the Autoregressive Conditional Heteroscedasticity (ARCH) model and its extensions. Since then, many researchers have applied these models to financial time series and a voluminous literature has emerged for modelling the temporal dependencies in financial market volatility (Bollerslev et al. 1992). The ARCH-type of models were designed to capture the effect of clusters in the volatility of asset returns.

Table 4.4 SADC exchange rates: mean equations

Angola Kwanza (sqrt)	Constant	AR(1)	AR(2)
ARIMA (2,1,0)(0,0,0)	0.072	0.385	0.185
t-statistic	3.097	4.715	2.266
Significance	0.002	0.000	0.025
	PP t = -14.629(0.000)	ADF t= -11.636(0.000)	
Botswana Pula (logs)	**Constant**	**MA(2)**	
ARIMA (0,1,2)(0,0,0)	0.006	-0.158	
t-statistic	3.050	-2.320	
Significance	0.003	0.021	
	PP t = -16.148(0.000)	ADF t=-15.664	
DRC Franc (logs)	**AR(2)**	**MA(2)**	
ARIMA (2,1,2)(0,0,0)	0.984	0.940	
t-statistic	47.074	20.004	
Significance	0.000	0.000	
	PP t = -12.016(0.000)	ADF t= -12.016(0.000)	
Madagascar Ariary	**MA(2)**		
ARIMA (0,1,2)(0,0,0)	-0.255		
t-statistic	-4.051		
Significance	0.000		
	PP t = -14.483(0.000)	ADF t= -6.890(0.000)	
Malawi Kwacha (sqrt)	**Constant**	**AR(1)**	
ARIMA (1,1,0)(0,0,0)	0.060	2.252	
t-statistic	3.853	3.799	
Significance	0.000	0.000	
	PP t =- 12.131(0.000)	ADF t=- 10.753(0.000)	

Table 4.4 *(Cont'd)* SADC exchange rates

Mauritius Rupee (logs)	**Constant**	**SAR(1)**	**SMA(1)**
ARIMA (0,1,0)(1,0,1)	0.004	-0.840	-0.760
t-statistic	3.146	-3.538	-2.730
Significance	0.002	0.000	0.007
	PP t = -17.760(0.000)	ADF t= -14.460(0.000)	
Mozambique Metical (logs)	**AR(1)**	**MA(1)**	**MA(2)**
ARIMA (1,1,2)(0,0,0)	0.993	0.727	0.200
t-statistic	125.898	11.124	3.085
Significance	0.000	0.000	0.002
	PP t = -14.847(0.000)	ADF= -5.721(0.000)	
Seychelles Rupee (logs)	**MA(1)**		
ARIMA (0,1,1)(0,0,0)	-0.146		
t-statistic	-2.279		
Significance	0.024		
	PP t = - 13.562(0.000)	ADF t=- 7.711(0.000)	
South Africa Rand (logs)	Constant		
ARIMA (0,1,0)(0,0,0)	0.005		
t-statistic	2.276		
Significance	0.024		
	PP t = - 14.770(0.000)	ADF t=- 14.642(0.000)	
Tanzania Shilling (logs)	Constant	MA(1)	
ARIMA (0,1,1)(0,0,0)	0.009	-0.144	
t-statistic	4.386	-2.228	
Significance	0.000	0.027	
	PP t = - 16.416(0.000)	ADF t=- 13.801(0.000)	
Zambia Kwacha (sqrt)	Constant	MA(13)	
ARIMA (1,1,13)(0,0,0)	28.703	0.151	
t-statistic	2.189	2.170	
Significance	0.030	0.031	
	PP=- 16.015(0.000)	ADF t=- 16.053(0.000)	

The ARCH model considers the variance of the current error term to be function of the variances of the previous time periods' error terms and relates the error variance to the square of a previous period's error. In particular, if the conditional variance at time t is related to the squared error at (t-1), we have what is called an ARCH (1) process and:

$$\sigma_t^2 = \alpha_0 + \alpha_1 e_{t-1}^2 \tag{4.2}$$

The ARCH (1) model says that when a shock happens in the last period (t-1) it will be represented by e_{t-1} having a large value and this will have a large impact on the conditional variance at time t. That is, when e_{t-1}^2 is large, the conditional variance at the next time period (t) will be large. In an ARCH (q) process, the conditional variance at time t is influenced by the squared error at times (t-1), (t-2)... (t-q) and:

$$\sigma_t^2 = \alpha_0 + \alpha_1 e_{t-1}^2 + \alpha_2 e_{t-2}^2 + \cdots + \alpha_q e_{t-q}^2 \tag{4.3}$$

In equation (4.3), the conditional variance depends on q lags of the squared errors. All of the α_i coefficients must be greater than zero (and less than 1) to ensure a positive conditional variance. In empirical applications of the ARCH model, a relatively long lag in the conditional variance equation is often called for. To avoid problems with negative variance parameter estimates a fixed lag structure is typically imposed (cf. Engle (1982)). ARCH methods have had wide application over the last ten years, particularly in the field of financial volatility.

However, ARCH models *per se* are now used with decreasing frequency due to a number of difficulties:

- How should the value of q - the number of lags- be determined? There is no clear best approach.
- The value of q required to capture all of the impact on the conditional variance might be very large. This would result in a complex ARCH model that is not parsimonious.
- The larger the value of q, the greater is the possibility that a negative conditional variance could be the result.

In this light, it seemed of immediate interest to extend the ARCH class of models to allow for both a longer memory and a more flexible lag structure. Econometric modelling of this volatility clustering phenomenon has been a very active area of research over the past decade. An extension of the ARCH (q) process was developed independently by Bollerslev (1986) and is called the generalised ARCH process or GARCH. A GARCH model allows the conditional variance to be dependent upon its own previous lags as well as the squared error terms of the ARCH models. In its simplest case, we have:

$$\sigma_t^2 = \alpha_0 + \alpha_1 e_{t-1}^2 + \beta_1 \sigma_{t-1}^2 \tag{4.4}$$

Equation (4.4) is referred to as GARCH (1, 1) and states that the conditional variance of the errors is a function of three components: an intercept term

(α_0), information about volatility during the previous time period (e_{t-1}^2) and the fitted conditional variance from the model during the previous period (σ_{t-1}^2). GARCH (1, 1) is often sufficient when modelling volatility over long sample periods (French et al., 1987; Franses and Van Dijk, 1996). The GARCH (p, q) model captures thick tails and other stylised facts such as non-trading periods and regular events. The ARCH coefficient (α_1) in Eq. (4.4) reflects the impact of news shocks in the short term; the GARCH coefficient (β_1) reflects the long term impact of news shocks. A GARCH (q, p) model has the form:

$$\sigma_t^2 = \alpha_0 + \alpha_1 e_{t-1}^2 + \alpha_2 e_{t-2}^2 + \cdots + \alpha_q e_{t-q}^2 + \beta_1 \sigma_{t-1}^2 + \beta_2 \sigma_{t-2}^2 + \cdots + \beta_p \sigma_{t-p}^2 \ldots \tag{4.5}$$

A potential limitation of applying the GARCH model to business and financial data is that it presumes that the impacts of positive and negative shocks are the same or symmetric. This is because the conditional variance in these equations depends on the magnitude of the lagged residuals, not their sign. Such a consideration led to the development of asymmetric volatility models, specifically the threshold GARCH (TGARCH) (Glosten et al. 1993) and the exponential GARCH (EGARCH) (Nelson, 1991). The threshold model is a simple extension of the GARCH scheme, with an extra term(s) added to account for possible asymmetries. The EGARCH class of volatility models can also accommodate asymmetry and specifies the conditional variance in a different way:

$$\ln(\sigma_t^2) = \alpha_0 + \alpha_1 \frac{|e_{t-1}|}{|\sigma_{t-1}|} + \beta_1 \ln(\sigma_{t-1}^2) + \gamma_1 \frac{e_{t-1}}{\sigma_{t-1}} \tag{4.6}$$

One reason why the EGARCH model has been popular in financial applications is that the logarithm of the conditional variance appears on the left side of Eq. (4.6), allowing for $\ln(\sigma_t^2)$ to be negative. It also permits asymmetries via the γ_1 term and if $\gamma_1 < 0$, this means that bad news leads to an increase in volatility. If $\gamma_1 = 0$, the model is symmetric. The selected ARIMA model specification serves as a mean equation to start the modelling procedure for ARCH family of models. The optimal volatility model should have the maximum Schwarz Bayesian Criterion (SBC) and the maximum log likelihood (LL) generated using the Berndt, Hall and Hall (1974) algorithm. In this chapter, all combinations of ARCH= 0, 1, 2 with GARCH= 0, 1, 2 were examined to identify the optimal volatility model for each exchange rate. Tables 4.5, 4.6, 4.7 and 4.8 present the optimal conditional variance equations associated with the mean equations presented earlier in this chapter. The models with the maximum SBC and LL statistic are reported in Tables 4.5 to 4.8. A Q-test was used to test the residuals for autocorrelation as proposed by Ljung and Box (1978). Correlograms were generated up to 24 lags and each single correlation coefficient was tested individually for the significance. Detected spikes were considered to enter the starting form of model (Brooks, 2008; Coshall, 2009). The following hypotheses were tested at 95% level of confidence:

H_0: The autocorrelation coefficient at lag s is zero.

H_1: The autocorrelation coefficient at lag s is different from zero.

As part of the diagnostic checking process, the residuals associated with a particular volatility model have to be checked for the absence of autocorrelation, which would indicate that the residuals behave like a white noise process. The Ljung-Box Q-statistic is used for this purpose as a *portmanteau* test, which has its null that all of the autocorrelations up to a lag of k are equal to zero and since the exchange rate data are monthly, k was chosen to equal 12. Q is asymptotically distributed as a chi-squared variable with k degrees of freedom. The Q-squared (denoted as QSQ in Tables 4.5 to 4.8) test was also applied to check the specification of the volatility models. Based upon the squared residuals, it examines whether there is any remaining ARCH in the volatility equation.

The Ljung-Box (1978) statistic tests Q(12) and QSQ(12) are also reported for up to twelve monthly lags. Findings from Tables 4.5, 4.6, 4.7 and 4.8 show that significant volatility models were obtained for most exchange rates, indicating that volatility is a big factor in the selected regional settings. In Table 4.5, EGARCH and GARCH were the best fitting models for four exchange and five rates respectively. Malaysia, the Philippines, Singapore and Thailand are countries where bad news have greater effect on exchange rates than do good news. Following the high amount of uncertainty that markets have been faced with during and after the AFC in 1997 (Please refer to Figures 42, 44, 45, 46 and 47 in Appendix 2), one would have expected this finding to be on a greater scale, particularly for countries like Indonesia.

Asymmetric models were found to be significant in the case of Indonesia but were outperformed by symmetric models. The latter finding might be explained by the fact that the Central Bank was very active in the FOREX market before and after the crisis which made the rupiah relatively stable; Indonesia used to be peg its currency to the dollar in early 90's but the authorities abandoned the policy of maintaining the currency within a set trading exchange rate band and adopted a free floating exchange rate arrangement. Judging from the plots of conditional variance overtime (Figures 40 to 48 in Appendix 2), ASEAN countries seem to have had stable currencies during the last decade and look like they have weathered the recent crisis comparatively well compared with to the rest of the world. In Table 4.6, all exchange rates in the CACM region involve GARCH volatility models. Negative shocks increase volatility in the exchange rates of Costa Rica colon and Honduras lempira more than would the positive shocks of same magnitude. GARCH models present the best fit to historical patterns of volatility in the CACM region and therefore provide the best fitting models for all exchange rates examined in Central America. Table 4.6 shows the particular importance of small lag volatility in the modelling of the behaviour of the present time period. As was the case for MERCOSUR, significant volatility models are obtained for all the currencies examined in the

Table 4.5 ASEAN exchange rates: variance equations

	α_0	α_1	β_1	β_2	$\emptyset_1$
Brunei Dollar					
GARCH(0,2)			1.996	-0.997	
t-statistic			1161.972	-580.670	
Significance			0.000	0.000	
		SBC=-4.095	QSQ(12)=		
	LL=443.439	Q(12)=7.920(0.637)	35.209(0.070)		
Cambodia Riel					
GARCH(0,1)	4146.102		0.873		
t-statistic	2.044		12.705		
Significance	0.040		0.000		
	LL=385.791	SBC=-3.496	QSQ(12)=		
		Q(12)=13.717(0.186)	7.350(0.770)		
Indonesia Rupiah					
EGARCH(1,2	-1.072	0.871	0.368	0.563	
)	-3.543	3.218	2.633	4.434	
t-statistic	0.000	0.001	0.008	0.000	
Significance	LL=392.741	SBC=-3.641	QSQ(12)=		
		Q(12)=10.034(0.438)	9.546(0.481)		
Laos Kip					
EGARCH(1,1			0.982		
)			147.378		
t-statistic			0.000		
Significance	LL=464.247	SBC=-4.233	QSQ(12)=		
		Q(12)=8.730(0.588)	14.487(0.152)		
Malaysia Ringgit					
EGARCH(0,2	-1.159		0.334	1.356	-0.500
)	-3.884		-3.873	-4.405	-4.405
t-statistic	0.000		0.000	0.000	0.000
Significance	LL=525.030	SBC=-4.936	QSQ(12)=		
		Q(12)=13.952(0.083)	15.358(0.053)		
Philippine Peso					
GARCH(1,2)	0.324	0.203	1.236	-0.479	-0.256
t-statistic	4.466	3.280	10.838	-5.468	-3.734
Significance	0.000	0.001	0.000	0.000	0.000
	LL=-366.685	SBC=3.653	QSQ(12)=		
		Q(12)=16.271(0.092)	10.202(0.423)		
Singapore Dollar					
EARCH(0,1)	-0.905		0.255		0.873
t-statistic	-1.999		2.049		13.853
Significance	0.045	SBC=-4.115	0.040		0.000
	LL=457.367	Q(12)=4.921(0.075)	QSQ(12)=1.914(0.67)		
Thailand Baht			1.048		-0.071
GARCH(1,0)			364.696		-13.440
t-statistic			0.000		0.000
Significance	LL=488.330	SBC=-4.442	QSQ(12)=		
		Q(12)=8.280(0.411)	4.830(0.300)		
Vietnam Dong					
GARCH(1,1)	-1809.401	-0.023	1.055		
t-statistic	-53.880	-10.176	6372.550		
Significance	0.000	0.000	0.000		
	LL=-1544.13	SBC=14.488	QSQ(12)=		
		Q(12)=12.743(0.310)	2.850(0.303)		

region highlighting the distinct relevance of the volatility for the region's exchange rates. There is some evidence of the presence of asymmetric parameters in Table 4.7 - in the MERCOSUR the magnitude of the response to a shock is greater to a response following positive news. Given the impact that Argentina's default had on the economies of the region in 2001, this comes as no surprise. International investors pulled out indiscriminately from neighbouring countries because of the uncertainty following the refusal of the

Table 4.6 CACM exchange rates: variance equations

	α_0	α_1	α_2	β_1	β_2	$\emptyset_1$
Costa Rica Colon						
GARCH (2,2)		0.116	0.284	1.435	-0.691	-0.109
t-statistic		-11.459	7.827	29.876	-19.236	-5.137
Significance		0.000	0.000	0.000	0.000	0.000
	LL=565.991	SBC=565.991	Q(12)= 9.247(0.599)	QSQ(12)= 11.524(0.400)		
Dominican Peso				2.258		
GARCH (0,1)	0.176			9.188		
t-statistic	7.804			0.000		
Significance	0.000					
	LL=-274.94	SBC=2.881	Q(12)= 4.469(0.762)	QSQ(12)= 9.730(0.340)		
Guatemala Quetzal				0.902		
GARCH (0,1)	0.003			31.731		
t-statistic	3.035			0.000		
Significance	0.000					
	LL=61.373	SBC=-0.452	Q(12)= 16.341(0.090)	QSQ(12)= 12.171(0.274)		
Honduras Lempira						
GARCH (0,2)				1.258	-0.375	
t-statistic				11.508	-4.743	
Significance				0.000	0.000	
	LL=515.840	SBC=-4.949	Q(12)= 5.206(0.179)	QSQ(12)= 8.245(0.230)		
Nicaragua Cordoba						
GARCH (2,1)		0.167	-0.214	1.026		-0.165
t-statistic		12316	-16124	58761		-5.316
Significance		0.000	0.000	0.000		0.000
	LL= 473.171	SBC=-4.523	Q(12)= 6.758(0.662)	QSQ(12)= 11.516(0.242)		

Argentinean government to pay an US $ 80 billion debt due to the IMF – debt crisis discussed in Chapter One. This knock-on effect has been strongly felt in Brazil, Chile and Uruguay. This makes the findings of this chapter particularly relevant because once again, it seems that exchange rates in the same region react in a similar fashion following a shock to the system. The collapse of one country plunges the neighbours in a crisis of their own and raises the fears of more uncertainty ahead which makes the exchange rate volatile.

EGARCH models seem to have performed particularly well in Latin America's MERCOSUR, having optimally modelled six exchange rates out of eight; the rest were optimally modelled by GARCH equations. Asymmetric responses to shocks are particularly relevant in this part of the world with associated significant parameters for Bolivia, Brazil, Colombia, Peru and Paraguay.

Table 4.7 MERCOSUR exchange rates: variance equations

	α_0	α_1	α_2	β_1	β_2	$\emptyset_1$
Bolivia						
Boliviano						
EGARCH(1,1)	-1.728	-0.308				0.227
t-statistic	-3.792	-4.079				3.854
Significance	0.000	0.000				0.000
	LL=	SBC=	Q(12)=			
	614.178	-5.563	14.733(0.195)			
Brazil Real						
EGARCH(1,2)	-1.203	-0.120		1.558	-0.899	0.218
t-statistic	-9.348	-2.166		32.223	-31.574	4.939
Significance	0.000	0.030		0.000	0.000	0.000
	LL=	SBC=	Q(12)=	QSQ(12)=		
	75.060	-0.716	5.914(0.822)	6.555(0.767)		
Chile Peso						
GARCH(1,2)		0.058		1.754	-0.861	
t-statistic		4.250		34.499	-18.247	
Significance		0.000		0.000	0.000	
	LL=	SBC=	Q(12)=	QSQ(12)=		
	475.536	-4.531	9.178(0.605)	6.889(0.808)		
Colombia						
Peso				0.688	-0.711	0.222
EGARCH(0,2)	-7.302			6.145	-3.842	1.981
t-statistic	-7.531			0.000	0.000	0.047
Significance	0.000			QSQ(12)=13		
	LL=	SBC=-	Q(12)=6.650	.129		
	461.252	4.482	(0.827)	(0.285)		
Paraguay						
Guarani						
EGARCH(2,2)	-7.241	-0.142	0.158	1.012	-0.982	
t-statistic	-69.155	-3.693	3.378	71.005	-62.886	
Significance	0.000	0.000	0.000	0.000	0.000	
		SBC=-	Q(12)=6.650	QSQ(12)=11		
	LL=498.43	4.482	(0.827)	.951		
	0			(0.125)		
Peru New Sol						
EGARCH(0,1)	-0.251			0.972		0.127
t-statistic	-6.462			190.330		2.811
Significance	0.000			0.000		0.004
	LL=	SBC=-	Q(12)=6.758	QSQ(12)=11		
	486.511	4.442	(0.662)	.516		
				(0.242)		
Uruguay Peso						
EGARCH(0,1)				0.991		0.387
t-statistic				106.517		3.349
Significance				0.000		0.000
	LL=486.23	SBC=-	Q(12)=8.881	QSQ(12)=		
	0	4.414	(0.448)	13.043(0.161)		
Venezuela						
Bolivar						
GARCH(1,2)		0.173		-0.074	0.860	
t-statistic		2.177		-10.761	70.528	
Significance		0.029		0.000	0.000	
	LL=271.74	SBC=	Q(12)=	QSQ(12)=		
	9	-2.804	8.371(0.593)	8.842(0.310)		

The picture is different in Africa's SADC as revealed in Table 4.8, since volatility models with small lags capture the behaviour of exchange rates in most sampled countries. The asymmetric effects seem to be subdued in the continent with significant parameters depicted only in the Democratic Republic of Congo and Madagascar. While Latin American and Asian countries were trying to fix their wrecked financial system during the decade leading to the 21st century, most nations in Africa were trying to come to terms with the psychological and physical wounds that perpetrated many nations across the region as a result of wars, civil wars and the Apartheid (in South Africa). EGARCH models capture the behaviour of the Angolan kwanza, DRC Franc and the Mauritian rupee. Other exchanges rates were optimally modelled by GARCH equations. The reader might notice that EGARCH seem to be popular in Latin America and to a lesser extent in Asia while GARCH seems to be triumphant in Central America and Africa. An interesting finding when this is related to what has been said earlier in this chapter about the link between the behaviour of an exchange rate and the stage of development of the country under investigation. Countries in Latin America and Asia seem to be "advanced" comparing to those in the African and the Central American blocs.

Table 4.8 SADC exchange rates: variance equations

	α_0	α_1	α_2	β_1	β_2	$\emptyset_1$
Angola						
Kwanza	-4.848	0.769				
EGARCH(1,0)	-14.856	5.121				
t-statistic	0.000	0.000				
Significance	LL=108.622	SBC=-1.317	Q(12)=12.308 (0.265)	QSQ(12)= 12.581(0.248)		
Botswana						
Pula		0.409	0.413	-0.501	0.416	
GARCH(2,2)		2.283	2.506	-4.329	4.901	
t-statistic		0.022	0.012	0.000	0.000	
Significance	LL=500.111	SBC=-4.477	Q(12)=10.921 (0.450)	QSQ(12)= 6.173(0.862)		
DRC Franc						
EGARCH(1,1)	-2.715	1.856		-1.031		
t-statistic	-8.097	6.070		-6.465	0.631	
Significance	0.000	0.000		0.000		
	LL=91.174	SBC=-1.115	Q(12)=6.410 (0.780)	QSQ(12)= 9.749(0.463)	10.385	
					0.000	
Madagascar						
Ariary				0.938		
GARCH(0,1)				20.362		
t-statistic				0.000		
Significance	LL=350.982	SBC=-3.190	Q(12)=7.290 (0.775)	QSQ(12)= 0.877(1.000)		
Malawi						
Kwacha		0.202	-0.228	1.055		
GARCH(2,1)		4551.772	-6004.189	19627.720		
t-statistic		0.000	0.000	0.000		
Significance	LL=104.509	SBC=-0.826	Q(12)=10.519 (0.484)	QSQ(12)= 4.865(0.937)		
Mauritius Rupee				-0.703		
EGARCH(1,1)	-14.489	0.619		-10.567		
t-statistic	-28.449	4.761		0.000		
Significance	0.000	0.000		QSQ(12)=		
	LL=545.850	SBC=-5.220	Q(12)=3.724 (0.959)	2.638(0.989)		

Table 4.8 (Cont'd) SADC exchange rates

Mozambique Metical					
GARCH(1,2)		0.169		1.458	-0.593
t-statistic		2.142		22.411	-14.315
Significance		0.000		0.000	0.000
	LL=463.013	SBC=-4.176	Q(12)=11.365 (0.330)	QSQ(12)= 2.072(0.996)	
Seychelles					
Rupee		0.535	-0.588	1.080	
GARCH(2,1)		2.629	-2.653	3831.9	
t-statistic		0.008	0.008	0.000	
Significance	LL=808.300	SBC=-7.394	Q(12)=14.755(0.194)	QSQ(12)=6. 629(0.828)	
South Africa Rand					
GARCH(2,1)		0.426	-0.466	1.051	
t-statistic		3.853	-4.242	7338.512	
Significance	LL=	0.000	0.000	0.000	
	470.91	SBC=-4.255	Q(12)=7.541 (0.820)	QSQ(12)= 12.477(0.400)	
Tanzania Shilling					
GARCH(0,2)				1.955	-0.968
t-statistic				72.738	-36.564
Significance				0.000	0.000
	LL= 483.254	SBC=-4.370	Q(12)=14.855 (0.189)	QSQ(12)= 15.656(0.150)	
Zambia					
Kwacha	1198.893	1.047		0.245	-0.073
GARCH(1,2)	3.843	4.056		26.652	-45.154
t-statistic	0.000	0.000		0.000	0.000
Significance	LL=	SBC=-3.200		QSQ(12)=5.	
	403.748		Q(12)=122.990 (0.293)	415(0.909)	

4.1.3 Volatility Forecasts

Table 4.9 presents the results of applying volatility models to forecast a set of more than 30 exchange rates in Africa, Asia, Central and Latin America. Volatility models performed particularly well in Central America with a mean absolute percentage error (MAPE) value of less than 10% in all five exchange rates examined in the region. MAPE is the measure chosen to assess the performance of forecasting models as it possesses the advantage of a unit-free measure for model adequacy (Lewis, 1982). From among the competing models, the one with the lowest MAPE is the best fit for the series under study. In the ASEAN region, ARIMA-volatility models performed particularly well with MAPE values of less than 5% (except in the case of the Philippines peso MAPE = 6.15% and Laos MAPE = 13.06%). Laos' kip was particularly volatile between 1997 and 2000 and this can be seen clearly in the variance plot graph in Figure 43 in Appendix 2. In the CACM region, volatility models perform well overall with MAPE values of less than 10% for the five exchange rates examined in the region. Furthermore, the MAPE values in this region have smaller spread compared with other regions, which hints at a particularly high degree of integration between the economies of Central America.

Table 4.9 Volatility Models Forecasting Performance

ASEAN	MAPE	CACM	MAPE	MERCOSUR	MAPE	SADC	MAPE
Brunei	2.50%	Costa Rica	3.10%	Bolivia	2.39%	Angola	7.84%
Cambodia	5.04%	Dominican Republic	2.18%	Brazil	3.72%	Botswana	5.95%
Indonesia	4.43%	Guatemala	5.73%	Chile	7.47%	DRC	*
Laos	13.06%	Honduras	7.23%	Colombia	15.61%	Madagascar	6.38%
Malaysia	1.46%	Nicaragua	7.94%	Paraguay	12.16%	Malawi	3.42%
Philippines	6.15%			Peru	4.94%	Mauritius	5.84%
Singapore	1.52%			Uruguay	*	Mozam-bique	3.32%
Thailand	*			Venezuela	5.62%	Seychelles	5.52%
Vietnam	2.81%					South Africa	9.44%
						Tanzania	6.57%
						Zambia	*

*No model found

In the SADC region, volatility models performed well overall with MAPE close to 10% for South Africa, the leading economy of the region. Volatility models did not perform as well in Latin America with a MAPE of 15.61% in Colombia and 12.16% in Paraguay which might be explained by the frequent Central Bank interventions of respective countries either because of a FARC militia attacks in the former or because of a political scandal in the latter. The internal strife is still evident in Colombia while Paraguay's political scene has been marked by numerous scandals. In fact, MERCOSUR suspended the membership of Paraguay from the bloc in 2012. In the SADC region, MAPE values seem to be consistent across countries. Forecasts generated using the ARIMA-volatility models have all registered MAPE values of less than 10% with the highest value registered in South Africa (9.44%) due to the particular volatility of the rand at the beginning of last decade (see Figure 71 in the Appendix 2). In fact, from the beginning of the year 2000, the rand depreciated sharply against the United States dollar from a level of 6.15 rands to the dollar at the end of 1999 to more than 7 rands to the US dollar (Metzger, 2008) which represents a depreciation of 15%. Table 4.9 provides a comparison of the volatility forecast performance in ASEAN, CACM, MERCOSUR and SADC countries.

4.2 Exponential Smoothing Models

4.2.1 Exponential Smoothing: Theory

The simple exponential smoothing model is a linear combination of historical realisations of variables. It assigns greater weight to newer observations, allowing old information to decrease in importance as the new data are obtained - unless the historical information still impacts the present (Brooks, 2008). Given that only previous values of the series of interest are used, the only question remaining is how much weight should be attached to each of the previous observations. Recent observations would be expected to have more power in forecasting future values of a series. In this case, a model that places more weight on recent observations than those further in the past would be desirable. On the other hand, observations in the past may still contain some information useful for forecasting future values of a series. An exponential smoothing model achieves this by imposing a geometrically declining weighting scheme on the lagged values of a series. Recent observations would be expected to have the most power in helping to forecast future values of a series. The simple, one parameter exponential smoothing model is applicable to series with no trend or seasonality and can be written as:

$$\hat{Y}_{t+1} = \hat{Y}_t + \alpha\,(Y_t - \hat{Y}_t) \tag{4.7}$$

Where $\hat{Y}_{t+1}$ is the forecasted value of the series at time (t+1), is the observed value of that series at time t and α is the smoothing or 'weighting' parameter $(0 \leq \alpha \leq 1)$ that is to be estimated. The 'optimal value' of α is defined as that which minimises the sum of the squares of the errors (SSE) and is found by means of a grid search of the form α = 0(0.1)1 or α = 0(0.01)1. High values of α in Eq. (4.7) imply that the impact of historical observations dies out quickly and vice-versa. Two other parameters, γ, a smoothing parameter for the trend and δ, a smoothing parameter for seasonal components, may be added to the simple model. Both parameters lie between 0 and 1 inclusive and their numerical values are also found by means of a grid search with the objective of minimising the sum of squared errors. In this respect, the 'Expert Modeller' facility of SPSS (Statistical Package for Social Sciences) software was used to establish optimal smoothing model and the results are presented in Table 4.10. This facility compares the simple smoothing model, Holt's linear trend models, the damped trend model, Winters' additive and multiplicative models. Holt's method allows the forecaster to use one smoothing parameter and is useful for data in a simple linear trend. Winter's Additive is applicable when the times series contains a constant seasonal component and a linear trend.

This method assumes that series can be best presented by three statistically correlated components (smoothed, seasonal and trend) and project forward the identified trend or seasonality. The damped trend model was introduced

Table 4.10 Exponential Smoothing Models

Currency	Model	α (level)	β (trend)	γ (season)
Singapore Dollar	Simple seasonal	0.900		0.000
Cambodia Riel	Winters' additive	1.000	0.001	0.001
Brunei Dollar	Simple seasonal	0.900		0.000
Indonesia Rupiah	Simple	1.000		
Laos Kip	Simple	1.000		
Malaysia Ringgit	Winters' additive	0.902		0.000
Philippine Peso	Winters' additive	1.000	0.001	0.001
Thailand Baht	Simple seasonal	0.999	0.000	1.000
Vietnam Dong	Winters' additive	0.988	0.001	0.999
Angola Kwanza	Holt	1.000	0.200	
Botswan Pula	Winters' additive	0.999	0.000	0.001
DRC Franc	Winters' additive	0.999	0.000	0.999
Madagascar Ariary	Winters' additive	1.000	0.001	0.001
Malawi Kwacha	Damped trend	0.999	0.286	0.789
Mauritius Rupee	Holt	0.898	0.000	
Mozambique Metical	Holt	1.000	0.001	
Seychelles Rupee	Simple	1.000	0.001	0.001
South Africa Rand	Simple	1.000		
Tanzania Shilling	Simple	0.902	0.000	0.001
Zambia Kwacha	Damped trend	0.939		
Bolivia Boliviano	Simple seasonal	1.000	0.001	0.001
Brazil Real	Winters' additive	0.901		0.000
Chile Peso	Winters' additive	1.000	0.001	0.001
Colombia Peso	Winters' additive	1.000	0.000	0.999
Paraguay Guarani	Damped trend	0.984	0.830	0.396
Peru New Sol	Winters' additive	1.000	0.044	0.999
Uruguay Peso	Damped trend	1.000	1.000	0.300
Venezuela Bolivar	Holt	0.999		1.000
Costa Rica Colon	Winters' additive	1.000	0.001	0.001
Dominican Peso	Damped trend	0.647	0.374	0.778
Guatemala Quetzel	Winters' additive	0.999	0.000	0.999
Honduras Lempira	Holt	0.993	0.000	1.000
Nicaragua Cordoba	Winters' additive	1.000	0.001	0.001

by Gardner and McKenzie (1985) and applies when the trend in a series fades away overtime. Birer el al. (2005) investigated the exchange rate between the US dollar and the Euro using different methods of forecasting and found that exponential smoothing results outperformed forecasts generated by other models. Taylor (2008) used exponential smoothing models to predict volatility in various market conditions. He attempted to predict volatility in financial returns and found that exponential smoothing gave encouraging results when compared to a variety of GARCH models. Codruta and Dezsi (2012) examined exchange rates of the Romanian Leu against the Euro, US dollar, British pound, Japanese yen, Chinese rembini and the Russian rouble using exponential smoothing techniques. Their findings confirm the performance of exponential smoothing models compared with ARIMA models because of the speed with which the former adapts to change. Needless to say, the literature on exponential smoothing in Finance seems to be surprisingly very limited compared with the one that uses ARIMA-volatility although smoothing techniques seem to outperform other forecasting models in this book. Therefore, the thesis fills this gap in the literature by assessing the performance of exponential smoothing models in forecasting exchange rates in the emerging world. The next section discusses the findings of applying exponential smoothing models to forecasts of exchange rates in ASEAN, CACM, MERCOSUR and SADC countries.

4.2.2 Exponential smoothing: results

Table 4.10 reports the optimal exponential smoothing models obtained for 35 exchange rates across all four regions. These findings show that the smoothing parameter (α) is very close to one for most exchange rates which confirms the high impact of the most recent observations on the present. This finding is valid for all smoothing models (simple, Holt and Winters). Interestingly, the exchange rates of Laos, Seychelles, South Africa and Tanzania have all been optimally forecasted by a simple smoothing model with no trend or seasonality. Laos, Seychelles, South Africa and Tanzania had their currencies pegged to the US dollar in the 1990's which itself was relatively stable during this period justifying the absence of any trend or seasonality. Winters' additive model with a strong smoothing component and a weak trend parameter performed particularly well compared with other models. This result is true regardless of the region investigated and is applicable to various exchange rates. This explains another characteristic of the exchange rate market which is the particular importance of recent past data in dictating the present over long periods of time. In the same line of thought, the damped trend model with a relatively strong trend component was an optimal model for only four exchange rates which are located in Central and Latin America; The Dominican Republic, Paraguay and Uruguay. For Peru, Colombia, Vietnam and Thailand, significant seasonal components were identified. Table 4.11 reports the forecasting accuracy of smoothing models in the prediction of exchange rates in the sampled countries. Exponential smoothing models seem to perform particularly well regardless of the region under study with a MAPE of less than 5% for all exchange rate (except Cambodia MAPE=5.03%). In the ASEAN countries, MAPE is around 1% in Brunei, Laos, Malaysia, Philippines, Singapore, Thailand

and Vietnam. Similarly in CACM countries, all exchange rate forecasts examined have a MAPE of less than 5% providing therefore the proof that exponential smoothing models can be particularly accurate in the forecasting exercise. This finding is an incentive for researchers who would like to venture in the forecast of exchange rates in the emerging world, especially in ASEAN and CACM regions, to use exponential smoothing techniques as the method clearly generates good results. This finding is given more impetus when the reader realises that exponential smoothing methods are widely under-used in Finance especially on the forecast of FOREX. The same is applicable in both MERCOSUR and SADC since exponential smoothing provided very accurate forecasts with MAPE values that range from 1.52% (Venezuela) to 4.81% (South Africa). A comparison between the performance of volatility, smoothing and Naïve I models (introduced in the next section) is provided towards the end of this chapter in order to demonstrate the strength of each method.

Table 4.11 Exponential Smoothing Models Forecasting Performance

ASEAN	MAPE	CACM	MAPE	MERCOSUR	MAPE	SADC	MAPE
Brunei	0.80%	**Costa Rica**	3.87%	**Bolivia**	1.72%	**Angola**	2.08%
Cambodia	5.03%	**Dominican Republic**	2.13%	**Brazil**	3.90%	**Botswana**	2.70%
Indonesia	2.90%	**Guatemala**	3.29%	**Chile**	3.36%	**DRC**	*
Laos	1.47%	**Honduras**	2.58%	**Colombia**	3.41%	**Madagascar**	2.56%
Malaysia	1.21%	**Nicaragua**	2.63%	**Paraguay**	2.36%	**Malawi**	1.55%
Philippines	1.77%			**Peru**	2.19%	**Mauritius**	2.50%
Singapore	1.91%			**Uruguay**	4.78%	**Mozambique**	2.78%
Thailand	1.77%			**Venezuela**	1.52%	**Seychelles**	2.23%
Vietnam	1.85%					**South Africa**	4.81%
						Tanzania	2.21%
						Zambia	4.41%

*No model found

Table 4.12 Naïve I Models Forecasting Performance

ASEAN	MAPE	CACM	MAPE	MERCOSUR	MAPE	SADC	MAPE
Brunei	2.02%	**Costa Rica**	8.18%	**Bolivia**	18.29%	**Angola**	4.48%
Cambodia	3.06%	**Dominican Republic**	2.76%	**Brazil**	8.49%	**Botswana**	12.18%
Indonesia	5.52%	**Guatemala**	3.92%	**Chile**	8.65%	**DRC**	*
Laos	9.86%	**Honduras**	2.88%	**Colombia**	6.84%	**Madagascar**	6.29%
Malaysia	2.69%	**Nicaragua**	4.28%	**Paraguay**	6.86%	**Malawi**	2.99%
Philippines	9.16%			**Peru**	2.5%	**Mauritius**	6.70%
Singapore	2.02%			**Uruguay**	4.81%	**Mozambique**	5.42%
Thailand	1.34%			**Venezuela**	2.86%	**Seychelles**	5.23%
Vietnam	3.43%					**South Africa**	15.91%
						Tanzania	8.98%
						Zambia	9.92%

4.3 Naïve I Models

Models that have become known as Naïve I can be included under the heading of time series models. Naïve I or "no change models" assume that a forecast of the series at a particular period equals the actual value at the last period available. For example, if annual data are considered, this model assumes that the forecast for the year 2009 should be equal to the actual value of 2008 and can be represented as follows:

$$\hat{Y}_{t+1} = Y_t \quad (4.8)$$

where Y_t is the observed value of the series at time t and Y_{t+1} the forecast value of the series at time (t+1). Similarly, for monthly data, the subscript changes to $\hat{Y}_{t+12} = Y_t$. Naïve I has been used in this research and its forecasting performance is reported in Table 4.12 which provides evidence that Naïve I models provide good forecasts in relation to the MAPE values (less than 10% except in Bolivia, 18.29%, Botswana, 12.18% and South Africa, 15.91%).

The fact that Naïve I models can provide accurate forecasts at times is a very important empirical finding in that a simple and easy model can generate good forecasts in the exchange rate market. More than 20 years ago, Dimson and Marsh (1990, 420) concluded in their study that despite the increased importance of the relatively complex models such as GARCH models, simplistic models seem to have gained ground in comparison. They stated that "with the increasing interest in using complicated econometric techniques for volatility forecasting, our research strikes a warning bell. For those who are interested in forecasts with reasonable predictive accuracy: the best forecasting models may well be the simplest ones". This book provides the proof that simple models can provide huge exploratory power, an assumption which can be easily verified across regions and continent with a quick glance at Table 4.12.

4.4 Structural Breaks

A problem with a stationary time series that is subject to a structural break (such as a change in intercept and/or trend) is that if the break is not catered for during model formulation, then application of a unit root test can lead to incorrect non-rejection of the null hypothesis of non-stationarity. It has become well recognised that unit root tests are biased in the face of structural breaks or unexpected shifts in time series data in general (Banerjee and Urga, 2005; Boero et al., 2010; Perron, 1989; Vogelsang and Perron, 1998) and for exchange rate series in particular (Barkoulas et al., 1999; Chowdhury, 2007, 2012; Sabaté et al., 2003). In such circumstances, unit root tests tend to have very low power.

An early approach to the structural break problem was that of Perron (1989), in which a single breakpoint was assumed and known to have occurred at time T_b. Three models were developed to cater for (A) a change in the level (or intercept) of the series effective at time $T_b + 1$, (B) a change in the growth rate (or slope) effective at time $T_b + 1$ and (C) a change in level and growth rate effective at time $T_b + 1$. The fact that the specification and choice of the breakpoint in these tests is dependent upon prior examination of the data has been criticised. It has been noted that exogenous predetermination of the breakpoint invalidates the distribution theory that underpins classical unit root testing (Christiano, 1992).

The work by Bai and Perron (1998, 2003 a, b) has greatly increased the scope of testing for structural breaks. They addressed the problem of testing for multiple structural changes under very general conditions on the data and the errors. In particular, they constructed the tests allowing for different serial correlation in the errors and different distribution for the data and the errors across segments. The method tests for multiple breaks of unknown break dates without imposing any prior beliefs. The break tests involve regressing the variable of interest (in this case exchange rates) on a constant and testing for breaks within that constant. First, the procedure assumes there is no break within the data against an alternate that there is up to b breaks in the data, where b is specified by the user. Furthermore, a minimum distance between breaks can also be specified. The early influential paper Perron (1989) tests null hypothesis of unit root under the assumption of known (exogenous, pre-tested) break date in both null and alternative hypotheses. Later Christiano (1992) criticises Perron's known date assumption as data mining. He argues that the data based procedures are typically used to determine the most likely location of the break, i.e. by pre-test examination of the data, and this approach invalidates the distribution theory underlying conventional testing. Zivot and Andrews (1992) and Perron (1997) proposed determining the break point endogenously from the data. However, these endogenous tests were criticised for their treatment of breaks under the null hypothesis. They do not allow for break(s) under the null hypothesis of unit root and derive their critical values accordingly. As a remedy of the limitations noted above, this book uses the Lee and Strazicich (2003) test which includes breaks under both the null and the alternative hypothesis, with rejections of the null unambiguously implying trend stationarity:

$H_0 =$ data are not trend stationary with breaks

$H_1 =$ data are trend stationary with breaks

The Lee and Strazicich (2003) test analyse two alternative models[15], Model A allows for two shift in the level of exchange rates while Model C includes two changes in level and trend. In Model A, the null and alternative hypotheses are given by equations (4.9) and (4.10) respectively:

$$y_t = \mu_0 + d_1 B_{1t} + d_2 B_{2t} + y_{t-1} + \vartheta_{1t} \qquad (4.9)$$

$$y_t = \mu_1 + \gamma_t d_1 D_{1t} + d_2 D_{2t} + \vartheta_{2t} \qquad (4.10)$$

Where $(\vartheta_{1t}, \vartheta_{2t})$ the error terms are stationary processes; $B_{jt} = 1$ for t= $T_{Bj} + 1$ (j=1, 2) and 0 otherwise and d= $(d_1, d_2)'$. In Model C, the null and alternative hypotheses are given by equations (4.11) and (4.12) respectively:

$$y_t = \mu_0 + d_1 B_{1t} + d_2 B_{2t} + \theta_1 D_{1t} + \theta_2 D_{2t} + y_{t-1} + \vartheta_{1t} \qquad (4.11)$$

$$y_t = \mu_1 + \gamma_t d_1 D_{1t} + d_2 D_{2t} + \varphi_1 DT_{1t} + \varphi_2 DT_{2t} + \vartheta_{2t} \qquad (4.12)$$

where the error terms $(\vartheta_{1t}, \vartheta_{2t})$ are stationary processes; $B_{jt} = 1$ for t= $T_{Bj} + 1$ (j=1,2) and 0 otherwise and d=$(d_1, d_2)'$. The L-S (2003) unit root test results[16] of Model A and C for ASEAN, CACM, MERCOSUR and SADC countries are reported in Tables 4.13 to 4.16. According to LM_T stats of Model A reported in Table 4.13 to 4.16, the null hypothesis cannot be rejected at 5% level of significance in the case of ASEAN, CACM, MERCOSUR and SADC countries. This indicates that data are not stationary. First order differencing (d=1) is required to make the data stationary. Same applies to the LM_T stats of Model C, where the null hypothesis cannot be rejected 1% level of significance in the case of ASEAN, CACM, MERCOSUR and SADC countries.

This indicates that data are not stationary. First order differencing (d=1) is required to make the data stationary. The volatility findings in this book should

[15] They omit an explicit discussion on model B arguing that it is commonly held that most economic time series can adequately be described by model A or C (L-S, 2003, 1083)

[16] The L-S (2003) unit root test results are generated by using GAUSS programming language

be considered with caution as evidence of structural breaks have been detected and further investigation on structural breaks is left for future work.

4.13 L-S test results for ASEAN countries

Country	Model A			
	LMT stats	*Break Dates*	*t stats Levels*	*Reasons*
Brunei	-2.784 [9]	1997M8 2005M4	-24.121* -24.199*	AFC
Cambodia	-2.720 [9]	1997M8 2005M4	-25.188* -25.040*	AFC
Indonesia	-2.833 [9]	1997M8 2005M4	-24.089* -24.121*	AFC
Laos	-2.865	1992M12 1996M8	6.042* 6.845*	Regime change
Malaysia	-1.933 [1]	1992M12 1996M8	6.059* 7.094*	Regime change
Philippines	-2.784 [9]	1997M8 2005M4	-24.121* -24.199*	AFC
Singapore	-1.900 [10]	1998M1 1998M9	-5.249* -1.757	AFC
Thailand	-2.833 [9]	1997M8 2005M4	-24.089* -24.121*	AFC
Vietnam	-1.506 [0]	1999M12 2000M12	4.625* 1.718	Currency re-valuation

The lag length of the *LMT* test is determined by a general to specific procedure choosing maximum lag on which the t-statistics are significant at the asymptotic 10% level, lag length chosen is in square. Critical values are available from Lee and Strazicich (2003, Table2). *Indicate 1% significance level **Indicate 5% significance level

Country	Model C				
	LMT stats	*Break Dates*	*Reasons*	*t-stats*	
				Levels	*Trends*
Brunei	-3.561 [2]	1997M8 2005M3	AFC	-12.770* 0.943	-0.031 -3.550*
Cambodia	-4.242 [5]	1997M8 2005M3	AFC	-12.924* 1.212	0.028 -4.118*
Indonesia	-3.572 [2]	1997M8 2005M3	AFC	-12.803* 0.901	-0.030 3.561*
Laos	-5.482 [8]	1996M4 2004M1	AFC	-0.023 0.710	4.286* -4.305*
Malaysia	-5.482 [8]	1996M4 2004M1	AFC	-0.023 0.710	4.286* -4.305*
Philippines	-3.561 [2]	1997M8 2005M3	AFC	12.770* 0.943	0.031 -3.550*
Singapore	-5.325 [12]	1997M8 2005M7	AFC	-0.426 2.231**	5.529* -5.075*

Thailand	-3.572 [2]	1997M8 2005M3	AFC	12.803* 0.901	-0.030 -3.561*
Vietnam	-5.624 [9]	1999M12 2007M8	Political instability	3.890* -0.467	4.593* -1.131

4.14 L-S test results for CACM countries

Country	Model A			
	LMT stats	*Break Dates*	*t-stats Levels*	*Reasons*
Costa Rica	-2.720 [9]	1997M8 2005M4	-25.188* -25.040*	Debt crisis
Dominican Republic	-2.784 [9]	1997M8 2005M4	-24.121* -24.199*	Debt crisis
Guatemala	-2.833 [9]	1997M8 2005M4	-24.089* -24.121*	Debt crisis
Honduras	-2.865 [9]	1997M8 2005M3	-24.366* -24.543*	Debt crisis
Nicaragua	-2.770 [9]	1997M7 2005M3	-24.540* -24.572*	Debt crisis

Model C				
LMT stats	*Break Dates*	*Reasons*	*t-stats*	
			Levels	*Trends*
-4.242 [5]	1997M8 2005M3	Debt crisis	-12.924* 1.212	0.028 -4.118*
-3.561 [2]	1997M8 2005M3	Debt crisis	-12.770* 0.943	-0.031 -3.550
-3.572 [2]	1997M8 2005M3	Debt crisis	-12.803* 0.901	-0.030 -3.561
-3.510 [2]	1997M8 2005M2	Debt crisis	-12.784* 1.066	-0.052 -3.507*
-3.772 [3]	1997M7 2005M2	Debt crisis	-12.889* 1.129	-0.014 -3.720*

The lag length of the *LMT* test is determined by a general to specific procedure choosing maximum lag on which the t-statistics are significant at the asymptotic 10% level, lag length chosen is in square. Critical values are available from Lee and Strazicich (2003, Table 2). *Indicate 1% significance level **Indicate 5% significance level

4.15 L-S test results for MERCOSUR countries

Country	Model A			
	LMT stats	*Break Dates*	*t-stats Levels*	*Reasons*
Bolivia	-2.978 [1]	1992M3	2.453**	Regime change
		1994M4	0.728	
Brazil	-2.436 [12]	1996M12	-1.687**	Debt crisis
		1999M8	1.877**	
Chile	-3.047 [1]	1992M3	2.478**	Regime change
		1992M5	1.532	
Colombia	-3.074 [1]	1992M3	2.418**	Regime change
		1994M4	0.869	
Paraguay	-3.055 [1]	1992M3	2.481**	Regime change
		1992M4	1.219	
Peru	-3.615 [9]	1992M3	2.605*	Regime change
		1994M12	0.631	
Uruguay	-2.788 [1]	1994M4	0.857	Debt crisis
		1998M7	0.806	
Venezuela	-2.957 [2]	1994M5	0.813	Debt crisis
		1998M8	0.759	

Model C				
LMT stats	*Break Dates*	*Reasons*	*t-stats*	
			Levels	*Trends*
-3.462 [1]	1994M2	Regime change	0.592	-2.428**
	1996M9		0.710	1.726
-5.199 [0]	1997M9	Debt	2.930*	4.310*
	2000M7	crisis	-0.691	-2.602*
-3.540 [1]	1994M2	Regime change	0.6135	-2.435**
	1996M9		-0.168	1.757
-3.580 [1]	1994M2	Regime change	0.620	-2.456**
	1996M9		-0.195	1.786
-3.557 [1]	1994M2	Regime change	0.645	-2.446**
	1996M9		-0.264	1.801
-4.235 [9]	2003M6	Debt crisis	0.772	-1.242
	2006M11		0.776	-3.003*
-4.905 [12]	1994M2	Debt crisis	0.849	-3.037*
	1996M9		-0.614	2.211**
-4.899 [12]	1994M2	Debt crisis	0.897	-3.144*
	1997M6		0.092	1.780

4.16 L-S test results for SADC countries

Country	Model A			
	LMT stats	*Break Dates*	*t stats Levels*	*Reasons*
Angola	-2.280 [10]	1998M2 1998M11	-2.680* 2.069**	Civil war
Botswana	-1.674 [11]	2000M5 2005M11	1.180 -0.531	Regime change
DRC	-2.184 [10]	1998M2 1998M11	-2.534** 2.072**	Civil war
Madagascar	-2.601 [2]	1996M7 2002M11	1.067 1.072	Regime changes
Malawi	-2.420 [0]	1993M4 1999M9	2.832* 2.780*	Regime change
Mauritius	-2.614 [2]	1996M6 2002M11	1.012 1.011	Regime change
Mozambique	-2.609 [2]	1996M6 2002M11	1.049 1.044	Debt crisis
Seychelles	-2.720 [9]	1997M8 2005M4	-25.188* -25.040*	Debt crisis
South Africa	-2.784 [9]	1997M8 2005M4	-24.121* -24.199*	Debt crisis
Tanzania	-2.865 [9]	1997M8 2005M3	-24.366* -24.543*	Debt crisis
Zambia	-2.770 [9]	1997M7 2005M3	-24.540* -24.572*	Debt crisis

The lag length of the *LMT* test is determined by a general to specific procedure choosing maximum lag on which the t-statistics are significant at the asymptotic 10% level, lag length chosen is in square. Critical values are available from Lee and Strazicich (2003, Table 2). *Indicate 1% significance level **Indicate 5% significance level ***Indicate 10% significance level

Model C				
LMT stats	*Break Dates*	*Reasons*	*t-stats*	
			Levels	*Trends*
-5.097 [0]	1997M9 2000M7	Civil war	2.959* -1.047	4.131* -1.554
-5.653 [10]	1999M12 2007M7	Regime change	4.366* -0.473	4.518* -0.984
-5.046 [0]	1997M9 2002M11	Civil war	3.246* 0.343	4.103 1.578
-2.887 [2]	1996M5 1999M8	Regime changes	-9.590* -0.285	-0.280 1.367
-2.863 [0]	1996M4 2006M6	Debt crisis	0.356 -0.211	-2.277* 1.522
-2.893 [2]	1996M4 1999M7	Regime change	-9.655* -0.282	-0.274 1.356
-2.886 [2]	1996M4 1999M7	Debt crisis	-9.672* -0.282	0.274 1.356
-4.242 [5]	1997M8 2005M3	Debt crisis	-12.924* 1.212	0.028 -4.118*
-3.561 [2]	1997M8 2005M3	Debt crisis	-12.770* 0.943	-0.031 -3.550*
-3.510 [2]	1997M8 2005M2	Debt crisis	-12.784* 1.066	-0.052 -3.507*
-3.772 [3]	1997M7 2005M2	Debt crisis	-12.889* 1.129	-0.014 -3.720*

4.5 Regional Comparisons

Table 4.17 provides a summary of the MAPEs of the volatility, exponential smoothing and Naïve I forecasts. Exponential smoothing fared very well in this research in terms of forecasting accuracy. This finding can be explained by the fact that one of the main characteristic of exponential smoothing is its ability to react to changes quickly compared with other time series methods. It should be noted that exponential smoothing performed well in Africa and Asia, two regions in the world well known for the sudden changes in their exchange rates (either because of unstable governments or exchange rate crises). Exponential smoothing models give more weight to the recent past as opposed to historical data. In the present study, this means that the impact of shocks to the exchange rate system fades away in the medium and long term while being significantly important on the short term. In addition, this reflects the nature of the exchange rate market which is described by practitioners as a market with short memory where traders ignore events that might have occurred within a similar pattern but belong to a different time period. Volatility and exponential smoothing methods consistently outperform Naïve I models.

As in the paper of Altavilla and De Grauwe (2010), historical data seems to be exceptionally important in dictating future changes not only in the foreign exchange market but in the financial market in general. This is what researchers in Finance denominate 'clusters' where positive changes are likely to be followed by positive changes and vice-versa. Taking into consideration the fact that the FOREX market is the most liquid market in the world, the effect of trends in one market are quickly compounded over the globe in a very short time which explains the pre-eminence of exponential smoothing as a first class forecasting method to capture such behaviour. The Naïve I model had some success in this research but was outperformed by volatility and exponential smoothing models. This can be explained by the fact that the period examined in the present study has been volatile by nature. Currency crises hit Southeast Asia in 1997 and shook economies and finances in that part of the world and elsewhere.

The crisis in Mexico and the inability of Argentina to pay back its debts to the IMF in 2001 spread panic in global financial markets and paralysed in the process the whole continent. Central American countries were governed by people who cared very little about currency stability and had other priorities in mind while the African continent was struggling to overcome its bloody conflicts and civil wars. Around the same period, South Africa whose currency is a legal tender for Lesotho, Namibia and Swaziland, was trying to heal the scars of the Apartheid regime and could hardly provide a leading role in matters related to exchange rate management. That said, the author of this book believes that the no-change Naïve I model still have a huge exploratory power over short horizons especially when markets are relatively stable. Last but not least, the forecasts generated by the best single model have all scored less than 5% MAPE with and an average of 2%. In other words, the margin of error between the real exchange rate value and the forecast is in average 0.02 (2%) for every one unit of a currency, an excellent approximation even by the standard of the FOREX market where changes are measured by basis point, 0.01(1%). Although this book is aimed mainly to policy makers, the findings are of particular relevance to traders in the quest to understand the mystery of the exchange rate market in the emerging world.

Table 4.17 Volatility, Exponential Smoothing and Naïve 1 Forecasting Competition

ASEAN	MAPE	CACM	MAPE	MERCOSUR	MAPE	SADC	MAPE
Brunei	ES (0.8%)	**Costa Rica**	Vol (3.1%)	**Bolivia**	ES (1.72%)	**Angola**	ES (2.08%)
Cambodia	N1 (3.06%)	**Dominican Republic**	ES (2.13%)	**Brazil**	Vol (3.72%)	**Botswana**	ES (2.7%)
Indonesia	ES (2.9%)	**Guatemala**	ES (3.29%)	**Chile**	ES (3.36%)	**Madagascar**	ES (2.56%)
Laos	ES (1.47%)	**Honduras**	ES (2.58%)	**Colombia**	ES (3.41%)	**Malawi**	ES (1.55%)
Malaysia	ES (1.21%)	**Nicaragua**	ES (2.63%)	**Paraguay**	ES (2.36%)	**Mauritius**	ES (2.5%)
Philippines	ES (1.77%)			**Peru**	ES (2.19%)	**Mozambique**	ES (2.78%)
Singapore	Vol (1.52%)			**Uruguay**	ES (4.78%)	**South Africa**	ES (4.81%)
Thailand	ES (1.77%)			**Venezuela**	ES (1.52%)	**Tanzania**	ES (2.12%)
Vietnam	ES (1.85%)					**Seychelles**	ES (2.23%)
						Zambia	ES (4.41%)

ES= Exponential smoothing; N1= Naïve 1; Vol= ARIMA-Volatility

4.6 Conclusions

The current study has examined volatility dynamics of exchange rates across parts of Africa, Asia, Central and Latin America. The relevance of volatility studies in these regional settings is unquestionable as significant volatility patterns have been found for most exchange rates examined. In a recent paper, Aghion et al. (2009) found that volatility of the real effective exchange rate is detrimental for productivity growth, especially for countries at relatively low levels of financial development. This is true of many countries sampled in this book which makes the study of exchange rates of particular relevance. Calvo and Reinhart (2002) showed that many emerging market countries resort to pegging strategies and regime changes, despite counter claims by the countries' monetary authorities that respective domestic currency floats freely. Although the claim by Calvo and Reinhart (2002) might be to some extent true, the main reason behind such a discrepancy is that policy makers in the emerging world are not equipped either with the understanding or the tools that will make them manage their exchange rates in an efficient way. Many of them still believe that forecasting volatility is a "notoriously difficult task" (Brailsford and Faff, 1996, 419). This chapter offers a very strong evidence that volatility exists and can be forecasted accurately. Exponential smoothing models have performed particularly well across continents while volatility models provided very good forecasts. Even the Naïve I model referred to as no change models in some text books, did surprisingly well in many occasions. The main finding of this chapter is that exponential smoothing method provides the most accurate forecasts comparing to the two other time series techniques used in this book. This raises many eyebrows as exponential smoothing has been largely under-used in Finance and particularly in exchange rate forecasts. This book makes a further contribution to literature since it forecasted future values of exchanges rates in the emerging world trading blocs using a set of time series models and because it provides empirical evidence that exponential smoothing forecast can be particularly accurate over and horizon of 24 months even during a period of instability. Forecasters would want to take note of that and integrate the method in their forecasting practice.

Gokcan (2000) suggested that volatility is related to the stage of market development. Risk or the uncertainty of returns in emerging markets is typically higher than those in developed markets. As such, volatility in emerging markets is generally larger and more persistent than in developed markets. The findings of this chapter confirm the assumption that volatility exist in developing countries and the patterns are similar for countries at the same stage of development regardless of the geographical location. Countries in Central America were found to respond to shocks in a similar fashion when compared to countries located in Southern Africa which makes the stage of development a relevant aspect to be taken into consideration in any future research that intend to venture on the examination of exchange rates in the emerging world. One explanation to higher volatility in the emerging world compared to the advanced world is the difference in the speed and reliability of information available to investors, which is associated with modes of telecommunication and possibly the accounting system in place. As such, a small and relatively under developed FOREX market should exhibit relatively larger volatility clustering. The general presumption is that an increase in exchange rate uncertainty will have an adverse effect on trade flows and consequently, the overall health of the world economy. Underdeveloped FOREX markets are characterised with high level of dollarisation, customer driven FOREX transactions (i.e. low level of speculative activity), low level of financial participation in the inter-bank market and the absence of forwards markets. Dollarization is very popular in many parts of Africa and Central America particularly during periods of political instability. Any future study examining volatility in these regional settings should take into consideration the existence of a black market parallel to the official currency market. There is an increasing need to incorporate the importance of modelling interventions and exchange rates as interdependent variables and more detailed information on intervention activity would make it possible to build and estimate more appropriately specified models of these relationships. Forecasting volatility is no longer a choice but a requirement for nations that want to strive in the 21st global and turbulent markets.

Chapter V. ARDL Cointegration Forecasting

Although cointegration has become a popular tool in the forecasting of financial series, it is still under-used in the examination of exchange rates. This is particularly true in emerging markets where little or non-macroeconomic data was available during the two decades leading to the 21st century. The present study investigates the determinants of exchange rate changes in selected regional settings. The majority of countries in Africa and Central America have never been investigated before in that respect while ARDL cointegration was hardly been used to capture the relationship between exchange rates and their determinants in most regional settings mentioned above. This is where the contribution of this chapter lies; providing empirical analysis for policy makers and international investors to identify factors that affect the size and the direction of exchange rate fluctuations in ASEAN, CACM, MERCOSUR and SADC countries. The findings of this chapter can be treated as an exploratory analysis or as a reference point for those who wish to delve on the study of exchange rates in the emerging world. Suffice it to say, the findings are relevant to policy makers who wish to strike a balance between monetary aggregates, trade welfare and sound macroeconomic policies in a turbulent 21st century.

The concept of cointegration is relatively new compared to other well established forecasting techniques like time series analysis. However, since the seminal work of Engle and Granger (1987), cointegration has become the prevalent tool of time series econometrics. Cointegration was introduced by Granger (1981) and elaborated further by Engle and Granger (1987), Engle and Yoo (1987), Johansen (1988) and Pesaran and Shin (1995, 1999). Cointegration examines whether a time series converges in the long-run, while allowing for the fact that it may not move in the same direction in the short-run. The ARDL form of cointegration of Pesaran and Shin (1995) is used in this research. It follows a two-step process. First, any long-run equilibrium relationships between exchange rates and economic aggregates are established and then an error correction model (ECM) is obtained - so called because short term deviations from equilibrium are corrected to achieve the long-run equilibrium. ARDL also quantifies the strength of the relationship between variables in the short and long term.

Chapter Three provided an overview of cointegration and ARDL applications in Finance followed by a section that examined the use of these techniques in the FOREX market with a particular focus on emerging countries. In this chapter, the ARDL cointegration method is used to identify the existence (if applicable), the size and the direction of relationships between exchanges rates and respective explanatory variables. Section 5.1 discusses the method and reviews the advantages of using such a model instead of other cointegration methods. Sections 5.2 and 5.4 analyse the results from local and regional angles while section 5.3 discusses the parameter stability tests. Section 5.5 concludes and makes recommendations for policy makers and international investors.

5.1 The ARDL Cointegration Method

Cointegration theory has led to a leap in the understanding of the non-stationary time series data. If non-stationary variables are entered into regression based analyses, we have what is known as the "spurious regression problem". This problem occurs when two or more variables are following similar trends. Newbold and Granger (1974) noted that there are three consequences of this: (i) estimates of the regression coefficients become inefficient (ii) forecasts based on the regression equations become sub-optimal and (iii) the usual significance tests of the coefficients become invalid. Within the framework of cointegration, there are two major "branches" namely the Engle and Granger method (1987), which is based on residual testing and the Johansen method (1988, 1991), based on likelihood-ratio tests.

Engle and Granger (1987) advanced cointegration theory and demonstrated that cointegration relationship has an error correcting form. The error correction representation simply means that the two variables can diverge in the short-run but will converge in the long-run. An ECM integrates the short-run dynamics with the long-run equilibrium without losing long-run information. The rationale behind this is intuitive; the bounding economic forces underlying two variables will keep their own movements within a boundary but short term dynamics may make them react independently in the short-run. There are many examples for these types of links and boundaries such as long-run and short-run interest rates, income and household expenditures, prices of the same commodities in markets that are located in different countries and the spot and future markets of financial assets (Brooks, 2008).

Despite its simplicity, the ARDL approach is not applied as often as the Johansen approach. In terms of methodology, the recently developed ARDL framework of Pesaran and Shin (1995, 1999), Pesaran and Pesaran (1997) and Pesaran et al. (2001), is used in this book to establish the direction of the relationships between exchange rates and selected macroeconomic variables. There are advantages to using this approach instead of the conventional Johansen (1988) method. The main one lies in the fact that it can be applied irrespective of whether the variables are stationary '*I*(0)',or require first level differencing '*I*(1)' (Pesaran and Pesaran 1997). Another advantage of this approach is that the model takes sufficient numbers of lags to capture the data generating process in a general-to-specific modelling framework (Laurenceson and Chai 2003). The reasons behind the choice of ARDL approach in this book can be summarised as follows:

1- The ARDL approach does not involve pre-testing of the variables, which means that a test on the existence of relationship between variables is applicable irrespective of whether the underlying regressors are purely *I*(0), purely $I(1)$ or mixture of both. The testing might only be needed if the researcher suspects that one of the variables requires second order differencing '$I(2)$'.

2- ARDL allows variables to have different optimal lags, which is impossible with the standard cointegration tests. This is particularly useful since explanatory variables used as determinants of exchange rates are expected to have different optimal lags.

3- The model could be used with limited sample data (30 to 80 observations), while other models require a larger set of data in order to identify any sort of relationships. This last feature is of particular relevance as countries like Angola and the Democratic Republic of Congo have only started recording economic data in the last couple of years and through ARDL, it would be possible to tease out potential relationships between exchange rates and the relative fundamentals even with the small amount of historical data available.

The simplest ARDL model would attempt to explain one variable from its own past and also includes current or lagged values of a second variable. Since lagged effects are possible, we say that the dynamic effects of a change in X_t upon Y_t can be modelled and explained as follows:

$$Y_t = \mu + \vartheta\, Y_{t-1} + \varphi_0 X_t + \varphi_1 X_{t-1} + e_t \qquad (5.1)$$

Where Y_t is the observed value of the Y series at time (t), Y_{t-1} is the observed value of the Y series at time (t-1), X_t is the observed value of the X series at time (t), X_{t-1} is the observed value of the X series at time (t-1) , e_t is an error term and μ, ϑ, φ_0, φ_1 are parameters of the model. If we subtract Y_{t-1} from both sides of Eq. (5.1) and use the notation ΔY_t to indicate the difference between the observed exchange rate values at time (t) and (t-1), then $\Delta Y_t = (Y_t - Y_{t-1})$. Therefore if we replace $(Y_t - Y_{t-1})$ by ΔY_t in Eq. (5.1) we will have:

$$\Delta Y_t = \mu + \vartheta\, Y_{t-1} - Y_{t-1} + \varphi_0 X_t + \varphi_1 X_{t-1} + e_t$$

$$\Delta Y_t = \mu + (\vartheta - 1) Y_{t-1} + \varphi_0 X_t + \varphi_1 X_{t-1} + e_t$$

$$\Delta Y_t = \mu + (\vartheta - 1) Y_{t-1} + \varphi_0 X_t - \varphi_0 X_{t-1} + \varphi_0 X_{t-1} + \varphi_1 X_{t-1} + e_t$$

$$\Delta Y_t = \mu - (1 - \vartheta) Y_{t-1} + \varphi_0\, \Delta X_t + (\varphi_0 + \varphi_1)\, X_{t-1} + e_t$$

$$\Delta Y_t = \varphi_0 \Delta X_t - (1 - \vartheta)\left[Y_{t-1} - \frac{\mu}{1-\vartheta} - \frac{\varphi_0 + \varphi_1}{1-\vartheta} X_{t-1}\right] + e_t$$

$$\Delta Y_t = \varphi_0 \Delta X_t - (1 - \vartheta)[Y_{t-1} - \alpha - \beta X_{t-1}] + e_t \qquad (5.2)$$

Where $\alpha = \frac{\mu}{1-\vartheta}$ and $= \frac{\varphi_0+\varphi_1}{1-\vartheta}$. ΔX_t which denotes the changes in the explanatory variable in the short term. For example, if we assume that current exchange rates Y_t) are affected by changes in trade (X_t) then the difference between the current and last time period level of trade is denoted as ΔX_t and an increase of one unit in (X_t) will have an immediate impact on (Y_t) of φ_0 units from Eq. (5.2). In other words, ΔX_t measures the short term change in exchange rate due to a change in the explanatory variable (in this example, trade). As stated earlier in this section, the ARDL modelling process involves establishing the error correction term which identifies by how much exchange rates deviate from their long-run equilibrium value. In Eq. (5.2) the adjustment parameter ECM is denoted by $(1-\vartheta)$ which should be significantly different from zero to validate the long-run relationship $[Y_{t-1} - \alpha - \beta X_{t-1}]$. A small ECM value indicates that exchange rates will return quickly towards long-run equilibrium whilst a large ECM value indicates that a shock to the system may have long-lasting effect on exchange rate values. To illustrate this, consider a particular ARDL model in which the Y_t variable is lagged by p time periods. Furthermore, assume that there are $k\ X_t$ variables which for simplicity are all lagged by q time periods. The particular error correction form for this ARDL scheme used is:

$$\Delta Y_t = \pi + \sum_{i=1}^{q=1} \beta_i \Delta Y_{t-i} + \sum_{i=1}^{q=1} \gamma_i \Delta X_{1,t-i} + \sum_{i=1}^{q=1} \tau_i \Delta X_{2,t-i} + \cdots + \sum_{i=1}^{q=1} \theta_i \Delta X_{k,t-i} + (\delta_1 Y_{t-1} + \delta_2 X_{1,t-1} + \delta_3 X_{2,t-1} + \cdots + \delta_k X_{(k,t-1]}) + e_t \quad (5.3)$$

Where $\sum_{i=1}^{q=1} \beta_i \Delta X_{t-i}$ indicate past changes in the dependent variable (exchange rates)

$\sum_{i=1}^{q=1} \gamma_i \Delta X_{1,t-i}$ indicate past changes in the first explanatory variable,

$\sum_{i=1}^{q=1} \tau_i \Delta X_{2,t-i}$ indicate past changes in the second explanatory variable

$\sum_{i=1}^{q=1} \theta_i \Delta X_{k,t-i}$ indicate past changes in the k explanatory variable and

$(\delta_1 Y_{t-1} + \delta_2 X_{1,t-1} + \delta_3 X_{2,t-1} + \cdots + \delta_k X_{(k,t-1]})$ the error correction model

The ARDL method developed by Pesaran, Shin, and Smith (2001) was used to establish cointegration relationships among the variables using the Microfit 4.0 for Windows software (Pesaran and Pesaran, 1997). As discussed earlier in this chapter, the ARDL method involves two steps. First, the existence of a long-run relationship among the variables in the model is determined. The existence of a long-run relationship is established by the bounds test based on a correctly specified and appropriate ARDL model and an associated unrestricted error correction model (Pesaran et al., 2001). The determination of an appropriate and correctly specified ARDL model is based on test criteria such as the SBC and various diagnostic tests for econometric problems. The unrestricted ECM is directly derived from the ARDL model. An ARDL model needs to exhibit no temporal autocorrelation. Additionally, an ARDL model needs to be homoscedastic and this was tested using the F-statistic test. Both statistics are reported in Tables 5.1 and 5.2. A few of the exchange rates analysed required the calculation of natural logarithms (logs) to come up with significant relationships between the dependent and the independent variables, while a time trend variable (T) was used to account for the possible effects a trend can have on exchange rates. A time trend is used if there is no other trending variable in the cointegrating relationship to cancel it out. In this case a trend is entered as one of the cointegrating variables.

2.7 5.2 ARDL Cointegration Findings (short and long-run relationships)

5.2.1 ASEAN

Cambodia's, Laos' and Myanmar's exchange rates were excluded from the analysis because no significant models were found over the sample period 1990-2009. Table 5.3 shows the results of using ARDL cointegration as a means to identify determinants of exchange rates for the remaining seven currencies of ASEAN. Table 5.3 also reports ECM values. Two explanatory variables stand out in this part of the world - GDP and exports. The empirical results yield long-run positive relationships between exports and the Malaysian ringgit (0.0001), exports and Philippines peso (0.0002), exports and Singapore dollar (0.0001) and exports and Thai baht (0.001). In other words, when the volume of exports increases by 1 unit, the exchange rate goes up by less than 0.001 units for all four currencies which might be considered as a small change by the standards of a trader since we are talking about a long term relationship here that is measured in terms of several months. When natural logarithms were used in the ARDL cointegration, the acronym (logs) is used.

Table 5.4 provides results for the investigation of short-run relationships between exchange rates and macroeconomic fundamentals in the ASEAN region. According to Duasa (2009), Malaysia was significantly affected by the terms of trade[17] during the AFC. There was an immediate impact of exchange rate shock on the volumes of exports and imports as the country heavily relies on international trade. Before the recession of 1997, Malaysia had a large trade surplus of US $4.0 billion which was wiped out to less than US $17.7 billion by 1998. Although the findings of this research support those of Duasa (2009), they show a weak relationship between exports and exchange rates not only in Malaysia but also in other ASEAN countries. This is one of the major findings of this research – changes in exchange rates have an immediate and strong impact on the terms of trade while the effects of changes in trade take more time to materialise in terms of changes in the exchange rate which explains relatively the small gradients between both variables. That said, the relationship

[17] Is the ratio of exports over imports, it measures the quantity of imports that can be purchased through the sale of fixed quantity of exports and hence is used as a proxy to measure the relative social welfare in a country (Duasa, 2009)

between GDP and exchange rates seems to be stronger than the one between trade and exchange rates. For example, an increase of 1% in the GDP of Indonesia leads to an increase of 0.013% on exchange rates in the long-run. Indonesia has weathered the global financial crisis relatively smoothly because of its heavy reliance on domestic consumption as the driver of economic growth (The Economist, 2011). During the AFC, the Indonesian rupiah lost over 75% of its value and the foreign denominated debts of Indonesia were multiplied by a factor of four which made it almost impossible not to be driven to insolvency by such a shock. This led to a rise in inflation exacerbating the financial crisis because it resulted in an increase on the interest rates. The relationship between exchange rates, inflation and interest rates was examined but yielded no significant results. The relationship between GDP and exchange rates reported in Table 5.3 would have been expected to be stronger were it not for the factors mentioned in the Economist (2011) which stated that Indonesia's development is hampered by the fact that a high share of the goods desired by consumers is imported, the economy being commodities-based, the poor infrastructure and corruption.

Table 5.1 ARDL Bounds F-tests for Cointegrating Relationships

Currency name	Specification	F-statistic
Angola Kwanza	Ex_{ANK} *(CPI)*	F(2, 97) 25.061*
Bolivia Boliviano	$logEx_{BOB}$ *(GDP, Gold)*	F(3, 225) 8.453*
Botswana Pula	$log\ Ex_{BWP}$ *(GDP)*	F(2, 161) 2.591**
Brazil Real	$log\ Ex_{BRL}$ *(Gold, TB)*	F(6, 181) 34.382*
Brunei Dollar	Ex_{BND} *(GDP)*	F(2, 65) 4.493**
Chile Peso	$log\ Ex_{CLP}$ *(Copper price, TB)*	F(2, 341) 3.559**
Colombia Peso	$log\ Ex_{COP}$ *(Interest Rate, TO)*	F(4, 171) 5.265*
DRC Franc	$log\ Ex_{CDF}$ *(log CPI)*	F(1, 166) 29.628*
Costa Rica Colon	$log\ Ex_{CRC}$ *(TO)*	F(2, 93) 2.789**
Dominican Republic Peso	$log\ Ex_{DOP}$ *(TB)*	F(2, 341)1.880**
Guatemala Quetzal	Ex_{GTQ} *(Imports, CPI)*	F(3, 340)1.729**
Honduras Lempira	$logEx_{HNL}$ *(CPI)*	F(3, 148)5.340*
Indonesia Rupiah	$log\ Ex_{IDR}$ *(GDP change)*	F(5, 122) 11.690*
Madagascar Ariary	$log\ Ex_{MGA}$ *(Capital Account)*	F(1, 342) 1.283**
Malawi Kwacha	$log\ Ex_{MWK}$ *(CPI)*	F(2, 260) 2.874**
Malaysia Ringgit	$log\ Ex_{MYR}$ *(Exports, Interest Rate)*	F(3, 236) 3.055**
Mauritius Rupee	$log\ Ex_{MUR}$ *(CPI)*	F(1, 342) 2.880*
Mozambique Metical	$log\ Ex_{MZN}$ *(logreserves, CPI, Interest Rate)*	F(5, 157) 7.741*
Nicaragua Cordoba	$log\ Ex_{NIO}$ *(TB)*	F(1, 186) 1.983**
Paraguay Guarani	$log\ Ex_{PYG}$ *(Exports, Imports)*	F(3, 52) 8.618*
Peru New Sol	Ex_{PEN} *(Capital Account, Interest Rate)*	F(3, 224) 17.778*
Philippines Peso	Ex_{PHP} *(Exports)*	F(2, 259) 2.097*
Seychelles Rupee	$log\ Ex_{SCR}$ *(Money Supply, Interest Rate)*	F(5, 127) 17.273*
Singapore Dollar	Ex_{SGD} *(Exports, Imports)*	F(3, 278) 3.803**
Tanzania Shilling	$log\ Ex_{TZS}$ *(Interest Rate)*	F(1, 152) 6.651**
Thailand Baht	$log\ Ex_{THB}$ *(Exports, Gold)*	F(4, 175) 4.107*
Uruguay Peso	$log\ Ex_{UYU}$ *(Gold, Interest Rate)*	F(4, 267) 27.327*
Venezuela Bolivar	$log\ Ex_{VEF}$ *(TB, Interest Rate)*	F(4, 211) 10.158*

*and ** denotes significance at 1% and 5 % level respectively

Table 5.2 Diagnostic Tests of Estimated Models

Currency name	Specification	X^2_{SA}	X^2_{NORM}	X^2_{HETER}
Angola Kwanza	ARDL(2,1)	6.727	145.822*	2.096
Bolivia Boliviano	ARDL(1,0,2)	14.726	12.629*	3.004
Botswana Pula	ARDL(1,0)	15.894	155.540*	0.520
Brazil Real	ARDL(3,3,0)	18.257	81.313*	3.654
Brunei Dollar	ARDL(1,0)	13.315	0.143	0.041
Chile Peso	ARDL(1,0,0)	13.037	158.35*	2.054
Colombia Peso	ARDL(2,0,0)	12.755	22.363*	1.645
DRC Franc	ARDL(1,1)	13.284	41.663*	2.020
Costa Rica Colon	ARDL(1,0)	15.366	27.421*	3.583
Dominican Peso	ARDL(1,0)	3.774	28.924*	1.428
Guatemala Quetzal	ARDL(1,0,0)	14.162	85.229*	0.128
Honduras Lempira	ARDL(1,0)	18.042	7.987*	1.027
Indonesia Rupiah	ARDL(1,4)	11.427	196.454*	0.211
Madagascar Ariary	ARDL(1,0)	13.055	34.052*	0.565
Malawi Kwacha	ARDL(2,0)	20.478	66.520*	0.738
Malaysia Ringgit	ARDL(1,0,0)	13.385	35.372*	2.065
Mauritius Rupee	ARDL(1,0)	13.291	77.950*	0.124
Mozambique Metical	ARDL(2,0,0)	19.711	162.639*	3.819
Nicaragua Cordoba	ARDL(1,0)	8.074	2.326	0.093
Paraguay Guarani	ARDL(1,0,0)	11.460	1.296	3.858
Peru New Sol	ARDL(1,1,1)	14.279	7.076**	1.456
Philippines Peso	ARDL(1,0)	15.421	107.772*	2.522
Seychelles Rupee	ARDL(2,3,0)	6.779	12.757*	1.762
Singapore Dollar	ARDL(1,0,0)	16.509	54.198*	0.980
Tanzania Shilling	ARDL(1,0)	18.043	37.887*	0.281
Thailand Baht	ARDL(2,0,0)	11.092	25.074*	2.707
Uruguay Peso	ARDL(2,0,0)	12.026	32.760*	2.134
Venezuela Bolivar	ARDL(1,0,1)	16.555	195.880*	0.076

* and ** denotes significance at 1% and 5% respectively

A long-term negative gradient of (-0.0001) defines the relationship between Brunei dollar exchange rates and the GDP volume. Crude oil and natural gas production account for just over half of GDP and more than 90% of exports in Sultanate of Brunei. Per capita GDP is among the highest in Asia, and substantial income from overseas investment supplements income from domestic production so the relationship between GDP and exchange rates would have been expected to be a lot stronger. As mentioned in Chapter Two, Brunei's Central Bank has maintained a Currency board arrangement as a policy to manage exchange rates. This means that the exchange rate is fixed and any appreciation of the currency should be backed by additional holdings of the key foreign currency which explains the weak relationship between GDP and exchange rates. In other terms, exchange rates fluctuations are not driven by macroeconomic changes such as GDP but are rather the result of Central Bank interventions.

Table 5.3 ASEAN Long-run Cointegration Coefficients

Variable	Coefficient	t-ratio	Significance
Brunei Dollar			
ARDL(1,0)			
Variable	Coefficient	t-ratio	Significance
GDP	-0.0001	-4.794	0.000
Constant	2.924	25.007	0.000
ECM(-1)	-0.127	-2.711	0.009
Indonesia Rupiah (logs)			
ARDL(1,4)			
Variable	Coefficient	t-ratio	Significance
GDP change	0.013	2.525	0.013
Constant	9.441	316.845	0.000
ECM(-1)	-0.222	-5.078	0.000
Malaysia Ringgit (logs)			
ARDL(1,0,0)			
Variable	Coefficient	t-ratio	Significance
Exports	0.00001	4.982	0.000
Interest Rate	-0.098	-2.483	0.014
Constant	1.166	16.871	0.000
ECM(-1)	-0.060	-2.843	0.005
Philippine Peso			
ARDL(1,0)			
Variable	Coefficient	t-ratio	Significance
Exports	0.0002	5.109	0.000
Constant	36.049	5.871	0.000
ECM(-1)	-0.028	-1.966	0.050
Singapore Dollar			
ARDL(1,0,0)			
Variable	Coefficient	t-ratio	Significance
Exports	0.0001	2.492	0.013
Imports	-0.0001	-2.671	0.008
Constant	2.797	17.672	0.000
ECM(-1)	-0.041	-2.973	0.003
Thailand Baht (logs)			
ARDL(1,0,0)			
Variable	Coefficient	t-ratio	Significance
Exports	0.001	6.406	0.000
Gold	-0.0003	-4.781	0.000
Constant	3.825	64.766	0.000
ECM(-1)	-0.114	-3.344	0.001
Vietnam Dong (logs)			
ARDL(1,0,0)			
Variable	Coefficient	t-ratio	Significance
CPI	0.005	4.175	0.000
Interest Rate	-0.019	-3.032	0.003
Constant	9.649	64.267	0.000
ECM(-1)	-0.055	-2.243	0.026

Table 5.4 ASEAN Short-run Cointegration Coefficients (none for Philippines and Vietnam)

Variable	Coefficient	t-ratio	Significance
Brunei Dollar			
ARDL(1,0)			
Variable	Coefficient	t-ratio	Significance
ΔGDP	-0.00001	-2.962	0.004
Constant	0.373	2.802	0.007
R-Squared	0.121		
R-Bar-Squared	0.094		
DW-statistic	2.310		
Log-likelihood	164.258		
Schwarz Bayesian Criterion	157.928		
Indonesia Rupiah (logs)			
ARDL(1,4)			
Variable	Coefficient	t-ratio	Significance
GDP change	-0.018	-2.511	0.013
Constant	2.098	5.071	0.000
R-Squared	0.325		
R-Bar-Squared	0.292		
DW-statistic	1.722		
Log-likelihood	179.389		
Schwarz Bayesian Criterion	162.407		
Malaysia Ringgit (logs)			
ARDL(1,0,0)			
Variable	Coefficient	t-ratio	Significance
ΔExports	0.000001	2.767	0.006
ΔInterest Rate	-0.005	-2.288	0.023
Constant	0.070	2.795	0.006
R-Squared	0.037		
R-Bar-Squared	0.025		
DW-statistic	1.909		
Log-likelihood	529.759		
Schwarz Bayesian Criterion	518.798		
Singapore Dollar			
ARDL(1,0,0)			
Variable	Coefficient	t-ratio	Significance
ΔExports	0.000004	2.357	0.019
ΔImports	-0.000005	-2.526	0.012
Constant	0.116	3.174	0.002
R-Squared	0.039		
R-Bar-Squared	0.029		
DW-statistic	2.150		
Log-likelihood	545.210		
Schwarz Bayesian Criterion	533.926		
Thailand Baht (logs)			
ARDL(1,0,0)			
Variable	Coefficient	t-ratio	Significance
ΔExports	0.0002	2.715	0.007
ΔGold	-0.00004	-2.627	0.009
Constant	0.436	3.387	0.001
R-Squared	0.085		
R-Bar-Squared	0.064		
DW-statistic	1.942		
Log-likelihood	353.362		
Schwarz Bayesian Criterion	340.380		

The interest rate shows up as a long-run explanatory variable for both Malaysia and Vietnam - there is a negative short and long-run relationship between exchange rates of the ringgit and interest rates with a gradient of (-0.098) and between exchange and interest rates in Vietnam with a gradient of (-0.019). In the case of Malaysia, the relationship between the exchange and interest rates is a lot stronger than the relationship between exports and exchange rates. Similarly for Vietnam, changes in interest rates significantly affect exchange rates compared with changes in the CPI (gradient of -0.019 as opposed to 0.053). As mentioned earlier in this section, there is both a short (0.0002) and long-run relationship (0.001) between Thailand's exports - mostly machinery and electronic components, agricultural commodities and jewellery- and exchange rates. With a well-developed infrastructure, a free-enterprise economy, generally pro-investment policies and strong export industries, Thailand enjoyed solid growth from 2000 to 2007 - averaging more than 4% per year, as it recovered from the AFC of 1997-98 (Employers' Confederation of Thailand, 2012).

In the Philippines, GDP grew by 7.3% in 2010 spurred on by consumer demand, a rebound in exports and investments. The economy has a minimal exposure to international markets which explains the lower dependence between exports and exchange rates (0.0002). The economy is relatively resilient and depends on domestic consumption, large remittances from five million overseas Filipino workers and a growing business process outsourcing industry (CIA, 2012). Interestingly, Malaysia and Vietnam are the only countries in the ASEAN area where monetary aggregates are significant explanatory variables. Additionally, those monetary aggregates seem to have a higher impact on exchange rates when compared with the impact of trade factors. The explanation for this is two-fold: both countries seem to have reached a certain level of development coupled with relatively sound macroeconomic fundamentals which allows them to let their exchange rates move in accordance with market forces. This is a proof that monetary theory of exchange rate determination holds in this part of the world. The reason why this assumption holds for Malaysia and not for a country like Singapore – classified as advanced by the IMF – is the fact that neither the Malaysian ringgit nor Singapore dollar are freely floating, although Singapore Central Bank seems more stringent in allowing exchange rate fluctuations because of the huge flow of capital to their financial hubs. In the last couple of years Singapore has become a popular financial hub in East Asia while Malaysia seems to be the natural destination of Islamic Banking investment. Both countries are managing the float of their exchange rates cautiously in regard of their respective monetary policy. Malaysia let the exchange rate fluctuate within a target zone with a series of controls and therefore monetary aggregates are thought to be significant exchange rates drivers. Malaysia is attempting to achieve high-income status by 2020 and to move farther up the value-added production chain by attracting more investments in Islamic finance, high technology industries, biotechnology, and services (CIA, 2012). This explains partly the reason why the authorities are prone to allow the exchange rate to move in accordance with monetary aggregates as an evidence of sound macroeconomic policies.

That said, exports - particularly of electronics, oil and gas, palm oil and rubber - remain significant drivers of the economy. As an oil and gas exporter, Malaysia has profited from higher world energy prices, which confirms the findings of Duasa (2009) who suggested that terms of trade are a particularly important factor in defining the size of the economic performance in Malaysia.

5.2.2 CACM

No previous study has been conducted in respect of the CACM countries; it is not possible to draw a parallel between the results in this book and those of the literature. Table 5.5 and 5.6 respectively identify drivers of exchange rate volatility in Central America and quantifies long-and-short-run relationships between these factors and exchange rates of CACM countries. An almost universal finding about the CACM countries is their heavy reliance on trade with the United States. In Table 5.5, a long term relationship is reported between exchange rates and either trade openness, trade balance, exports and/or imports for all CACM countries except Honduras. The countries in Table 5.5 and 5.6 are all signatories of the CAFTA-DR (Dominican Republic-Central America Free Trade Agreement) treaty, an FTA with the United States launched following the initiative of President Bush in 1990. The region covered by CAFTA-DR became in 2008 the third-largest Latin American export market for the United States right after Mexico and Brazil. Combined, the small Central America countries plus the Dominican Republic are a larger export market for US goods, than Russia, India, or Turkey (Eguizabal, 2010). Contrary to what the small size of the region's economies would suggest, as a whole it constitutes a relatively important market for the US buying US $25 billion of goods a year. Despite being the smallest country in terms of geography in Central America, El Salvador has the third largest economy in the region (Eguizabal, 2010). However, with the adoption of the US dollar as its currency in 2001, El Salvador lost control over monetary policy and therefore any changes in exchange rates might not relate to changes in either trade or monetary aggregates locally but probably to changes elsewhere (i.e. the US economy). Therefore the author of this book decided not to investigate the relationship between exchange rates and macroeconomic fundamentals in El Salvador.

There is a long-run relationship between trade balance and exchange rates of the Dominican peso and Nicaragua Cordoba. The Dominican Republic economy is highly dependent on the US; the destination for nearly 60% of its exports (Eguizabal, 2010). The picture is different in Guatemala where the effect of changes in imports is as important to the determination of the exchange rates but with a different sign. In Table 5.5 and 5.6, the coefficients of the short and long term relationships are respectively of (-0.0004) and (-0.021) which means that an increase in the terms of imports drives exchange rates down in Guatemala - the most populous country in Central America with a GDP per capita roughly one-half that of the average for Latin America and the Caribbean (Fajnzylber and Lopez, 2008). There is a negative short term (-0.070) and long term relationship (-2.447) between trade openness and the exchange rate of Costa Rica colon. Data for Costa Rica are only available from 2001 until the end of 2009 where a long term relationship was established between the exchange rate and trade openness. Honduras, the second poorest country in Central America suffers from extraordinarily unequal distribution of income, as well as from high underemployment (Fajnzylber and Lopez, 2008). While historically dependent on the export of bananas and coffee, Honduras has diversified its export base to include apparel and automobile equipment. Nearly half of Honduras's economic activity is directly tied to the US, with exports accounting for 30% of GDP and remittances for another 20% (CIA, 2012).

Table 5.5 CACM Long-run Cointegration Coefficients

	Costa Rica Colon (logs)		
	ARDL(1,0)		
Variable	Coefficient	t-ratio	Significance
Trade Openness	-2.447	-3.169	0.002
Constant	8.197	16.538	0.000
ECM(-1)	-0.029	-2.375	0.020
	Dominican Peso (logs)		
	ARDL(1,0)		
Variable	Coefficient	t-ratio	Significance
Trade Balance	0.004	2.701	0.007
Time Trend	0.002	6.697	0.000
ECM(-1)	-0.023	-2.133	0.034
	Guatemala Quetzal		
	ARDL(1,0,0)		
Variable	Coefficient	t-ratio	Significance
CPI	0.233	4.258	0.000
Imports	-0.021	-2.557	0.011
Constant	3.636	2.478	0.014
ECM(-1)	-0.019	-1.718	0.049
	Honduras Lempira (logs)		
	ARDL(1,0,0)		
Variable	Coefficient	t-ratio	Significance
CPI	-0.042	-2.019	0.045
Time Trend	0.027	2.375	0.019
Constant	4.425	5.488	0.000
ECM(-1)	-0.048	-2.143	0.034
	Nicaragua Cordoba (logs)		
	ARDL(1,0)		
Variable	Coefficient	t-ratio	Significance
Trade Balance	-0.012	-3.817	0.000
ECM(-1)	0.004	4.626	0.000

The relationship between the exchange rate and trade balance yielded no significant long or short-run results. However, there is a short and long term relationship between the exchange rate of the lempira and the CPI. The gradients are respectively of -0.043 for the long term and -0.002 for the short

Table 5.6 CACM Short-run Cointegration Coefficients

Costa Rica Colon (logs)			
ARDL(1,0)			
Variable	Coefficient	t-ratio	Significance
Δ*Trade Openness*	-0.071	-1.951	0.049
Constant	0.239	2.431	0.017
R-Squared	0.056		
R-Bar-Squared	0.036		
DW-statistic	1.828		
Log-likelihood	251.829		
Schwarz Bayesian Criterion	244.983		
Dominican Peso (logs)			
ARDL(1,0)			
Variable	Coefficient	t-ratio	Significance
Δ*Trade Balance*	0.0001	2.568	0.011
Time Trend	0.0005	2.646	0.009
R-Squared	0.010		
R-Bar-Squared	0.005		
DW-statistic	1.981		
Log-likelihood	391.759		
Schwarz Bayesian Criterion	382.988		
Guatemala Quetzal			
ARDL(1,0,0)			
Variable	Coefficient	t-ratio	Significance
Δ*CPI*	0.004	1.982	0.048
Δ*Imports*	-0.0004	-2.158	0.032
Constant	0.072	2.651	0.008
R-Squared	0.015		
R-Bar-Squared	0.006		
DW-statistic	1.819		
Log-likelihood	60.498		
Schwarz Bayesian Criterion	48.817		
Honduras Lempira (logs)			
ARDL(1,0,0)			
Variable	Coefficient	t-ratio	Significance
Δ*CPI*	-0.002	-3.573	0.000
Time Trend	0.001	3.755	0.000
Constant	0.216	3.072	0.003
R-Squared	0.097		
R-Bar-Squared	0.079		
DW-statistic	1.632		
Log-likelihood	436.034		
Schwarz Bayesian Criterion	425.986		

Nicaragua Cordoba (logs)			
ARDL(1,0)			
Variable	Coefficient	t-ratio	Significance
Δ*Trade Balance*	0.00005	2.241	0.026
R-Squared	0.010		
R-Bar-Squared	0.005		
DW-statistic	1.741		
Log-likelihood	541.038		
Schwarz Bayesian Criterion	535.801		

term which means that inflation does have a significant negative effect on the exchange rate of the country. Nicaragua, the poorest country in Central America and the second poorest in the southern hemisphere, has widespread unemployment and poverty (Eguizabal, 2010). Textiles and apparel account for nearly 60% of the country's exports. This study found a relationship between trade balance and the exchange rate of the Nicaragua cordoba. The long term relationship has a coefficient of -0.012 whilst the short term relationship has a coefficient of 0.00005. The next section discusses the ARDL findings in Latin America's MERCOSUR.

5.2.3 MERCOSUR

Bolivia is one of the poorest and most socially unequal countries in South America, with a GDP per capita of US $4200 - around one-eleventh that of the United States (Stobart, 2011). However, the country recorded the highest growth rate in South America in 2009 which explains the strong relationship between exchange rate and GDP. A positive gradient of (0.261) defines the long-run relationship between exchange rate of Bolivia boliviano and GDP as shown in Table 5.7. During 2010, an increase in world commodity prices resulted in the biggest trade surplus in history. However, a lack of foreign investment in the key sectors of mining and hydrocarbons and higher food prices pose challenges for the Bolivian economy. In addition to the GDP relationship, there is a long term relationship between the bolivar exchange rates and the reserves of gold in Bolivia with positive gradients respectively of (0.002) and (0.0001). Both relationships illustrate the general trend between mineral exports and exchange rates in MERCOSUR since significant relationships between the two have been identified also in Brazil and Uruguay. Peru is the world's sixth largest producer of Gold and Colombia exports 48 tonnes every year (CIA, 2012)

Brazil adopted the 'Real plan' and launched a new currency on July 1st 1994, bringing down in the process an inflation of more than 1000% to the low double digits. A new unit of account, the unit of Real Value, was introduced and was equivalent to one U.S. dollar. The behaviour of the new currency, the real, was examined using ARDL model from 1994 to 2009. Gold reserves and trade balance are both cointegrated with the exchange rate of the Brazilian real. The long term relationship between gold and the exchange rate yielded a positive gradient of (0.0006) whilst the short term relationship yielded a gradient of (0.0001). Surprisingly, the relationship between the exchange rate and trade balance is relatively weak with a gradient of (0.0002) for the long term and an even weaker gradient for the short term when we consider that Brazil is already the world's largest exporter of coffee, sugar, chickens, beef and orange juice (CIA, 2012). This is due to the fact that the Central Bank sets parity for the value of the real in terms of the US dollar. The currency was reclassified by the IMF from "independent floating" to "managed floating" as the authorities intervene occasionally in the FOREX market. This weak relationship contradicts the assumption that the country's currency will get stronger because of its commodities-led trade following the soaring Asian demand for exports from its farms and mines. It also exports vast amounts of soya and iron ore, as well as other ores, metals and is a host of the world's second largest mining company. Oil accounts for 12% of Brazilian GDP, a four-fold increase since 1997 (Cordoba, 2012). Characterised by large and well developed agricultural, mining, manufacturing and service sector, Brazil's economy outperforms that of all other South American countries - it is also expanding its presence in global markets. Brazil was one of the last countries to enter the global downturn started by the financial sector in 2007, and one of the first to come out of it (The Economist, 2010). The Central Bank's headline interest rate is 8.75%, one the highest rates in the world (The Economist, 2009). Despite slower growth in recent years, Brazil overtook the United Kingdom as the world's sixth largest economy in terms of GDP. That said, no relationships were found between the exchange rate and GDP, interest rates or even imports and exports.

Chile is a market-oriented economy characterised by a high level of foreign trade and a reputation for strong financial institutions and sound policy that have given it the strongest sovereign bond rating in South America. A cointegration relationship was found between the price of copper and the exchange rate of the peso. This short term relationship has a negative gradient (-0.0001) whilst the long term gradient has a positive sign (0.058) as reported in Table 5.8. This is very good news for the government in Chile since copper alone provides one-third of government revenue. In addition, there is a long-run relationship between exchange rates and trade balance (0.003) which comes with no surprise since exports account for more than one-fourth of GDP, with commodities making up some three-quarters of total exports (CIA, 2012). With an annual production of 48 tonnes of gold in 2009, Colombia's exchange rate would have been expected to be cointegrated with gold reserves (Klodt and Lehment, 2009). However, the only significant relationship identified was of the interest rate with a negative coefficient in the long term (-0.011) which means that for every one unit increase of the interest rate, the exchange rate will drop by 0.011 unit. The US-Colombia FTA was ratified by the US congress in 2011 making Colombia the third largest Latin American exporter of oil to the US (Villarreal, 2012). The government has signed FTAs with a number of countries including Canada, Chile, Mexico, Switzerland, the EU, Venezuela, South Korea, Turkey, Japan and Israel. All three major ratings agencies have upgraded Colombia's investment grade. The relationships involving GDP, terms of trade and exchange rates yielded no significant results which can be due to the fact that the country has been through periods of instability throughout much of the last two decades. The government has been fighting the FARC guerrilla consistently and such events seem to have overshadowed any cointegration relationships between economic aggregates and the exchange rates.

Landlocked Paraguay has a market economy distinguished by a large informal sector, featuring re-export of imported consumer goods to neighbouring countries, as well as the activities of thousands of microenterprises and urban street vendors (CIA, 2012). A large percentage of the population, especially in rural areas, derives its living from agricultural activity, often on a subsistence basis making the country the sixth largest soya producer in the world (World Bank, 2011). Because of the importance of the informal sector, accurate economic measures are difficult to obtain.

Table 5.7 MERCOSUR Long-run Cointegration Coefficients

Variable	Coefficient	t-ratio	Significance
Bolivia Boliviano (logs)			
ARDL(1,0,2)			
Variable	Coefficient	t-ratio	Significance
GDP	0.261	2.508	0.013
Gold	0.002	2.688	0.008
ECM(-1)	0.004	5.451	0.000
Brazil Real (logs)			
ARDL(3,3,0)			
Variable	Coefficient	t-ratio	Significance
Gold	0.0006	3.313	0.001
Trade Balance	0.0002	2.489	0.014
ECM(-1)	-0.026	-3.799	0.000
Chile Peso (logs)			
ARDL(1,0,0)			
Variable	Coefficient	t-ratio	Significance
Copper Price	0.058	4.128	0.000
Trade Balance	0.003	2.860	0.004
ECM(-1)	0.003	4.166	0.000
Colombia Peso (logs)			
ARDL(2,0,0)			
Variable	Coefficient	t-ratio	Significance
Interest Rate	-0.011	-2.277	0.024
Trade Openness	-10.295	-3.617	0.000
Constant	8.688	91.278	0.000
ECM(-1)	-0.067	-3.120	0.002
Paraguay Guarani (logs)			
ARDL(1,0,0)			
Variable	Coefficient	t-ratio	Significance
Exports	-0.0004	-3.061	0.003
Imports	-0.0002	-3.520	0.001
Constant	9.193	341.264	0.000
ECM(-1)	-0.383	-4.758	0.000
Peru New Sol			
ARDL(1,1,1)			
Variable	Coefficient	t-ratio	Significance
Interest Rate	-0.00005	-4.564	0.000
Capital Account	0.00004	3.103	0.002
Constant	4.440	3.293	0.001
ECM(-1)	-0.018	-1.947	0.049
Uruguay Peso (logs)			
ARDL(2,0,0)			
Variable	Coefficient	t-ratio	Significance
Interest Rate	0.014	2.519	0.012
Gold	-0.003	-3.029	0.003
Constant	3.498	7.781	0.000
ECM(-1)	-0.007	-3.560	0.000

Table 5.7 *(Cont'd)* MERCOSUR Long-run Cointegration...

	Venezuela Bolivar (logs)		
	ARDL(1,0,1)		
Variable	Coefficient	t-ratio	Significance
Interest Rate	0.019	2.786	0.006
Trade Balance	0.0002	2.562	0.011
Time Trend	0.024	15.695	0.000
Constant	-6.637	-12.033	0.000
ECM(-1)	-0.072	-3.149	0.002

On a per capita basis, real income has stagnated at 1980 levels. Relationships were found between imports, exports and the exchange rate of the Guarani. In terms of exports, the long term relationship registers a negative coefficient of (-0.0004) whilst the short term relationship has a coefficient of (-0.0001). Imports have a long term cointegrating relationship that involves a coefficient of (-0.0002) and a coefficient of (-0.0001) for the short-run. The reader will note that both exports and imports short term coefficients reported in Table 5.8 are equal.

As any other small economy in the region, Peru is heavily dependent on trade (International Trade Centre, 2012). The economy grew by almost 6% per year during the period 2002-06, with a stable exchange rate and low inflation (World Bank, 2011). The wealth of its gold mines is one of the reasons why the economy grew by close to 9% in 2010 following the soaring price of gold of which Peru is the world's sixth-biggest producer (The Economist, 2010). Relationships between the Peru New Sol, GDP, trade balance and trade openness were investigated but no significant statistical model was found. A short term relationship was found between interest and exchange rates although it has a weak coefficient of (-0.00005). One can argue that the effect of a change in the interest rate can hardly be felt on the exchange rate of the New Sol and the currency is clearly affected by factors that are not identified in the present ARDL model such as the one suggested Jaramillo and Severan (2012) – PPP. No relationship was found between the exchange rates and the CPI though. In Uruguay, there are negative long term (-0.003) and short term (-0.00002) relationships between exchange rates of the peso and gold reserves. In addition, there is a positive long term relationship (0.014) between the exchange and the interest rates. The latter relationship has a negative sign in the short term (-0.0001). Venezuela remains highly dependent on oil revenues that account for roughly 95% of export earnings (Rodriguez et al. 2012) which explain the positive significant long term (0.0002) and short term (0.00001) relationships between the trade balance and the exchange rate of the bolivar. Fuelled by high oil prices, record government spending helped to boost GDP by about 10% in 2006, 8% in 2007 and nearly 5% in 2008 before a sharp drop in oil prices caused a contraction in 2009-10 (Rodriguez et al. 2012). No significant relationships were found between the exchange rates and the GDP though. However, there is a positive long term relationship (0.019) between the interest and exchange

Table 5.8 MERCOSUR Short-run Cointegration Coefficients

	Bolivia Boliviano (logs)		
	ARDL(1,0,2)		
Variable	Coefficient	t-ratio	Significance
Δ*GDP*	-0.001	-2.301	0.022
Δ*Gold(-1)*	0.0001	3.592	0.000
R-Squared	0.101		
R-Bar-Squared	0.085		
DW-statistic	1.844		
Log-likelihood	632.659		
Schwarz Bayesian Criterion	619.075		
	Brazil Real (logs)		
	ARDL(3,3,0)		
Variable	Coefficient	t-ratio	Significance
Δ*Gold*	0.0001	4.820	0.000
Δ*Gold(-2)*	-0.0001	-4.080	0.000
Δ*Trade Balance*	0.000006	2.013	0.046
R-Squared	0.534		
R-Bar-Squared	0.515		
DW-statistic	1.813		
Log-likelihood	234.42		
Schwarz Bayesian Criterion	213.297		
	Chile Peso (logs)		
	ARDL(1,0,0)		
Variable	Coefficient	t-ratio	Significance
Δ*Copper Price*	-0.0001	-2.411	0.016
Δ*Trade Balance*	-0.00001	-2.669	0.008
R-Squared	0.020		
R-Bar-Squared	0.014		
DW-statistic	1.838		
Log-likelihood	617.011		
Schwarz Bayesian Criterion	608.251		
	Colombia Peso (logs)		
	ARDL(2,0,0)		
Variable	Coefficient	t-ratio	Significance
Δ*Trade Openness*	-0.697	-2.558	0.011
Constant	0.588	3.125	0.002
R-Squared	0.109		
R-Bar-Squared	0.088		
DW-statistic	1.982		
Log-likelihood	366.594		
Schwarz Bayesian Criterion	353.668		
	Paraguay Guarani (logs)		
	ARDL(1,0,0)		
Variable	Coefficient	t-ratio	Significance
Δ*Exports*	-0.0001	-3.083	0.003

Table 5.8 *(Cont'd)* MERCOSUR Short-run...

ΔImports	-0.0001	-2.463	0.017
Constant	3.527	4.743	0.000
R-Squared	0.332		
R-Bar-Squared	0.293		
DW-statistic	1.760		
Log-likelihood	132.843		
Schwarz Bayesian Criterion	124.792		
	Peru New Sol		
	ARDL(1,1,1)		
Variable	Coefficient	t-ratio	Significance
ΔInterest Rate	-0.00005	-4.564	0.000
ΔCapital Account	-0.00004	3.103	0.002
Constant	0.080	3.692	0.000
R-Squared	0.193		
R-Bar-Squared	0.175		
DW-statistic	1.828		
Log-likelihood	262.706		
Schwarz Bayesian Criterion	246.418		
	Uruguay Peso (logs)		
	ARDL(2,0,0)		
Variable	Coefficient	t-ratio	Significance
ΔGold	-0.00002	-2.046	0.042
ΔInterest Rate	0.0001	3.590	0.000
Constant	0.026	3.033	0.003
R-Squared	0.290		
R-Bar-Squared	0.279		
DW-statistic	1.943		
Log-likelihood	570.066		
Schwarz Bayesian Criterion	556.51		
	Venezuela Bolivar (logs)		
	ARDL(1,0,1)		
Variable	Coefficient	t-ratio	Significance
ΔInterest Rate	0.005	5.348	0.000
ΔTrade Balance	0.00001	2.411	0.017
ΔTime Trend	0.001	3.226	0.001
Constant	-0.479	-3.247	0.001
R-Squared	0.162		
R-Bar-Squared	0.142		
DW-statistic	2.170		
Log-likelihood	264.284		
Schwarz Bayesian Criterion	248.158		

rates. Venezuela's government adopts a multiple exchange rate policy for the management of its currency and the parallel market is very active, which might explain the weak relationship between the bolivar and exports. The parallel market rate is sometimes 100% more than the official market rate. The next section presents the results of applying ARDL cointegration to the exchange rates of the SADC region.

5.2.4 SADC

Angola's high growth rate in recent years was driven by high international prices for its oil. Located on the Atlantic coast in the southern part of Africa, the Republic of Angola is the second largest oil producer in Africa (Staines, 2012). Angola became a member of OPEC in late 2006 and in late 2007 was assigned a production quota of 1.9 million barrels a day (bbl/day). Oil production contributes about 85% of GDP; Diamond exports contribute an additional 5% (CIA, 2012). There is no cointegration between trade balance, interest rate, exports and the exchange rate of the Angolan Kwanza. It means that there exist no direct relationships between the kwanza exchange rates and these economic aggregates. However, there is a unique relationship between the exchange rate and the CPI. In the short term, the exchange rate is positively cointegrated with the CPI (1.481) while this relationship turns negative in the long term (-0.287) as indicated in. This might be explained by the fact that there has been huge flow of capital towards the country mainly by international firms who intend to invest in the oil industry and all sorts of companies who see in Angola a future African diamond. This translates to huge capital flows that pushed the prices up and weaken the currency in the process. The short term relationship is very strong and means that for every one unit increase in the CPI, the exchange rate will increase on average by 1.48 units. The immediate effect of the capital flows into the country is to drive up the exchange rate as the demand for the currency increases. This latter finding, if viewed in conjunction with long term coefficient of (-0.287), partially explains why Luanda was declared the most expensive capital in the world in 2011 (World Bank 2011-2012). The higher the prices, the greater the currency loss in terms of the PPP which again leads to an increase in the prices.

In Botswana, diamond mining has fuelled much of the expansion in the economy and accounts for more than one-third of GDP, 70-80% of export earnings and about half of the government's revenues (CIA, 2012). Relationships between exchange rates of the Botswana Pula and exports, trade balance and interest rates yielded no statistical significant results. Instead, the best forecasting model has been generated via the long-run relationship between the GDP and the exchange rate. Capital account data are not available. GDP by volume is cointegrated both in the short (0.000002) and long term (0.00004) with the Pula exchange rate. Although this relationship is positive, it is very weak and shows that the macroeconomic fundamentals in Botswana provide little insight about the behaviour of exchange rates in this country. In nearby DRC, much economic activity still occurs in the informal sector. This may explain the fact that no relationship was found between exchange rates of the Franc and trade balance, GDP and interest rates. Most export income comes from the mining sector but no significant relationship was found between exports and the exchange rates. There is a relationship between the DRC Franc exchange rate and the CPI. In the short term, the cointegration coefficient is (-0.231) and (1.715) in the long term. The DRC signed a Poverty Reduction and Growth Facility with the IMF in 2009 and received US $12 billion in multilateral and

Table 5.9 SADC Long-run Cointegration Coefficients

Botswana Pula (logs)			
ARDL(1,0)			
Variable	Coefficient	t-ratio	Significance
GDP	0.00004	4.666	0.000
Constant	1.606	14.238	0.000
ECM(-1)	-0.046	-2.215	0.028
Madagascar Ariary (logs)			
ARDL(1,0)			
Variable	Coefficient	t-ratio	Significance
Capital Account	0.039	3.005	0.003
ECM(-1)	0.002	4.293	0.000
Malawi Kwacha (logs)			
ARDL(2,0)			
Variable	Coefficient	t-ratio	Significance
CPI	0.046	4.573	0.000
ECM(-1)	0.010	3.329	0.001
Mauritius Rupee (logs)			
ARDL(1,0)			
Variable	Coefficient	t-ratio	Significance
CPI	0.023	2.278	0.023
ECM(-1)	0.002	2.569	0.011
Mozambique Metical (logs)			
ARDL(2,0,0,0)			
Variable	Coefficient	t-ratio	Significance
Log Capital Reserves	0.496	14.266	0.000
CPI	-0.034	-2.959	0.004
Interest Rate	0.022	3.969	0.000
Time Trend	0.027	3.479	0.001
ECM(-1)	-0.047	-3.043	0.003
Tanzania Shilling (logs)			
ARDL(1,0)			
Variable	Coefficient	t-ratio	Significance
Interest Rate	0.268	5.327	0.000
ECM(-1)	0.002	3.582	0.000
DRC Franc (logs)			
ARDL(1,1)			
Variable	Coefficient	t-ratio	Significance
Log CPI	1.714	4.709	0.000
ECM(-1)	-0.012	-3.277	0.001
Seychelles Rupee (logs)			
ARDL(2,3,0)			
Variable	Coefficient	t-ratio	Significance
Interest Rate	0.107	8.152	0.000
Money Supply	0.0002	6.302	0.000
ECM(-1)	-0.026	-2.224	0.028

Table 5.10 SADC Short-run Cointegration Coefficients

Variable	Coefficient	t-ratio	Significance
Angola Kwanza			
ARDL(2,1)			
Variable	Coefficient	t-ratio	Signifi-cance
ΔCPI	1.481	4.2171	0.000
R-Squared	0.343		
R-Bar-Squared	0.322		
DW-statistic	2.062		
Log-likelihood	-219.361		
Schwarz Bayesian Criterion	-228.572		
Botswana Pula (logs)			
ARDL(1,0)			
Variable	Coefficient	t-ratio	Significance
ΔGDP	0.000002	2.208	0.029
Constant	0.075	2.303	0.023
R-Squared	0.031		
R-Bar-Squared	0.019		
DW-statistic	2.070		
Log-likelihood	339.514		
Schwarz Bayesian Criterion	331.864		
Madagascar Ariary (logs)			
ARDL(1,0)			
Variable	Coefficient	t-ratio	Significance
ΔCapital Account	-0.00009	-2.239	0.026
R-Squared	0.003		
R-Bar-Squared	0.0008		
DW-statistic	1.830		
Log-likelihood	541.913		
Schwarz Bayesian Criterion	536.072		
Malawi Kwacha (logs)			
ARDL(2,0)			
Variable	Coefficient	t-ratio	Significance
ΔCPI	-0.0004	-2.188	0.030
R-Squared	0.021		
R-Bar-Squared	0.014		
DW-statistic	1.992		
Log-likelihood	354.738		
Schwarz Bayesian Criterion	356.380		
Mozambique Metical (logs)			
ARDL(2,0,0,0)			
Variable	Coefficient	t-ratio	Significance
ΔLog Capital Reserves	0.023	3.449	0.001
ΔCPI	-0.001	-3.975	0.000
ΔInterest Rate	0.001	3.942	0.000
Time Trend	0.001	4.108	0.000

Table 5.10 *(Cont'd)* SADC Short-run

R-Squared	0.197		
R-Bar-Squared	0.172		
DW-statistic	1.863		
Log-likelihood	380.675		
Schwarz Bayesian Criterion	365.393		
Tanzania Shilling (logs)			
ARDL(1,0)			
Variable	Coefficient	t-ratio	Significance
ΔInterest Rate	-0.0005	-2.589	0.011
R-Squared	0.041		
R-Bar-Squared	0.035		
DW-statistic	1.804		
Log-likelihood	366.071		
Schwarz Bayesian Criterion	361.034		

bilateral debt relief in 2010 (CIA, 2012). A significant cointegrating relationship was found between capital accounts and the exchange rate of Madagascar's Ariary. This relationship has a gradient of (0.00009) in the short term and of (0.040) in the long term.

Madagascar followed a World Bank and IMF-led policy of privatisation and liberalisation that placed the country on a slow and steady growth path from an extremely low level. Agriculture, including fishing and forestry, is a mainstay of the economy, accounting for more than one-fourth of GDP. However, the relationship between GDP, exports, CPI and the exchange rates yielded no significant results. In Malawi, there is a cointegrating relationship between the exchange rate and the CPI. This relationship has a positive coefficient of (0.047) in the long term and a negative coefficient of (0.0004) in the short term. Additionally, although agriculture accounts for more than one-third of GDP and 90% of export revenues (CIA, 2012), no relationship between exports and the exchange rate was found. A huge flow of capital would normally affect the exchange rate one way or another. Similarly, changes in interest rates are likely to affect the behaviour of the currency. Both relationships between exchange rates, the capital account and interest rates were examined for the kwacha but yielded no significant results, which is the reason why the author of this book believes exchange rates are manipulated in Malawi.

The economy of Mauritius relies largely on sugar, tourism, textiles, apparel and financial services. Investment in the banking sector alone reached over US $1 billion in 2010 (CIA, 2012). The relationship between exports, trade balance, interest rate and growth domestic product was examined and yielded no significant results. There is a positive long term relationship (0.024) between the exchange rate of the Mauritian Rupee and the CPI as Mauritius depends on international markets when it comes to energy and raw materials. Mozambique remains dependent upon foreign assistance for more than half of its annual budget and the majority of the population remains below the poverty line.

Ideally, the relationship between international aid and exchange rates should have been investigated but this was not possible due to the unavailability of data. Furthermore, no GDP or trade data are available for Mozambique. However, there is a negative long term (-0.034) and short term (-0.001) relationship between the exchange rate and the CPI in Mozambique. In addition, there is a positive long term relationship between the exchange and interest rates (0.022). Seychelles adopted fixed exchange rates untill mid-1996 which is why this study investigates the period post-1996. Growth has been led by the tourism sector and by tuna fishing. In recent years, the government has encouraged foreign investment to upgrade hotels and other services. There are significant positive long-run (0.107) and short-run (0.002) relationships between exchange and interest rates in Seychelles. In addition, money supply seems to be positively cointegrated with the exchange rate on the long term (0.0002) whilst negatively cointegrated with the exchange rate in the short term (-0.00002).

Recent banking reforms in Tanzania have helped increase private-sector growth and investment. In fact there is a consistent positive relationship between the interest and exchange rates. When the interest rate increases by 1 unit, the exchange rate appreciates by 0.27 units on average. This is the highest gradient found for SADC countries with a macroeconomic aggregate. In the short term, this relationship is of negative nature and has a coefficient of (-0.0005). No relationship has been found between GDP and the exchange rates of the Tanzania Shilling. Despite the fact that the country has registered an average GDP growth of 7% per year from 2000-2008 (CIA, 2012) it still relies on international aid from the World Bank, the IMF and bilateral donors. As a matter of fact, in 2008 Tanzania received the World's largest Millennium Challenge Compact grant, worth US $698 million (World Bank, 2011). As per South Africa's exchange rate, it was not possible to generate a significant model since the rand series failed the test of heteroscedasticity and autocorrelation which means that no significant relationships have been identified for South Africa Rand. The next section discuss the parameter stability tests, CUSUM and CUSUM SQ.

5.3 Parameter Stability Tests

A number of test statistics are available which are designed to examine whether the parameters of an estimated ARDL model are stable, in the sense that these parameters are constant over time. Various testing procedures are available for assessing parameter stability during the sample period. They involve computing recursive estimates of the model at hand (Vogelvang, 2005).

Recursive estimation involves computing the parameters of a model by repeatedly adding one observation and then re-estimating these parameter values at each step. One starts with a sub-sample of the gathered data that runs from the first reading up to the first point at which the sample size is deemed to be large enough for reasonable inferences to be made. The parameters of the model are estimated based on this subset of the data. Note that if the researcher's model contains K parameters to be estimated, then the first K +

1 observations is the smallest number of readings that can be used for estimation purposes (Vogelvang, 2005). The next observation is now added, the first K + 2 observations used to re-run the model and the model parameters re-estimated. The recursive procedure continues until the entire sample of N readings is exhausted, whereby (N – K) estimates of the model parameters are generated overall.

Formal statistical tests of parameter stability may be generated based on recursive estimation. Two such, the CUSUM (cumulative sum) test and the CUSUM of Squares test (CUSUM SQ) of Brown et al. (1975), are widely used to assess model stability and are available as part of the ARDL routine in the Microfit software package (Cameron, 2005). Both tests are based on the residuals derived from the researcher's model from each sub-sample. These are referred to as recursive residuals, which are based on predicting the dependent variable for the sample period of duration K + 1 from the model derived using the sample period of K. They are one-step-ahead forecasting errors and are conventionally standardised to have a zero mean and unit variance. The cumulative sum of the standardised recursive residuals, W_n or the CUSUM, can be written as:

$$W_n = {}^{1}/_{\hat{\sigma}} \sum_{j=K+1}^{n} r_j \qquad (5.4)$$

where $\hat{\sigma}$ is the standard error of the model fitted to the entire sample of N observations, r_j is the standardised recursive residual based on j observations and n = K + 1, K + 2, ..., N (Quantitative Micro Software, 2004). If the recursive residuals are independently and randomly distributed with zero mean, then W_n should not exhibit a tendency to cumulate as the researcher rolls through the sample. The expected value of W_n under model stability is, therefore, $E(W_n) = 0$ (Johnston and DiNardo, 1997). Its variance is approximately equal to the number of residuals being summed, since each independent residual has unit variance (Greene, 2003). Analysis of the behaviour of W_n is usually by graphical means. The key point is whether departures of W_n from zero falls outside of a pair of (typically) 5% significance lines, the distance between which increases with the number of residuals used for the computation of W_n. If W_n strays outside of these significance lines at a particular point, then there is evidence that the model parameters are not constant during the sample period and that there is a structural break in the data at that point in time. The CUSUM of Squares test (CUSUM SQ) involves the cumulative sum of the squared recursive residuals. The statistic S_n is computed:

$$S_n = \left(\sum_{j=K+1}^{n} r_j^2\right) / \left(\sum_{j=K+1}^{N} r_j^2\right) \text{ for } n = K+1, K+2, \ldots, N \qquad (5.5)$$

which has an expected value that ranges from zero at n = K + 1 to one at n = N. The significance of the departure of S_n from its expected value is again assessed graphically according to whether or not its value crosses the pair of significance lines. Movement outside of these lines is indicative of parameter or variance instability. If S_n lies within these lines, it suggests that the residual variance is stable. If the CUSUM and CUSUMSQ tests reveal model instability at break points, then the model at hand should be modified by the introduction of variables which might account for the observed instability. CUSUM and CUSUM SQ graphs have been generated for all ARDL models examined in this book. According to the CUSUM and CUSUMSQ graphs, there is a stable long-run equilibrium in almost all exchange rates examined except for countries where the AFC hit (Indonesia, Malaysia, Philippines, Singapore and Thailand), countries that suffered from the aftermath of debt crises (Brazil and Uruguay) and those who experience exchange rate regime changes and unstable governments (Madagascar, Mozambique, Malawi and Mauritius).

5.4 Regional Comparisons

By using the ARDL technique, this study has been able to identify some of the determinants of exchange rates changes even for series with limited sample data such as DRC and Angola. Additionally, for most exchange rates, ARDL identified at least two determinants of exchange rates as the technique enables different variables to have different optimal lags, an advantage comparing to other cointegration techniques. The CPI is the most commonly occurring explanatory variable for the SADC countries. That is, inflation is a major factor in the exchange rate determination in this part of the world. In comparison with more developed economies where inflation can generally be predicted, the nature of SADC economies makes it very difficult to identify either the size of inflation trends.

Many of the countries studied in this book - particularly Angola and DRC - had been ravaged by war throughout most of the period of the study (1990-2009). Whilst this chapter is being written, there are still confrontations between different factions in DRC which result in clashes every now and then and mainly feed into the uncertainty of the economic scene. These clashes sometimes transcend to neighbouring countries which makes a whole region prone to instability. Quantitative analysis should be used in conjunction with judgmental forecast which incorporates non-quantitative variables such as political instability. This is particularly relevant in countries like Zimbabwe in Africa, Myanmar in Asia or even Venezuela in Latin America. In such contexts it is up to the researcher to make sure that he is acquainted with the research background and which the will lay the foundation for tools like ARDL analysis to assess potential relationships, ceteris paribus. For countries where there exists a long-run relationship between the exchange and the interest rates, the size and the direction of the relationship varies. Countries like Seychelles and Tanzania have entered an era of relative stability since their respective exchange rates seem to respond to the natural forces of the market. Changes in the money supply and the interest rate affect changes in exchange rates in the Seychelles Rupee while Tanzania interest rate affect significantly exchange rates. Another factor to be taken into consideration when examining the SADC countries is data availability. The author of this book had a limited choice when it comes to investigating exchange rates in Africa in respect of potential economic aggregates. The scarcity of data in this part of the world was the reason behind the limited number of non-trade variables used for this region.

That said, short-and long-run relationships that have been reported for SADC and other regions were statistically validated. The exploratory power of the present work, it is hoped, will lay a platform for future researchers that intend to investigate the exchange rates in sub-Saharan Africa.

The present research suggests that in CACM countries, trade is the factor that respective governments in Central America should look at, ahead of an exchange rate examination. The eminence of the trade factors in Central America illustrates the effect that the FTA with US is having on the economies of the region. The ARDL findings confirm the positive effect of liberal trade agreements between the United States and the countries in the region. The ARDL results also confirm the expectation of analysts that the signing of CAFTA-DR agreement in 2003 would deepen the integration of the region with the US market (Eguizabal, 2010). The heavy reliance of CACM countries on trade, remittances and aid from the US makes the study of their exchange rates very tricky.

In the ASEAN region, trade and inflation appear as significant explanatory variables in the long term along with the GDP volume. Although Tang (2007) and Abdullah (2010) both found a relationship between the ASEAN exchange rates, interest rates, GDP and money supply this study had only found a strong relationship between trade variables and the exchange rates of ASEAN countries. Judging from the small ECM calculated for ASEAN currencies, exchange rates slowly return to equilibrium following a shock to the system. This is true particularly in countries where the AFC hit very hard mainly in Indonesia, Malaysia, Thailand and Singapore. The fact that inflation and interest rate have been identified as determinants for Vietnam's Dong exchange rate proves that this country is entering an era of relative stability with sound macroeconomic fundamentals. Vietnam has very good economic prospects as the country plays host to many multinational companies who chose to leave China because of the continuous increase in labour cost. Cambodia and Vietnam are the two countries in Southeast Asia that are expected to grow by a percentage close to a double digit in the coming couple of years. Studies such as the present one provide an insight to policy makers and investors alike for a better understanding of exchange rate fluctuations and their determinants, a much needed knowledge for a better management of the commercial transactions.

The analysis of the MERCOSUR trading bloc shows that most countries in Latin America emerged from the era of uncertainty and volatility following the crisis in 2001 and are now making steady progress towards market economy where exchange rates are decided by macroeconomic fundamentals. According to the findings of this research, trade plays very little role in the determination of exchange rates (similarly for monetary aggregates) which can be justified by the interference of the authorities in the exchange rates following the huge flow of FDI into countries such as Brazil which led to overheating of the economy and can hurt exports if its effects are not levelled up. MERCOSUR exchange rates are different from ASEAN's in that the former take more time to return to equilibrium following a shock to the system. This might be due to the fact that the Latin American continent was hit by several crises during the period that this study covers compared to Southeast Asia. Furthermore, few countries in Latin America such as Paraguay and Colombia still suffer from stints of political instability. In that respect, MERCOSUR region share some similarities with the SADC region where exchange rates take considerable time to adjust to equilibrium. CACM exchange rates take as much time as ASEAN exchange rates to return to equilibrium - an interesting finding given the fact that both regions are far apart from each other. One would expect that Central and Latin America would behave similarly following a shock to the system. This chapter provides evidence that even regions in different geographical areas can behave similarly as a response to bad news in the market.

5.5 Conclusions and Recommendations

This chapter examined for the first time the relationship between exchange rates and fundamentals in Central America under the auspices of CACM and identified quantitative and non-quantitative factors that explain changes in exchange rates. The same was achieved for Latin America's MERCOSUR, Africa's SADC and Asia's ASEAN. Exchange rates were examined in line with the three popular theories of exchange rate determination, the traditional model, the monetary model and the parity conditions models and for every currency - the strength of short and long-run relationship between the exchange rate and macroeconomic fundamentals was identified. The author believes that there is still a useful role for trade flows in the asset approach to exchange rate since trade flows have implications for financial asset flows. If balance of trade deficits are financed by depleting domestic stocks of foreign currency and trade surpluses are associated with increases in domestic holding of foreign money, we can see the role of the trade account. If the exchange rate adjusts so that the stocks of domestic and foreign money are willingly held, then the country with a trade surplus will be accumulating foreign currency. As holdings of foreign money increase relative to the local currency, the relative value of foreign money will fall or the foreign currency will depreciate.

This chapter examined trade and non-trade variables that can be identified as drivers of exchange rate fluctuations in four continents. Traditionally, studies that used ARDL cointegration for exchange rate determination investigated the relationship of the latter with macroeconomic variables – namely interest rates, trade balance, inflation rates and GDP changes. This means that by nature, ARDL cannot be applied to countries that do not record the progress of their macroeconomic performance. Therefore, if the ARDL cointegration method delivers good results for any currency, then this is a sign that the country in question has reached a certain stage of development where we can make sense and work out relationships between its aggregates. In this research, fundamentals that cause changes in the exchange rates of the emerging world have been discussed. As news related to money supplies, trade balances, or fiscal policies is received by the market, exchange rates will change to reflect this news. We might think of the discussion being macroeconomic, as such news affects the entire economy and other prices change along with exchange rates. However, there is also a micro-level, at which exchange rates are determined by interactions among traders. Beyond the macro-news or public information shared by all, there is also inside information which favours those that have access to it over others. Understanding the "market microstructure" allows us to explain the evolution of the FOREX market in a more specific sense, in which FOREX traders adjust their bid and ask quotes throughout the business day and in the absence of any macro news. In general, exchange rates examined in this study seem to have been influenced mainly by the trade openness variable and this assumption is valid across all regions.

Traditionally, exchange rates were determined by the flow of currency through the FOREX market. The focus of attention is on the trade account mainly because when the traditional theory of exchange rate determination was developed, capital flows were restricted enough so as not to enter the argument. Capital flows were treated as exogenous shocks rather than as being endogenous to the model. This approach is very different from the modern asset view of the exchange rate where the exchange rate is treated as the price of an asset (relative price of two monies). This seems to be particularly true for ASEAN and CACM countries where trade aggregates do appear to affect significantly the behaviour of exchange rates. Only recently, the CACM countries registered negative growth rate because their main trading partner (the US) experienced a dip in domestic demand. Future researchers, who intend to investigate the CACM area, will have to understand the nature of these markets first. There would be between 1.5 million and 2.5 million Salvadorans, 1 to 1.5 million Guatemalans and close to one million Hondurans who work illegally in the US although it is very difficult to come to reliable estimates (Eguizabal, 2010). The involvement of some of these illegal immigrants in drug trade and gangster activities is a variable to be taken into consideration when looking at fluctuations of exchange rates. One future line of research can use ARDL to assess whether there is a relationship between the flux of migrants and exchange rates. Furthermore, an examination of the exchange rate of CACM countries and the US dollar might be a pre-requirement to explain the impact of the fluctuations of the US dollar on the currencies of these countries. The present research assesses the strength of relationship between exchange rates and macroeconomic fundamentals in the emerging world and a future line of research could seek a comparison between the findings of this study and those that examine developed countries.

For statistical modelling purposes, this research used various sample periods (from 1990 to 2009) to assess possible long-run cointegration relationships between series of exchange rates and of explanatory variables. This means that for every exchange rate, the period examined is slightly different from the rest of the sample. For example, Brazil data were analysed from 1994 onwards since this date marks the introduction of a new currency, the real. The same thing applies to exchange rate determinants since the data for some of them were not available in 1990. The Seychelles data was analysed from 1996 since this is the year where the Central Bank allowed the currency to float. There is sometimes a tendency for time series modelling to be led by the technique, rather than any real relationship between the random variables in a multivariate system. This highlights the importance of a deep understanding of the research background and mainly the purposes that the study at hand would want to serve which explains the attempt by the author to investigate thoroughly economic and sometimes political and social aspects that are deemed to affect the behaviour the exchange rates. This chapter provides the reader with the knowledge needed to understand the background of ARDL cointegration studies in selected regional settings. For every country, information deemed to have a potential impact on to the exchange rate was provided, when available. For most regions, growth rates, currency regimes, major economic and political events were examined to prepare the foundations on which the ARDL findings need to be analysed. For example, Venezuela late president decided to end abruptly the peg of the bolivar to the dollar towards the end of last decade which explains why the exchange rate became volatile since then and which would not have been possible without a thorough investigation of both the exchange rate itself and economic sources on Venezuela and Latin America.

Another line of research that might be followed is the examination of the performance of exchange rates of the main trading partner for the country under study. Because of the increasing integration of ASEAN countries and the ever growing presence of China in the region, it would be interesting to see whether changes in the Chinese Yuan Rembini affect or even dictate changes in exchange rates of countries in the region. This is of particular importance when we note the fact that Indonesia is already using the Chinese currency for its international transactions and the fact that China loosened its monetary policy recently and allowed the Yuan to appreciate against the US dollar. According to the Economist (2011), China is considering the prospect of playing a bigger role in the international currency market by using its currency in international trade and enticing its partners to behave in a similar fashion. Interestingly, this is of particular relevance to SADC countries too. Given the fact that China has become the major trading partner of Africa and the biggest investor in the continent, the study of the Chinese currency ahead of the study of exchange rates of the region seems more like a pre-requirement. It is the belief of the author of this book that the currency war between the Yuan and the US Dollar will not abate anytime soon and the future of research belong to those who can understand the relationships between different currencies and those who can quantify the strength of these relationships in numerical terms.

Furthermore, it would be of particular interest for SADC countries to examine whether the switch from the Euro has made countries that had their currencies pegged to European currencies more volatile. For example, some researchers might be interested in looking at exchange rates of currencies that were pegged to the French Franc before the introduction of the Euro and compare it with the period of peg against the Euro which might of big relevance for Africa where many French colonies are located (an examination of the CFA Franc might be relevant in that respect).

Having used the ARDL cointegration method in this chapter the author would like to highlight the huge exploratory power this method has. Other researchers might choose to combine this method with a time series method to provide more accurate forecasts, since most of the economies are not mature and the exchange rate is not only affected or dictated by the traditional economic aggregates. Also, since a number of countries in this study seem to be dependent on the US, it would be interesting to check for relationships between the parity of the present currencies with the US dollar exchange rates.

Chapter VI Combination Forecasting of Exchange Rates

Combination Forecasting has hardly been applied to FOREX although it has been widely used in many fields related to business economics and finance. Among the popular uses of combination methods are: tourism demand forecasting (Fritz et al., 1984; Coshall and Charlesworth, 2011; Shen et al., 2011), employment growth forecasting (Rapach et al., 2010), political risk (Bunn and Mustafaoglu, 1978), portfolio choice (Dunis et al., 2001), asset returns (Fang and Xu, 2003), interest rate forecasting (Greer, 2005), forecasting the amount of cash withdrawals from ATM machines (Andrawis et al., 2011), inflation forecasting (Bjørnland et al., 2010), S&P volatility forecasting (Becker and Clements, 2008), inflation and output growth forecasting (Kapetanios et al., 2008) and forecasting macro-economic variables (Terui and van Dijk, 2002).

Chapter Three provided a review of the literature on combination forecasting since 1989, the year when Clemen (1989) wrote his annotated bibliography on the topic. A review of combination forecasting applications in finance with a particular focus on exchange rates was also presented. This chapter introduces the two methods of combination forecasting used in this book with a discussion of the merits of each approach. These are the equal weights and the variance-covariance methods which are discussed in Section 6.1. The results of applying combination forecasting techniques to a set of more than 30 exchange rates using one, two, three and four-way combination methods are presented in section 6.2. The following section (6.4) examines the findings from a regional perspective, a task that has never been attempted in none of the selected regional settings. The chapter concludes with an assessment of the value of combination forecasting to the study of exchange rates with recommendations relevant to policy makers and other market players.

6.1 Combination Forecasting Methods

The equal weights method

In this book, the equal weights and the variance-covariance method were used to forecast the exchange rates of selected currencies in Africa, Asia, Central and Latin America. The literature uses equal weights and simple average interchangeably to refer to the combination method where the researcher adds up two or more forecasts and divides the result by the number of forecasts. Newbold and Granger (1974) took up this theme empirically and demonstrated that the performance of a weighted average forecast can indeed be superior to individual forecasts using a simple average. According to De

Menezes et al. (2000), simple average has the virtues of impartiality, robustness and a good "track-record" in economic and business forecasting added to its simplicity. This research combines the forecasts of time series and cointegration models. The simple average combination of forecasts generated from ARIMA, Exponential Smoothing, Naïve I and ARDL method can be presented as follows:

$$\hat{Y}_{combined,t} = k_1\hat{Y}_{Volatility,t} + k_2\hat{Y}_{ES,t} + k_3\hat{Y}_{Naive1,t} + k_4\hat{Y}_{ARDL,t} \qquad (6.1)$$

Where $\hat{Y}_{combined,t}$ is the combination result at time (t) and $k_1 = k_2 = k_3 = k_4$ are the weights of every single forecast with and $\sum_{i=1}^{4} k_i = 1$ and $k_1 = k_2 = k_3 = k_4 = ¼$, while $\hat{Y}_{volatility,t}$ are volatility forecasts at time (t), $\hat{Y}_{ES,t}$ are Exponential smoothing forecasts at time (t), $\hat{Y}_{Naïve,t}$ are NaïveI forecasts at time (t) and $\hat{Y}_{ARDL,t}$ are ARDL forecasts at time (t). The rationale behind the equal weights method is to prove that you can outperform single models and provide more accurate forecasts by simply averaging out the forecasts generated from single models. The idea of forecast averaging presented above, laid the platform for more combination methods which meant that other models were developed later to account for the complexity of modern time series and the variance-covariance method presented in the next section is one such example.

The variance-covariance method

Bates and Granger (1969) noted that the complexity of economic systems means that different forecasts tend to exploit different information. Earlier researchers noticed the strong performance of average forecasts and Bates and Granger (1969) extended this idea by weighting the forecasts in different ways on the basis of their past performance. The weights of the various forecasts were restricted to sum up to one in the simple average combination method. The variance-covariance combination method assigns unequal weights to each single model forecast based on its historical performance. The size of the weights attached to a forecast indicates the relative importance of that model in the combination. In this research, every two, three and four-way combination of the four models (ARIMA-Volatility, Exponential Smoothing, Naïve I and ARDL) were computed for the 32 exchange rates examined. A total of 15 forecasts were thus calculated for each exchange rate. There then follows an assessment of each forecast to identify the optimal method that generates the minimum absolute percentage error (MAPE), the measure of forecasting performance used throughout the thesis. In sum, 11 forecasts were generated via the variance-covariance method, one forecast from equal weights method and four single model forecasts. The following is a demonstration of the calculation of the weights (*) used in the variance-covariance method. For simplicity, the variance-covariance method will be illustrated for two time series and later extended to four. We start by identifying the error term of the combination forecast such as:

$$e_{combined,t} = Y_t - \hat{Y}_{combined,t} \quad (6.2)$$

where $e_{combined,t}$ denotes the difference between observed values and combined forecast. Since we know that the sum of the weights should be equal to 1 ($\sum_{i=1}^{2} k_i = 1$) we can assume that the forecast errors from the combined forecasts are:

$$e_{combined,t} = Y_t - (k * \hat{Y}_{1,t} + (1-k) * \hat{Y}_{2,t}) \quad (6.3)$$

In a two-way combination, the weight assigned to the second combined forecast $(1-k)$ is equal to the difference between 1 and the way assigned to the first forecast (k). The sum of the weights is always equal to one and $0 < k < 1$. The forecast error calculated from the first model at time t is the difference between the real and the forecast value generated by this model. The same thing applies to the second model and both are presented respectively in equations (6.4) and (6.5):

$$e_{1,t} = Y_t - \hat{Y}_{1,t} \quad (6.4)$$

$$e_{2,t} = Y_t - \hat{Y}_{2,t} \quad (6.5)$$

$$\hat{Y}_{1,t} = Y_t - e_{1,t} \quad (6.6)$$

$$\hat{Y}_{2,t} = Y_t - e_{2,t} \quad (6.7)$$

Eq. (6.6) denotes the model one forecast at time (t) which equals the difference between observed exchange rates and respective errors while (6.7) denotes the model two forecast at time (t) which equals the difference between observed exchange rates and respective errors. If we replace $\hat{Y}_{1,t}$ and $\hat{Y}_{2,t}$ in equation (6.3) with their values in equation (6.6) and (6.7), we will have the following:

$$e_{combined,t} = Y_t - k\,(Y_t - e_{1,t}) - (1-k)(Y_t - e_{2,t})$$
$$e_{combined,t} = Y_t - k\,Y_t + k\,e_{1,t} - Y_t + e_{2,t} + kY_t - k\,e_{2,t}$$
$$e_{combined,t} = k\,(e_{1,t} - e_{2,t}) + e_{2,t}$$
$$e_{combined,t} = ke_{1,t} + (1-k)\,e_{2,t} \quad (6.8)$$

The variance of the combined forecast errors in Eq. (6.8) can be presented as follows

$$Var(e_{combined,t}) = Var(ke_{1,t}) + Var((1-k)\,e_{2,t}) + 2k\,(1-k)\,Cov(e_{1,t}e_{2,t}) \quad (6.9)$$

where Cov $(e_{1,t}e_{2,t})$ represents covariance of the forecasting errors from the two models. If we develop Eq. (6.9) we get:

$$Var(e_{combined,t}) = k^2\,Vare_{1,t} + (1-k)^2 Vare_{2,t} + 2k(1-k)cov(e_{1,t} + e_{2,t})$$

$$= \mathrm{k}^2\,\mathrm{Var}\,\mathrm{e}_{1,t} + \mathrm{Var}\,\mathrm{e}_{2,t} - 2\mathrm{k}\,\mathrm{Var}\,\mathrm{e}_{2,t} + \mathrm{k}^2\,\mathrm{Var}\,\mathrm{e}_{2,t} + 2\mathrm{k}\,\mathrm{cov}(\mathrm{e}_{1,t} + \mathrm{e}_{2,t}) - 2\mathrm{k}^2\,\mathrm{cov}\,(\mathrm{e}_{1,t} + \mathrm{e}_{2,t})$$

The first derivative of the variance of the combined errors is equal to:

$$\frac{d\,Var}{d\,k} = 2k\,Vare_{1,t} - 2Vare_{2,t} + 2k * Vare_{2,t} + 2cov\,(e_{1,t} + e_{2,t}) - 4k * cov(e_{1,t} + e_{2,t}) \qquad (6.10)$$

The second derivative should be > 0, since we are looking to minimise the error term. Consequently, we need to establish the value of that solves the equation which states that the first derivative is equal to zero:

$$2k\,Vare_{1,t} - 2Vare_{2,t} + 2k * Vare_{2,t} + 2cov\,(e_{1,t} + e_{2,t}) - 4k * cov(e_{1,t} + e_{2,t}) = 0$$

$$2k\,[Vare_{1,t} + Vare_{2,t} - 2cov\,(e_{1,t} + e_{2,t})] - 2Vare_{2,t} + 2cov\,(e_{1,t} + e_{2,t}) = 0$$

$$2k\,[Vare_{1,t} + Vare_{2,t} - 2cov\,(e_{1,t} + e_{2,t})] = 2 \quad (Vare_{2,t} - cov\,(e_{1,t} + e_{2,t}))$$

$$k\,[Vare_{1,t} + Vare_{2,t} - 2cov\,(e_{1,t} + e_{2,t})] = Vare_{2,t} - cov\,(e_{1,t} + e_{2,t})$$

$$k^* = {Vare_{2,t} - cov\,(e_{1,t} + e_{2,t})} \Big/ {Vare_{1,t} + Vare_{2,t} - 2cov\,(e_{1,t} + e_{2,t})} \qquad (6.11)$$

The above result is based on the combination of two methods. Li (2007) and Coshall (2009) neglected the sample covariance term in Eq. (6.11) since they described the calculation of 'optimal weight' as over-complex. Instead $Vare_{1,t}$ *and* $Vare_{2,t}$ were replaced with $\sum_{t=1}^{t} e_1^2$ and $\sum_{t=1}^{t} e_2^2$; as this book combines four models. So we will have $\sum_{t=1}^{t} e_3^2$ and $\sum_{t=1}^{t} e_4^2$ as well.

6.2 Study Findings

The aim of the present chapter is to combine time series and econometric forecasts to assess the accuracy of composite forecasting against the arguments of previous researchers who used combination techniques. It should be noted, though, that combining exchange rate forecasts in the regions selected in this book has never been attempted in the past and therefore the author believes that the present work in general and this chapter in particular is a big contribution to knowledge on this topic and fills a gap in the literature. Out-of-sample forecasts obtained from the four models combined via the equal weights and variance-covariance methods were generated over a 24 months period starting from January 2008. MAPE was computed for forecasts generated by the models considered singly, combined in pairs, in threes and all four together. The findings of this research are unique and hence drawing any parallels with other findings in the literature is not possible due to the absence of similar research related to the same regional settings.

MAPE values reported in Tables 6.1, 6.2, 6.3 and 6.4 show that overall, exponential smoothing models outperformed forecasts generated by other single models (Volatility, Naïve1 and ARDL). This is true for almost all the currencies examined, regardless of the region. This finding supports those in the literature which state that time series methods generate good forecasts in the FOREX market. Importantly, it highlights the failure of ARDL as a single model and it questions the view that exchange rate fluctuations might be explained by macroeconomic variables or economic fundamentals. That finding comes almost 30 years after the work of Meese and Rogoff (1983) who found that structural models perform poorly in a horizon of 1 to 12 months for the Dollar/Pound, Dollar/Mark, Dollar/Yen exchange rates as well as the trade weighted Dollar exchange rate. They concluded that the ability of economic fundamentals to predict exchange rates -particularly in the short-run is limited and that for some assets, in particular, exchange rate, prices and fundamentals are largely disconnected. This book provides evidence that the assumptions made by Meese and Rogoff (1983) in the developed world are valid for the developing world. The ARDL model fails to be optimal when considered alone and is outperformed throughout the study by forecasts generated via time series methods, mainly exponential smoothing. This suggests that, in general, exchange rates are influenced by factors other than macroeconomic fundamentals and as such, ARDL models would not adequately explain the short-run changes that characterise the FOREX market. Overall, combined forecasts outperformed single-model forecasts on 23 occasions. Only two of them were based on equal weight methods. 12 of these 23 forecasts were based on two-way variance-covariance methods while eight were based on the three-way variance-covariance combinations. Four-way variance-covariance combinations outperformed other forecasts only in Tanzania with a MAPE of 1.94%.

The exchange rates of Nicaragua Cordoba, Paraguay Guarani, Venezuela Bolivar, Madagascar Ariary, Mozambique Metical, Zambia Kwacha, Brunei Dollar, Laos Kip and the Philippines Peso were optimally forecasted by a non-combination method. Given that MAPE values below 10% are regarded as "highly accurate forecasting" (Lewis, 1982), all of the reported models - bar the weighted average combination involving Bolivia, Peru and Venezuela (MAPE= 10.87%, 17.07% and 12.46% respectively) - have generated acceptable forecasts of exchange rates. Therefore the findings of this research seem to be in line with Clemen's (1989), MacDonald and Marsh's (1994), Shahriari's

(2011), Altavilla and De Grauwe's (2010) and Anastakis and Morts' (2009) who all agree that combining the forecasts is appropriate when the researcher knows little about the series he is trying to forecast.

Table 6.1 MAPE values and associated models derived from statistically-based combined forecasts for ASEAN countries

ASEAN			Equal-Weights	Variance-covariance		
Currencies		Single model	4 models	Two-way models	Three-way models	Four -way models
Brunei Dollar	Exp.	0.80	1.89	Exp-N1(0.86)	Vol-Exp-ARDL (0.93)	1.02
Indonesia Rupiah	Exp.	2.90	5.43	Vol-Exp (2.71)	Vol-Exp-ARDL (2.76)	2.87
Laos Kip	Exp.	1.47	7.79	Vol-Exp (1.50)	Vol-Exp-Naive1 (1.57)	*
Malaysia Ringgit	Exp.	1.21	1.18	Naive1-ARDL (1.25)	Exp-Naive1-ARDL (0.55)	1.14
Philip-pines Peso	Exp.	1.77	5.47	Exp-N1(1.77)	Vol-Exp-Naive1 (1.89)	2.01
Thailand Baht	Na-ive 1	1.34	3.36	Exp-N1(1.08)	Vol-Exp-Naive1 (1.10)	1.09
Singapore Dollar	Vol.	1.52	1.09	Vol-ARDL (1.29)	Vol-Exp-ARDL (1.42)	1.57
Vietnam Dong	Exp.	1.85	2.15	Vol-Exp (1.80)	Vol-Exp-Naive1 (2.06)	*
Cambodia Riel	Na-ive 1	3.06	3.53	Exp-N1(2.57)	(no Volatility models)	*

(*) No ARDL model established due to data unavailability

Averaging out the forecasts provided only optimally forecasted exchange rates for Singapore Dollar and Angola Kwanza. Simply averaging out the forecast yields good results but is clearly outclassed by the forecasts generated by the best single model and the variance-covariance combinations. This later finding replicates the one of Hibon and Evgeniou (2005) who concluded in their empirical results that managers and researchers should be cautious as combinations are no better than the best individual forecasts. Researchers ought to use the best single forecast model if they have prior knowledge of it. Simply averaging out the forecasts of the Angolan Kwanza and Singapore Dollar yields an impressive MAPE of 1.11% and 1.09% respectively. Tables 6.1, 6.2, 6.3 and 6.4 report the models with minimum MAPE values for both combination methods and single models. The models with the best overall minimum MAPE value for each destination are presented in bold.

Table 6.2 MAPE values and associated models derived from statistically-based combined forecasts for CACM countries

CACM			Equal Weights	Variance-covariance		
Currencies		**Single model**	**4 models**	**Two-way models**	**Three-way models**	**Fou-way models**
Costa Rica Colon	Vol.	3.10	4.09	Vol-ARDL (2.90)	Exp-Naive1-ARDL (0.92)	3.02
Guatemala Quetzal	Exp.	3.29	4.03	Exp-Naive1 (3.06)	Exp-Naive1-ARDL (1.53)	3.55
Honduras Lempira	Exp.	2.58	3.58	Exp-Naive1 (2.35)	Vol-Exp-Naive1 (2.40)	*
Nicaragua Cordoba	Exp.	2.63	4.46	Exp-Naive1 (2.95)	Vol-Exp-Naive1 (3.19)	*
Dominican Peso	Exp.	2.13	5.10	Exp-ARDL (2.05)	Vol-Exp-Naive1 (2.13)	2.14

(*) No ARDL model established due to data unavailability

Table 6.3 MAPE values and associated models derived from statistically-based combined forecasts for MERCOSUR countries

MERCOSUR			Equal Weights	Variance-covariance		
Currencies		**Single model**	**4 models**	**Two-way models**	**Three-way models**	**Four-way models**
Bolivia Boliviano	Exp.	1.72	10.87	Vol-Exp (1.75)	**Exp-Naive1-ARDL (1.11)**	1.95
Brazil Real	Vol.	3.72	5.35	Vol-Naive1 (3.55)	**Exp-Naive1-ARDL (1.92)**	3.82
Chile Peso	Exp.	3.36	4.80	Exp-Naive1 (3.23)	**Exp-Naive1-ARDL (3.03)**	3.36
Colombia Peso	Exp.	3.41	5.82	**Exp-Naive1 (3.37)**	Vol-Exp-ARDL(3.42)	3.65
Paraguay Guarani	Exp.	**2.36**	6.31	Exp-Naive1 (2.43)	Vol-Exp-Naive1 (2.68)	*
Peru Nuevo Sol	Exp.	2.19	17.07	Exp-Naive1 (1.74)	**Vol-Exp-ARDL(1.73)**	1.91
Uruguay Peso	ARDL	4.71	4.07	**Exp-ARDL (0.47)**	Exp-Naive1-ARDL (2.82)	4.71
Venezuela Bolivar	Exp.	**1.52**	12.46	Exp-Naive1 (1.52)	Vol-Exp-Naive1 (1.54)	*

(*) No ARDL model established as the data was unavailable

6.3 Regional Analysis

Overall, variance-covariance combination of time series and econometric models worked particularly well in Central and Latin America. Tables 6.1 and 6.2 illustrate the dominance of these combination methods over single forecasting models. Variance-covariance three-way combinations provide the most accurate forecasts for the exchange rates of Costa Rica Colon and Guatemala Quetzal. Similarly, variance-covariance two-way combinations are optimal models for the exchange rates of both Honduras Lempira and the Dominican Republic Peso. It is worth mentioning that exponential smoothing forecasts outperformed both combination method forecasts only on one occasion in Central America (Nicaragua Cordoba) but was a component in the combinations that provided optimal forecasts for all other five exchange rates. The story repeats itself in Latin America, where the variance-covariance method provides the most accurate forecasts on six occasions (out of nine). Two and three-way variance-covariance forecasts outperformed the results generated by other methods. Again, the exponential smoothing model was a component in all optimal combinations whilst it outperformed -as a single model- combination models on two occasions (Paraguay Guarani and Venezuela Bolivar).

Table 6.4 MAPE values and associated models derived from statistically-based combined forecast for SADC countries

SADC Currencies		Single model	Equal Weights 4 models	Variance-covariance Two-way models	Three-way models	Four models
Angola Kwanza	Exp.	2.08	**1.11**	Exp-N1(1.91)	Vol-Exp-Naive1 (1.87)	1.92
Botswana Pula	Exp.	2.70	5.79	**Vol-ARDL (0.99)**	Vol-Exp-Naive1 (2.96)	3.18
Madagascar Ariary	Exp.	**2.56**	7.24	Vol-Exp (2.82)	Vol-Exp-ARDL (3.02)	3.37
Malawi Kwa-cha	Exp.	1.55	1.69	**Vol-Exp (0.93)**	Vol-Exp-Naive1 (1.46)	*
Mauritius Ru-pee	Exp.	2.50	3.36	**Exp-Naive1 (2.44)**	Exp-Naive1-ARDL (2.52)	2.62
Mozambique Metical	Exp.	**2.78**	4.76	Vol-Exp (3.03)	Vol-Exp-ARDL (3.24)	3.68
South Africa Rand	Exp.	4.81	8.36	**Exp-Naive (4.58)**	Vol-Exp-Naive1 (4.78)	*
Tanzania Shil-ling	Exp.	2.12	3.85	Vol-Exp (2.12)	Vol-Exp-Naive1 (1.95)	**1.94**
Zambia Kwa-cha	Exp.	**4.04**	8.42	Exp-Naive (4.14)	-	*

The picture is slightly different with both SADC and ASEAN. Although the variance-covariance combinations fared well in both regions, their performance is clearly outclassed by results in Central and Latin America. The method provides optimal models on 10 occasions (out of 19) with almost all optimal models being two-way rather than three-way combinations. Although exponential smoothing forecasts provided low MAPEs, there is a resurgence of volatility models as consistent components in the combination exercise. This might be explained by the continuous impact of crises in Asia from the mid 1990's to early 2000's and the instability of many African economies during the two decades leading to the 21st century. These findings support those of Armstrong's (1989) who stated that combination forecasts produce consistent but modest gains in accuracy. According to the MAPE values reported in Tables 6.3 and 6.4, variance-covariance combination models outperform single ones consistently but do so within small margins for Asian and African countries. For Central and Latin America, combined forecasts outperform their single counterparts by an average MAPE of 2% which is a significant improvement for traders. One wonders whether these small improvements are significant for other market players. From a trader's point of view, a forecast improvement of one basis point (0.01) makes a big difference because of the huge daily volume of transactions. Other market players, such as policy makers, might be interested in the trend forecast (in terms of increase or decrease) rather than an accurate value of exchange rates over the forecast period. The aims and the objectives of any FOREX analysis should state clearly whom the forecasts will benefit to avoid misconceptions and misinterpretations of the outcomes.

In the SADC region equal weights forecasts yield on average twice the MAPEs generated by the best single forecast models. For MERCOSUR exchange rates, equal weight forecasts yield on average three times the MAPEs generated by the best single model forecasts. Similarly for ASEAN and CACM, simply averaging out the forecasts yields between two and three times the MAPEs generated by single model forecasts. The simple average combination approach is not the method to use if the researcher seeks optimal forecasts. Rather, simply averaging combination is the method to use for exploratory purposes and when the material at hand does not offer any clue towards the best single forecast method that would be needed for modelling purposes.

ASEAN

Myanmar currency was removed from the analysis because it was pegged to the American dollar for the best part of the last three decades. Consequently, combination forecasting results were generated for nine exchange rates in the ASEAN region. Table 6.1 presents the MAPE results of the various forecasting models, both single and combined. The table gives the MAPE values of the optimal single model forecast, the equal weights model and the optimal two, three and four-way combination forecasts. All single model forecasts generated for the ASEAN currencies have MAPE values lower than 5%. The single model forecasts outperformed other model forecasts in the case of the Brunei Dollar, the Lao Kip and Philippine Peso. The variance-covariance combination method outperforms other approaches in the case of the Indonesian Rupiah, the Malaysian Ringgit, the Thai Baht, the Vietnamese Dong, the Cambodian Riel and the Singapore Dollar. Exponential smoothing is a component in all these combinations and therefore this means that it is a key method in combining ASEAN currencies.

Table 6.1 provides evidence that combination forecasting can outperform forecasts generated from single models, although single model MAPEs are almost as good as MAPEs generated from combination forecasting methods. Indonesia, Cambodia and the Philippines were not politically stable during most of the historical period covered in this study. Combination models provided optimal forecasts for these currencies which demonstrates the power combination has in the forecasting of the changing behaviour of exchange rates over time when they are affected by various factors that might be captured by different components in the combination. On the other hand, the fact that equal weights provided the highest MAPE for a few currencies means there is at least one model component in combination that does not fit the data and therefore contributes negatively to the combination forecast. This shows the danger of choosing a single model when the researcher is uncertain about which method to adopt and it highlights the importance of combination methods. The next section presents the results of applying combinations techniques to the forecast of the exchange rates of the CACM region, followed by a similar discussion for both the MERCOSUR and SADC.

CACM

The variance-covariance method performed particularly well in Central and Latin America as the respective two and three-way combination models outperformed the forecasts generated by other models. For both Honduras and Nicaragua, exponential smoothing models combined with the Naïve I model outperformed other forecast models, whilst for the remaining currencies the combination of ARDL, Naïve I and exponential smoothing outperformed other single and combination methods. Close monitoring of the exchange rate fluctuations from international institutions makes it very unlikely that these currencies are driven solely by macroeconomic fundamentals because of the relative frailty of economic aggregates in developing countries. Instead, because Central American countries adhere to a tight agenda dictated by offices in Washington and Paris, the exchange rate is likely to deviate from equilibrium in the short term in the belief that in the long term, the country will have sound macroeconomic fundamentals on which the exchange rate will depend. From a single model perspective, the exponential smoothing method consolidates its good performance and provides good forecasts with overall MAPE values of less than 5% that outperforms all other single model forecasts. The equal weights method generates good forecasts too, although none of them is the most accurate. This is also valid for the variance-covariance four-way combination method.

The economy of Central America is highly dependent on the US, the prime destination for its exports and the source of large remittances which amount sometimes to almost half of exports and three-quarters of tourism receipts for a number of Central American states. The signature of the US-Central American-Dominican Republic Free Trade Agreement (DR-CAFTA) which came into force on 1 January, 2009 is likely to exacerbate this dependence. Analysts believe that the DR-CAFTA will lead to increased FDI in key sectors of the economy, including the insurance and telecommunications sectors recently opened to private investors. Panama and Belize adopt the American dollar as legal tender and therefore have no control over their monetary policy, illustrating a financial as well as an economic dependence on the US; hence both their exchange rates were omitted from the analysis. Apart from trading with the US, Central America also generates income from tourism which constitutes the largest source of foreign currency for both Belize and Costa Rica. More than 50% of the population of Honduras and Nicaragua live below the poverty line and it is no surprise that they are recipients of aid from the World Bank's "Highly Indebted Poor Countries" initiative.[18]

MERCOSUR

Of the eight currencies studied in Latin America, combination forecasting was the optimal model in six. Four of these optimal forecasts were based on the three-way and two based on the two-way variance-covariance combinations. The ARDL models seem to perform particularly well in Latin America when combined with other time series models. In almost all the optimal combined forecast, ARDL was a persistent component of the combination and this applies to both the two-way and three-way variance-covariance combinations. In addition, those forecasts have an average MAPE value of 2% and therefore the forecasts generated are deemed to be very accurate. The equal weights method generates the least accurate forecasts in this region which translates into high MAPE values (Bolivia Bolivar, 10.87%; Peru New Sol, 17.07%). Similarly, the variance-covariance four-way combinations did not show up as an optimal model in any of the currencies examined but they did generate good forecasts overall (with MAPEs less than 5%).

The variance-covariance method provided more accurate forecasts than the simple average method. However, this method offers only a slight improvement in accuracy when compared to the best single forecasting model. This raises the question as to the relevance of combining forecasts if the results are almost similar to those we can obtain through the use of the best single forecast model. Obviously the most straightforward answer to this question depends on whether we know what the best single forecast method is. In other words, if the researcher is aware of the best single forecast method to use he is left with the choice to decide whether the slight improvement in accuracy is significant in the context of his study. It should be noted that for this region, the ARDL method outperformed other single method forecasts just once. In fact, ARDL optimally forecasts Uruguay Peso with a very good MAPE (4.71%). However, this performance is overshadowed by the very accurate results of the two-way combination (Exp-ARDL, 0.47%) and the three-way combination (Exp-Naïve 1-ARDL, 2.82%). Notwithstanding the fact that the combination

[18] The HIPC Initiative was launched in 1996 by the IMF and World Bank with the aim of ensuring that no poor country faces a debt burden it cannot manage. Since then the international financial community, including multilateral organizations and governments, have worked together to reduce to sustainable levels the external debt burdens of the most heavily indebted poor countries (IMF, 2013).

model provides a more accurate forecast, the reader will notice that the ARDL is a component in all three best performing models. This is another highlight of the findings of this research: Macroeconomic aggregates can provide key information for the forecasting of exchange rates in the MERCOSUR assuming an element of past behaviour is taken into consideration in the analysis in the shape of a time series forecast. The next section discusses the results of applying combination methods to the forecasting of the exchange rates of the SADC countries.

SADC

The Namibian dollar, Lesotho loti and Swaziland lilangeni were removed from the analysis because they are pegged on a par with the South African Rand and their respective Central Banks have little freedom in steering monetary policy one way or the other. All three countries form a Common Monetary Area (CMA) with the South African rand as a lead currency. This is meant to reduce transaction and information costs (Metzger, 2008).

The author of this book decided not to study the Zimbabwe Dollar because of the huge manipulation of the currency by Zimbabwe Central Bank motivated by a political agenda rather than a financial or economic one. The exponential smoothing model outperformed other single models in the forecasts of SADC exchange rates. Out of ten exchange rates examined in the SADC region combination forecasting outperformed single model forecasts on six occasions. The variance-covariance method performed particularly well in the forecasts of the Botswana Pula, Malawi Kwacha, Mauritius Rupee and South Africa Rand with an average MAPE of 2%. There is a stark difference between the performance of both two-way and three-way variance-covariance combination methods. In fact, the latter was outperformed by other models for all exchange rates studied in the SADC region. Three-way combination fails to provide an optimal model although the forecasts provided are accurate (MAPE of less than 5%). This is an interesting result if we take into consideration the fact that three-way combination did very well in Central and Latin America.

A simple average approach to combination forecasting was the optimal model on one occasion which is quite a contrast with the view in the literature which stipulates that simply averaging out forecasts provides better forecasts than any other single forecast (see Section 3 and 4, Chapter Three). The average MAPE calculated from equal weights combination forecasts in SADC is about 7%. Although this is quite a good performance, researchers and practitioners alike are better off using other combination methods that provide a lot more accurate results. That said; simply averaging out the forecast did extremely well in the forecast of Angola Kwanza (MAPE 1.11%). This might be explained by the fact that the exchange rate in Angola is affected by an array of factors including volatility, political instability, the huge flow of capital and the like. In other words, different models are required to capture the effects of these various factors. Currency fluctuations in Africa are affected by factors that go beyond economic aggregates and time series axioms. Politics plays a major role in the way governments manage their finances (i.e. exchange rate) and those who are interested in forecasting SADC currencies should equip themselves with background knowledge about these countries and especially learn more about the beliefs and ambitions of their policy makers.

African countries like Madagascar, Malawi, Mozambique, Tanzania and Zambia are all signatories of the "Highly Indebted Poor Countries" initiative. This initiative by the World Bank makes exchange rates of these countries dependent on the tight agenda international institutions dictate to them. In other words, the exchange rate is not free to move in one direction or another based on the soundness (or not) of macroeconomic fundamentals. Instead, exchange rates are manipulated in a way to allow these institutions to implement policies that they believe would help indebted countries to overcome obstacles peculiar to their own development. Four-way combination does not provide the most accurate forecast in SADC (except for the Tanzanian Shilling). This corroborates the finding of Hibou and Evgeniou (2005) who stated that sophisticated combination models do not lead to the best forecasts.

6.4 Conclusions and Implications for Policy Makers

One of the main findings of this research is that simply averaging out forecasts does not seem to be the optimal model for the panel of currencies examined. Out of more than 30 currencies, the equal weights method generated the most accurate forecast for the Angola Kwanza (1.11%) and the Singapore Dollar (1.09%) while simply averaging out forecasts did not match the performance of other forecasting models for any of the currencies studied in Central and Latin America. Overall, this means that the findings of this research differ from those in the literature, where researchers state that simply combining forecasts is the best method of combination and that simple combination forecast is more accurate than single model forecasts.

A second important finding of this chapter, which is in line with the literature is that over-sophisticated combination methods do not always generate the best forecasts (Altavilla and De Grauwe, 2010). On only one occasion did the four-way variance-covariance combination method produce the lowest MAPE (Tanzanian Shilling, 1.94%). A third important finding of the combination exercise is the fact that exponential smoothing methods performed extremely well, evidenced by MAPE values of less than 5% in most cases. Exponential smoothing models seem to reflect the constant changing behaviour of the exchange rates in Africa, Latin America and Asia. Given the relative ease with which one can generate exponential smoothing forecasts, the model can be used as an exploratory approach for key players to gauge the sentiment of the exchange rate market.

Interestingly, exponential smoothing performed well across the four continents. All forecasts generated by this method provided accurate results with a margin of error of less than 5%. The variance-covariance combination of exponential smoothing with ARDL yielded the best results in Latin and Central American whilst the variance-covariance combination of time series models provided the most accurate forecasts in Africa and Asia. In the context of this study, explanatory variables for exchange rates in Africa and Asia were not always available in the two decades leading up to the 21st century. That said, in the light of the results shown in the MAPE tables, there is a clear correlation between the behaviour of the exchange rates in Central and Latin America. Furthermore, it seems there are common trends between countries in different regions (i.e. Africa and Asia) but which are in the same stage of development. The ARDL model provides very good results when combined with the time series method in Central and Latin America whilst the exchange rates in Africa and Asia are best forecasted using a combination of time series techniques.

A further important finding of this chapter is the fact that variance-covariance combination performed particularly well overall. Variance-covariance two-way combinations outperformed other combination models in the ASEAN and SADC region, while variance covariance three-way combination was the best performer in Central and Latin America. Furthermore, although the ARDL model did not provide the most accurate forecast when used as a single model, it was a component/element in every single combination model. Most of the currencies analysed in this book belong to countries in their early stages of development and therefore the behaviour of exchange rates depends on macroeconomic fundamentals and on historical data. One might argue that this assumption is valid for any currency whether in a developed or under developed country.

The fact that the ARDL model outperformed single and combination models only once in over thirty currencies is a signal that the currencies examined cannot be predicted only by looking at interest rates, inflation rates, money supplies and trade balances because most markets in the four regions have not matured yet. In DRC, the Philippines, Cambodia, Colombia, Honduras and Nicaragua, the state is still struggling to ensure stability in the face of the resurgence of rebels, separatists, drug gangs and/or armed opposition (CIA, 2012). Additionally, Bolivia, DRC, Honduras, Madagascar, Malawi, Mozambique, Nicaragua, Tanzania and Zambia are all members of the "Highly Indebted Poor Countries" club (IMF, 2013). The ARDL approach did not come up in any of the combinations in the HIPC group while exponential smoothing fared very well in these countries. In practice, it seems unlikely that any of these currencies will exhibit a sudden sweeping change because of the tight terms that come with any debt contract. This might, therefore, explain the encouraging performance of exponential smoothing as a simple model in these currencies. The recent past is the most important element to be taken into consideration and this makes the Naïve 1 model relevant because the changes in the currency value from month to month will be small as the fluctuations in economic aggregates (i.e. exchange rates) are tightly monitored by international lending institutions mainly the IMF and the World Bank. The MAPE results in Tables 6.1, 6.2, 6.3 and 6.4, provide the bedrock of an analysis that will be useful for key players in the FOREX market (policy makers and traders to name a few). The empirical results of this chapter provide evidence that most of the combined forecasts based on the variance-covariance method perform better than the individual forecasts. The simple average combination method - which attaches the same weight to each of the individual forecasts - was widely applied due to its relative simplicity as reported in the forecasting literature (for example Makridakis and Winkler 1983; Fang 2003; Hibon and Evgeniou 2005). But its performance was limited in this research because although it provided good forecasts other single and combination models proved much better. These findings confirm those of Hibon and Evgeniou (2005) in which they examined only the simple average combination method and concluded that the advantage of combination is to decrease the forecasting risk but not to significantly outperform the best single forecast. Results of this chapter also show that most of the combined forecasts based on the variance-covariance method perform better than the individual forecasts. This is in line with the study of Makridakis and Winkler (1983) who applied several versions of the variance-covariance weighting method to examine the performance of the combined forecasts and found similar results. Studying how to choose between methods and their combinations is an important aspect of practical research and clearly it may not always be best to combine forecasts (Hibon and Evgeniou, 2005).

Indeed, simply averaging out the forecasts is outperformed as a method by the optimal single model for almost every currency examined in this research. In other words, although combination forecasting has proved to be popular, the choice of the combination technique and the components of the combination itself seem to dictate the ensuing results. This means that if the forecaster has background knowledge about the exchange rate to forecast, using the best single method might yield more accurate results than simply averaging out the forecasts. In respect of the ARDL model, the author believes that there are factors inherent to this research which makes the above method seem less attractive than previously thought. The choice of significant explanatory variables – namely interest rates, money supply, trade balance and GDP growth - was not possible for some countries because data was not available. The author of this book believes that ARDL will yield better results when future researchers can access all potential explanatory variables; assuming they use periods where countries are relatively stable and immune from non-regular manipulation of their exchange rates for reasons completely disconnected from finance and economics.

The successful combination of time series models and econometric models is clear in this research. The ARDL approach works well when combined with other approaches. This was most apparent in Central and Latin America. Furthermore, even for ASEAN and SADC currencies, the ARDL model was a consistent component of second and third best combination models. It is a fact that ARDL as a single model was the best forecast only once, which opens the question about the extent to which explanatory variables have the power to predict exchange rate movements in the regional settings chosen for this research. One could argue that a traditional choice of explanatory variables based on the monetary theory of exchange rates where interest rates, money supply, trade openness and inflation rate should provide a clear insight into the behaviour of exchange rates. The nature of the countries being examined in this study makes this task difficult. Even if the data of such aggregates was available, a number of these countries mainly in Africa and Central America and Latin America are still struggling with unstable governments.

Chapter VII Conclusions, Summary and Recommendations for Policy Makers

7.1 Main Findings

This book used time series, cointegration and combination methods to examine and forecast the exchange rates of the ASEAN, CACM, MERCOSUR and SADC countries. This is the first attempt in the literature to compare exchange rates based on a regional approach and on such a large scale. Many of the exchange rates examined in the ASEAN, CACM, MERCOSUR and SADC regions were never investigated before using the techniques mentioned above. Findings were presented in such a way to highlight the power these methods can have in the forecasting of exchange rates in the emerging world.

Given the dependent nature of many developing economies, the exchange rate is probably the most important asset price that respective governments have to manage. Consequently, understanding and forecasting exchange rate behaviour is particularly important to policy makers and other market players who have to integrate volatility in the modelling process. The finding that statistically significant volatility models have been generated for most exchange rates examined in this book is a fact that speaks for itself. This book started by making an assumption that volatility is an important concept in the study of exchange rates in the emerging world - a topic that has been overlooked for some time. Based on the findings discussed in Chapter Four, the author confirms that the forecast of the volatility of exchange rates in the emerging world is an important theme, to which attention should be directed. Significant volatility models were generated for all exchange rates investigated in this book. Volatility parameters were identified as a precursor to exchange rate forecasts for the sampled countries. The accuracy of the forecasts generated via volatility models was measured and compared with other forecasting techniques to assess their performance on a regional basis. The results provided evidence that asymmetric volatility models reflecting the greater impact of bad news is an aspect that transcends the locality of a country and was a recurring pattern in countries from Central America to Southeast Asia.

This book also used exponential smoothing techniques to model more than 35 exchange rates in four trading blocs across continents. No previous research covered such a large scope. It provided evidence that exponential smoothing models can generate very accurate forecasts and can outperform forecasts of other time series and econometric methods. Clearly, this family of models has potential in forecasting exchange rates in the emerging world. The Naïve 1 method is another technique that receives very little attention because of its simplicity. Nonetheless, this research proved that Naïve1 model can provide quite accurate forecasts and can be used as an exploratory method for those with limited resources and knowledge of time series techniques. Mean absolute percentage error was employed as a forecasting evaluation technique to judge the relative performance of three competing models. The forecasting models included time series models (ARIMA-Volatility, exponential smoothing and Naïve 1), a cointegration model (ARDL) in addition to combination models (equal weight and variance-covariance combination techniques).

By using the ARDL cointegration method, Chapter Five provided a thorough examination of the various determinants of exchange rates in the emerging world. For every single exchange rate, at least one exchange rate determinant was identified. The choice of explanatory variables was different between countries which reflect the specifics of every exchange rate. The relationship between exchange rates, GDP, money supply, interest rate, inflation and trade was investigated due to their popularity in the literature. The forecasts generated on the basis of changes in selected variables were computed while short-and long-run relationships were identified. In addition an error correction model measuring the speed that exchange rates require to return to long-run equilibrium following a shock was used. Overall, trade activity seemed to be particularly important in the determination of the changes in exchange rates in all four regions. This finding came as no surprise, since many of the countries examined in this research rely heavily on trade.

As Taylor and Sarno (2002, 4) stated in their book "While macroeconomic fundamentals appear to be as important determinants of exchange rate movements over relatively long horizons and in economies experiencing pathologically large movements in such fundamentals (such as during a hyperinflation), there seems to be substantial and often persistent movements in exchange rates which are largely unexplained by macroeconomic fundamentals". This was particularly true in this book as the ARDL cointegration forecasts were outperformed by time series and combination methods. However, ARDL forecasts are particularly useful when combined with other techniques such as time series. This is exactly what the combination method, discussed and applied in Chapter Six, has proven. Combination techniques were used to forecast the future behaviour of exchange rates in selected regions in Africa, Asia, Central and Latin America. The results show that combination forecasts outperformed time series and econometrics forecasts in about 70% of cases. This finding is one of the major contributions of this book to knowledge since it provides empirical evidence that composite methods are particularly useful in exchange rate forecasts, especially in the emerging world. The variance-covariance method of combination performed particularly well across regions, although different sets of combinations were required in different continents.

The reason behind the choice of a regional approach in the examination of exchange rates in this book had a purpose. The financial crisis in Southeast Asia and the debt crisis in Latin America made markets almost unpredictable. The spillover of such crises had effects that few market players had expected. The strong integration of financial markets was criticised as the prime factor that exacerbated the crisis, while Central Bank interventions in a number of countries was promoted as a magic tool (that did not work) to ensure stability of returns. In fact, many studies have noted an increased interdependence of financial markets within and outside Latin America (see for example Choudhry, 1997; Edwards and Susmel, 2001; Fernandez-Serrano and Sosvilla-Rivero, 2003). Only a few studies have indicated that these interdependencies are weak (Edwards and Susmel, 2001; Berg et al., 2003) which explains to some extent the unanimous reaction to shocks in Latin America's MERCOSUR. This book provided a regional analysis of exchange rates in four different geographical settings and shows that exchange rates in the same region tend to respond to shocks in a similar fashion. Furthermore, countries at the same stage of development, particularly in Central America and sub-Saharan Africa have a lot in common when it comes to the behaviour of their exchange rates. An obstacle the author was faced with is the fact that boundaries between the auction market, interbank market, bureau market and parallel market (this is where the currency can be bought or sold) are not clearly defined in most emerging markets. This will test the willingness of any government to monitor currency fluctuations and should account for factors that usually do not apply to the study of advanced world currencies. For example, the parallel market was dominant in Angola and Cambodia during the 1990's while bureau markets were very active in Mozambique Mauritius and Brazil during the same period (Johnston and Swinburne, 1999). This means that the official rate announced by the Central Bank does not reflect the real value of the currency, since different markets have different rates. Although this might be true for several countries, the trend nowadays is to make sure that the official rate reflects exactly the performance of the currency on both local and international levels. The reason behind this is simple: most countries examined in this book are part of what we refer to since the turn of the century as the emerging markets bloc. They are striving to prove to the outside world that they have now left the era of tyranny and moved on to an era of stability and transparency that will make them attractive to international investors and partners alike.

The FOREX market is not efficient in the sense that both risk neutrality and rational expectations appear to be rejected by data (Sarno and Sarno 2002, 2). Although there is some truth in this statement, this research was able to identify factors that influence the behaviour of exchange rates and forecast accurately a set of exchange rates of countries across the globe. This work laid the foundations for a solid understanding of the behaviour of exchange rates in the four trading blocs chosen as a framework for this book. Models can either be used to generate forecasts from 2014 onwards or findings can be directly incorporated in the decision making process at the top strategic level. The present work stressed the importance of the adoption of a regional perspective in the study of exchange rates in the emerging world.

7.2 ASEAN

Exponential smoothing outperformed other single models in the forecasts of ASEAN currencies, reflecting the power that time series have in integrating recent changes when modelling exchange rate behaviour. Naïve I was the best forecast model for two exchange rates in the region providing evidence that the simplicity of the method does not undermine its exploratory power. Nonetheless, combination methods, especially the variance-covariance techniques, seem to have provided the most accurate forecasts in the ASEAN region and in the process, it outperforms the best single forecasts (i.e. exponential smoothing). Most optimal combinations were of time series models. A combination of an ARDL and a time series model provided the best forecast on only one occasion. Based on the ARDL analysis in Chapter Five, trade and economic variables are the main determinants of exchange rate changes in the ASEAN region.

Southeast Asia is infamous for its financial crisis that hit in 1997 and wiped out the efforts of the economies of the regions to improve living standards and macroeconomic fundamentals. The exchange rate lesson was learned the hard way by countries struck by the currency crisis. The crisis illustrates how little control government has when they open up their economies to international capital prematurely without an extensive examination of exchange rate fluctuations. According to Sarno and Taylor (2002, 4), the recent and emerging literature on FOREX microstructure in some measure reflects an attempt by researchers in international Finance to understand the deviations from macroeconomic fundamentals; as does this book. Clearly, the fact that the ARDL model did not perform as well as time series techniques in the ASEAN region provides evidence of the presence of extraneous variables. These include the transmission of information between market participants, the behaviour of market agents, the relationship between information flows, the importance of order flows, the heterogeneity of agents' expectations and the implications of such heterogeneity for trading volume and exchange rate volatility. Although governments should be playing an active role in the examination of exchange rates in this part of the world they will have to strike a balance between regulation and the need to allow their financial services industries to develop without over-burdensome restrictions.

The ASEAN is one of the most successful trading blocs on earth. The member countries are combining forces to emulate the European Union to adopt a single currency before the end of the decade. True, the ASEAN has its geographic advantages as the region sits astride the Pacific and the Indian Ocean. Moreover, the area boasts rich natural resources, low-cost labour forces and extensive trade links with the rest of the world. Although some ASEAN countries like Singapore and Malaysia have sound economic fundamentals, there are still aspects related to the economy and especially to exchange rates that need to be looked at if member countries are to succeed in achieving their single currency target. As discussed in Chapters Four and Five: although most ASEAN members seem to manage the floating of their exchange rates, they still fall short of coordinating their respective monetary policies. This means that respective Central Banks decide on the fluctuations at the margins of the currency which leads to various monetary policies being adopted across the board. In other words, if the ASEAN countries intend to have a single currency by 2020, closer coordination is required in terms of interest rates, inflation rates and money supply to lay the foundations of monetary union.

This book showed that there are still big gaps between the economic might of countries like Singapore and Malaysia compared to countries like Myanmar, Laos and Cambodia. These gaps should be addressed sooner rather than later as they widen every day, especially given the unstable situation in Myanmar where the government seems to adopt an ethnic cleansing policy towards the Muslim Rohingya minority. Since its inception in August 1967 in Bangkok, the ASEAN adopted a non-interference policy towards its members' national affairs in the belief that its focus should be on economic development and that countries should be able to manage their own internal affairs. Although this policy paid dividends and made the ASEAN one of the most successful trading blocs in the world, it is widely criticised by analysts (The Economist, 2011). Consequently it becomes a challenge to centralise any decision related to economy and monetary policy let alone monetary union. In fact, during the Asian economic integration summit hosted by ASEAN and held in Bangkok, Yukio Hatoyama, prime minister of Japan (the region's largest economy) said that the ASEAN should have a common currency and aspire to lead the world (The Economist, 2009). By 2015 a single market and production base are to be established while the AEC addresses the development gaps and accelerates the integration of Cambodia, Myanmar, Laos and Vietnam through the Initiative for ASEAN Integration.

Indonesia is one of the fastest growing nations in the ASEAN region. It is the world's third largest democracy and registers the highest growth rate after India and China (The Economist, 2009). As the most populous country in Southeast Asia and its biggest economy, Indonesia has always played a dominant role in the ASEAN (The Economist, 2009). As the ASEAN moves towards greater economic integration, Indonesia has a real chance to position itself as a main economic hub. Officials like to cite the example of the assembly of cars in Java for the ASEAN market by German company Volkswagen as one example of this (which makes this study important to multinational companies too). The size of the domestic market makes Indonesia the logical destination for foreign investors looking for a base within the ASEAN from which to attack the regional market. Indonesia was considered a basket case not so long ago but is now seen as an extra 'I' in the BRIC group of big, fast-growing emerging markets. Two-way variance-covariance combinations provided the optimal forecasting model for the exchange rate of the Indonesian rupiah, with three and four-way the second and third best, respectively.

7.3 CACM

Central America has been ignored by researchers for many years because of the very unstable political situation in the region and it is the belief of the author that one of the main contributions of this book is an assessment of the performance of exchange rates in CACM countries during a period of 20 years, together with an analysis of the factors that affect their volatility as well as a successful attempt to generate empirical forecasts. Significant volatility models generated good forecasts for the exchange rates of the CACM countries (plus the Dominican Republic). As with the ASEAN, exponential smoothing models provided the most accurate single forecasts. Combination methods fared well in generating good forecasts for all CACM countries except for Nicaragua. One interesting fact about this finding is that combination of time series techniques and cointegration are a dominant combination model in this part of the world. This is an interesting finding if one recalls that for the ASEAN most optimal combinations were of time series techniques. In fact, this reflects the over-dependency of Central American countries on trade mainly with the United States as all exchange rate determinants identified for this region are trade components (exports, trade balance and trade openness).

The Central America Free Trade Agreement bolstered this strong relationship between exchange rates and trade. In fact, the CACM envisaged a similar agreement with the European Union which tested out the region's resolve since a wider discussion about the necessary macroeconomic reforms was initiated putting sustainable development and social equity issues back on the table. The lessons learned from the CAFTA-DR negotiations provided the region with an opportunity to initiate negotiations of an Association Agreement with the European Union which many analysts suspect will be difficult and complex. However, if all goes well, it could have a very positive impact on Central American integration. Although the United States and Europe seem to play crucial roles in Central America, new actors like Mexico and Brazil are becoming increasingly important.

As per the ASEAN, the CACM region suffers from a huge gap between its member countries. Costa Rica is one of the world's oldest democracies while Nicaragua is the poorest country in mainland Latin America which explains why almost half Guatemala's children are chronically malnourished (The Economist, 2011). Conflicts in both El Salvador and Nicaragua and political unrest elsewhere left the region in confusion and disarray. Although the civil wars that ravaged Central America in the 1970's and 1980's are over, exchange rate behaviour remains most unpredictable. This is due particularly to the frailty of the economies which generate most of its income from trading activities with the US in the shape of outsourcing companies. In the 1990's, foreign investors set up textile factories to benefit from the low cost of labour to supply the US market with goods. The fact that Central America depends on imported oil and food makes them vulnerable to fuel and commodity price volatility. This is associated with increasing poverty in the continent. Costa Rica was the first country to consolidate its FOREX market in 1983, devalue the currency and establish a crawling peg tied to the US dollar and periodically adjusted by inflation differentials. Costa Rica is richer, more democratic and more stable than its Central American neighbours.

As part of the 1992 agreement that ended the country's civil war, El Salvador and Guatemala emerged from gruesome civil wars in the early 1990's which explains why they maintained multiple exchange rates and other controls until 1989 when they consolidated their FOREX markets and established a managed float. Honduras did so in 1990. Nicaragua is a case apart. A study by the United Nations Economic Commission for Latin America and the Caribbean (ECLAC, 2006) found that an increase in remittances is the main factor behind the real appreciation recorded by the exchange rates of Guatemala and Honduras between the early 1990's and mid-2006 (24% and 18% respectively). Combination of time series and econometric models in the CACM region provided the best forecasting results for five economies in the region and the second best forecast in Nicaragua. As a single model, exponential smoothing fared particularly well in Central America. Due to the importance of ARDL forecast in the combination exercise in Central America, future researchers might decide to assess the relationship between exchange rates and remittances in Central America.

7.4 MERCOSUR

Most countries in Latin America seem to have sound economic policies. With money cheap and returns poor in the developed world, Latin America is set to become a prime destination for investors. Although this is supposed to be a good omen for the continent, it is more a difficulty for a few countries in the region as more cash inflows mean ever appreciating currencies. Between 2009 and 2011 the Brazilian real appreciated by 38% against the US dollar, making it hard for exporters to compete with cheap markets and consequently finding their products priced out of international markets (The Economist, 2011). The forecasting of exchange rates has never been more relevant to economies in this part of the world. Deeper integration means that the economies of the region have to unify their exchange rate policies in the future and this is one of the main contribution to knowledge in this region: improving the understanding of the behaviour of the exchange rates in Latin America's MERCOSUR ahead of the single currency project. What has been said about Central America in terms of the relevance of combination methods based on both time series and ARDL techniques is valid for Latin America too as variance-covariance combination forecasts outperformed most other forecasts in the region. As a single model, exponential smoothing performed well by generating accurate forecasts for the exchange rates of MERCOSUR countries. Overall, two and three-way combinations seem to be the most recurrent combination in the MERCOSUR region while other types of combinations (four-way and equal weights) seem to be outclassed in terms of accuracy. This latest finding can be verified across other regions (mainly the ASEAN and the CACM). One of the interesting features depicted by ARDL cointegration in the MERCOSUR is the relationship between commodities and exchange rates. The valuation of gold reserves in Bolivia, Brazil and Uruguay has yielded significant long term relationships as with the copper price in Chile. Although some countries like

Uruguay get very little publicity, their economic progress is no less impressive than their benchmarks – Brazil and Chile.

In the MERCOSUR, political agendas seem to overshadow the drive towards a unified monetary policy that would lead to more stable inflation rates and less volatile exchange rates. Earlier this year, analysts accused the governments in Venezuela and Argentina of miscommunication of data related to their macroeconomic performance. Inflation is thought to be over 20% in Argentina while government authorities argue that it is around 10% (CIA, 2012). A wave of nationalisation by late president Chavez of Venezuela has provided a living example of the restricted relevance that quantitative analysis might have in the forecast of exchange rates in some contexts. In Brazil, one would have expected that trade and monetary aggregates are key to exchange rate determination since the country is now the sixth largest economy in the world ahead of the UK. According to the Economist (2011), the "sub-salt" fields that Brazil is developing are thought to hold over 13 billion barrels/day of oil. By 2020, Petrobas, the country's government controlled oil firm, will be pumping 4m barrels/day, double today's amount. Energy prices might have a stronger relevance to the value of the currency in the future. One reason why Brazil does not seem to be affected by the terms of trade is its diversified portfolio of trade, oil, minerals and services. Nonetheless, Latin America in general is uncomfortably dependent on commodities. In the past decade they accounted for 52% of the region's exports, while in East Asia they account for less than 30% of total exports illustrating the difference between the economies of the two regions. Brazil aims to be the world's leading food exporter in 2025 (World Bank, 2011)

Critics have accused the MERCOSUR of becoming politicised and moving away from its free-trade origins. Talks to secure a trade accord with the EU began in 1999 but were suspended in 2004. The two blocs agreed to resume negotiations on a free trade agreement at talks in Madrid in May, 2010 despite opposition from several key European nations including France. MERCOSUR and CAN (Andean Community of Nations) leaders signed an agreement to form a third organisation, UNASUR, in May 2008. UNASUR is meant to encompass trade, security, and political issues, much like the European Union. Some analysts believe that the UNASUR could eventually replace the MERCOSUR. In fact, the Union of South American Nations is an inter-governmental union integrating two existing customs unions – the MERCOSUR and the CAN - as part of a continuing process of South American integration. The UNASUR gained full legality in 2011 and the 12-members announced their intention to model the new community after the European Union including a single market by 2014, a common currency, a parliament and a passport by 2019. The combined population of UNASUR is estimated to be more than 400 million. It contains the 10 members and associate members of the MERCOSUR in addition to Guyana and Suriname.

7.5 SADC

This book examined exchange rate fluctuations in the SADC region from 1990 to 2009. Exchange rates were first analysed on an individual basis followed by a regional comparison to assess the degree of financial integration in the trading bloc. Forecasts were generated using time series, econometric and combination approaches. The performance of the forecasting techniques was then compared across regions. The author believes that there will be increasing interest in studies like this one as capital holders around the globe are looking for business opportunities away from Europe.

The exponential smoothing model provided the most accurate forecasts for all SADC exchange rates. Two-way combinations outperformed other combinations techniques in the composite forecasts of the currencies of the region. An interesting feature of the ARDL results that pertain to the SADC is the importance of inflation rates as determinants of the changes in exchange rates. The author supports the work of Adeneyi et al. (2011) in that the interest of policy makers in these countries should focus on whether the potential gains from regional economic integration in Africa are offset by the disparities that may come from the emergence of potential winners and losers from such an agreement. The differential impact of this policy of real depreciation across countries implies that appropriate and better policy coordination among these countries is necessary for ease of collective action and hence the sustainability of the trading bloc. Such policies should engender incentives that are compatible with the growth and developmental objectives of member states.

The CFA zone is the oldest North-South monetary arrangement which is deeply embedded in the colonial past. West African countries have had their common currency – CFA – pegged to the French Franc since mid-1940 and to the Euro since its introduction in 1999. Although these countries constitute a substantial part of the world sample of fixed exchange rate countries and form the West African Economic and Monetary Union, the author chose not to examine them because the countries in question have little say in either fiscal or monetary policy where Central Banks are mainly dependent on the instructions of the Banque de France. Recently WAEMU countries have shifted briskly away from France and other Euro areas towards Brazil, India and China (Ngouana, 2012). This highlights a new trend in Africa of less dependence on the west and increasing cooperation with the east, mainly China. One of the novel elements of this research was that its results are relevant to an understanding of the current trends in international markets in that emerging market economies are moving towards regional integration and that the importance of major currency fluctuations like the US Dollar and the Euro are slowly fading away and making way for a new thinking targeting a regional currency union in Asia, Latin America and Africa.

The talk in Africa is of a virtuous cycle in which growth feeds expertise which feeds investment. Some of this new prosperity is the result of better economic policies but more is the consequence of a boom in commodity prices that has spurred investment in mining and drilling as well as in office towers, bridges and roads. The IMF and some oil majors have made a good start by pressing governments to publish details of their revenues from natural resources.

Having been the world's biggest gold producer for more than a century, South Africa has fallen behind China, Australia and America. Some of its mines are nearing the end of their productive lives. Gold continues to be an important contributor to the economy earning 49 billion Rand in FOREX in 2011 and is the country's second most important mineral after platinum, in which South Africa is the global leader. Unsurprisingly, findings in Chapter Five show a significant long-standing relationship between gold reserves and exchange rate fluctuations. In fact the country has fabulous mineral wealth with 90% of the world's known platinum reserves, 80% of its manganese, 70% of its chrome and 40% of its gold as well as rich coal deposits; (The Economist, 2010).

South Africa is still the biggest player in sub-Saharan Africa as the core of the CMA based on an agreement signed in 1986 with Lesotho, Swaziland and Namibia. This agreement formalised an existing de facto monetary integration as the South African currency had been serving as a legal tender in Lesotho and Swaziland since the 1920's. Botswana participated in the CMA negotiations in the 1970's, but it opted out in favour of a managed floating of its currency, the Pula. Since then, Botswana has pegged the Pula to a trade-weighted basket of rand and SDR whose specific composition is not disclosed. However, the South African Rand has a large weight in this basket. Exports from all CMA members, with the exception of Swaziland, are overwhelmingly directed to the rest of the world, in particular the EU and the United States. With regard to imports, however, Lesotho, Namibia and Swaziland are highly dependent on South Africa which accounts for 70% or more of each of these countries' total imports (Metzger, 2008, 52). Swaziland, renowned as Africa's last absolute monarchy, has been in a state of emergency for the past 37 years. Political parties are banned, critics are systematically arrested and beaten up by police and freedom of expression is severely curtailed. Ministers, judges and local chiefs are all appointed by the king. Moreover, member countries can draw on a pool of FOREX reserves that is managed by the South African Reserve Bank. Lesotho, Namibia and Swaziland may hold additional FOREX for direct and immediate needs of which up to 35% may be held in currencies other than the South African Rand. Their Central Banks and authorised dealers have free access to the FOREX market in South Africa. Finally, while there are no restrictions on capital movement within the CMA, a common exchange control system vis-a-vis the rest of the world is administered by the South African Reserve Bank in cooperation with Central Banks of the other members.

References:

Abdullah, H. (2010). Re-examining the demand for money in ASEAN-5 countries. *Asian Social Science,* 6(7), 146-155.

AbuDalu, A. and Almasaeid, S.W. (2011). The purchasing power parity of ASEAN-5 against Europe exchange rate: Evidence using autoregressive distributed lag. *Scholarly Journal of Business Administration,* 1(3), 54-62.

Achsani, N.A. (2010). Stability of money demand in an emerging market economy: An error correction and ARDL model for Indonesia. *Research Journal of International Studies,* 3, 54-62.

Adebeyi, M. A. (2007). An evaluation of foreign exchange intervention and monetary aggregates in Nigeria (1986-2003). *Munich Personal RePEc Archive,* 3817, 1-20.

Adedayo, A.O. (2012). Exchange rate pass-through in Nigeria: Dynamic evidence. *European Journal of Human and Social Sciences,* 16(1), 785-801.

Adeneyi, O., Omisakin, O. and Oyinlola, A. (2011). Exchange rate and trade balance in West-African monetary zone: Is there a J-curve. *The International Journal of Applied Economics and Finance,* 5(3), 167-176.

Adeneyi, O., Omisakin, O. and Yaqub, J. (2012). Oil price-exchange rate in Nigeria: Further evidence from an oil exporting economy. *International Journal of Humanities and Social Science,* 2(8), 113-121.

Adom, A.D., Morshed, A. K. M. and Sharma, S.C. (2012). Sources of real exchange rate volatility in Africa: the case of ECOWAS. *African Development Review,* 24(1), 79-92.

Adom, P.K., Bekoe, W., Akoena, S.K. (2012). Modeling aggregate domestic electricity demand in Ghana: An autoregressive distributed lag bounds cointegration approach. *Energy Policy,* 42, 530-537.

Aghion, P., Bacchetta, P., Ranciere, R. and Rogoff, K. (2009). Exchange rate volatility and productivity growth: The role financial development. *Journal of Monetary Economics,* 56, 494-513.

Aguiar, M. and Broner, F.A. (2006). Determining underlying macroeconomic fundamentals during emerging market crises: Are conditions as bad as they seem? *Journal of Monetary Economics,* 53(4), 699-724.

Aguirre, A., Ferreira, A. and Notini, H. (2007). The impact of exchange rate volatility on Brazilian manufactured exports. *Economica,* 53(1-2), 1-19.

Aiolfi, M. and Timmermann, A. (2006). Persistence in forecasting performance and conditional combination strategies. *Journal of Econometrics,* 135(1-2), 31–53.

Akgul, I. and Sayyen, H. (2008). Modelling and forecasting long memory in exchange rate volatility vs. stable and integrated GARCH models. *Applied Financial Economics,* 18, 463-482.

Adeneyi, O., Omisakin, O. and Spence-Hilton, R. (1984). Effects of exchange rate uncertainty on German and U.S. trade. *Federal Reserve Bank of New York Quarterly Review,* 9, 7-16.

Akinlo, A. E. (2006). The stability of money demand in Nigeria: An autoregressive distributed lag approach. *Journal of Policy Modelling,* 28(4), 445-452.

Alberg, D., Shalit, H. and Yosef, R. (2008). Estimating stock market volatility using asymmetric GARCH models. *Applied Financial Economics,* 18, 1201-1208.

Alexander, C. (1995). Common volatility in the foreign exchange market. *Applied Financial Economics,* 5(1), 1-10.

__________ (1998). *Risk management and Analysis: Measuring and Modelling Financial Risk.* Wiley: London.

__________ (1999). Optimal hedging using cointegration. *Philosophical transactions of the Royal society,* 357, 2039-2058.

__________ (2001). *Market Models: A Guide to Financial Data Analysis.* Wiley: Chichester.

Alexander, C. and Dimitriu, A. (2005). Indexing, cointegration and equity market regimes. *International Journal of Finance and Economics,* 10(5), 213-231.

Alexander, C. and Riyait, N. (1992). The world according to GARCH. *Risk magazine,* 5(8), 120-125.

Altavilla, C. and De Grauwe, P. (2010). Forecasting and combining competing of exchange rate determination. *Applied Economics,* 42, 3455-3480.

Anastasakis, L. and Mort, N. (2009). Exchange rate forecasting using a combined parametric and nonparametric self-organising modelling approach. *Expert Systems with Applications,* 36, 12001-12011.

Andrade, S.C. and Tabak, B.M. (2001). Is it worth tracking dollar-real implied volatility? *Revista de Economia Aplicada*, 5, 67-89.

Andersen, T.G. and Lund, J. (1997). Estimating continuous-time stochastic volatility models of the short-term interest rate. *Journal of Econometrics*, 77, 343-377.

Anderson, T.G. and Bollerslev, T. (1998). Answering the sceptics: Yes, standard volatility models do provide accurate forecasts. *International Economic Review*, 39, 885-905.

Andrade, S. C. and Tabak, B. M. (2001). Is it worth tracking dollar/real exchange rate volatility? *Revista de Economia Aplicada*, 5, 471-529.

Andrawis, R.R., Atiya, A.F. and El-shishiny, H. (2011). Forecast combinations of computational intelligence and linear models for the NN5 time series forecasting competition. *International Journal of Forecasting*, 27, 672-688.

Arestis, P., Ferreiro, J. and Serrano, F. (2006). *Financial developments in national and international markets*. Palgrave Macmillan: Basingstoke.

Arezki, R., Dumitescu, E., Freytag, A. and Quintyn, M. (2012). Commodity prices and exchange rate volatility: Lessons from South Africa's capital account liberalisation. *IMF Working Paper*, 12/168, 1-18.

Arize, A.C. (1994). A Re-examination of the demand for money in small developing economies. *Applied Economics*, 26(3), 217-228.

_________ (1995). The effects of exchange rate volatility on US exports: An empirical investigation. *Southern Economic Journal*, 62, 34-43.

Arize, A.C., Osangm, T. and Slottje, D.J. (2000). Exchange rate volatility and foreign trade: Evidence from thirteen LDCs. *Journal of Business & Economic Statistics*, 18, 10-17.

Armstrong, J.S. (1983). Commentary on the Makridakis time series competition: M-competition. *Journal of Forecasting*, 2, 259-311.

Armstrong, J.S. (1989). Combining forecasts: The End of the beginning or the beginning of the end. *International of Journal Forecasting*, 5, 585-588.

Armstrong, J.S. (2001). Combining forecasts chapter principles of forecasting. In *Handbook for Researchers and Practitioners*. (Ed.) Scott, J. A. Kluwer Academic Publishers: Norwell.

ASEAN (2008). *The ASEAN Charter*. ASEAN Secretariat, Jakarta.

ASEAN (2008). *ASEAN Economic Community Blueprint*. ASEAN Secretariat, Jakarta.

ASEAN (2009). *Roadmap for an ASEAN Community 2009-2015*. ASEAN Secretariat, Jakarta.

ASEAN (2010). *ASEAN Economic Community Scorecard: Charting Progress towards Regional Economic Integration*. ASEAN Secretariat, Jakarta.

ASEAN (2012). *Economic Community Scorecard: Charting Progress towards Regional Economic Integration*. ASEAN Secretariat, Jakarta.

Assenmacher-Wesche, K. and Pesaran, H. (2008). Forecasting the swiss economy using VECX models: An exercise in forecast combination across models and observation windows. *Swiss National Bank Working Papers*, 3, 1-38.

Asseery, A. and Peel, D.A. (1991). The effects of exchange rate volatility on exports-some new estimates. *Economic Letters*, 37, 173-177.

Atkins, F.J. and Coe, P.J. (2002). An ARDL bounds test of the long-run Fisher effect in the United States and Canada. *Journal of Macroeconomics*, 24(2), 255-266.

Auboin, M. and Ruta, M. (2011). The Relationship between exchange rates and international trade: A review of economic literature. *Staff Working Papers*, 17, World Trade Organisation.

Azali, M., Wong, K.S., Lee, C. and Shafinaz, A. (2007). The ASEAN-5 future currency: Maastricht criteria. *Munich Personal RePEc Archive Paper*, 10272, 1-13.

Bacchetta, P. and van Wincoop, E. (2006). Can information heterogeneity explain the exchange rate determination puzzle. *American Economic Review*, 96, 552-576.

Bache, I.W., Brubakk, L., Jore, A.S., Maih, J. and Nicolaisen, J. (2010). Monetary policy analysis in practice - an integrated approach for conditional forecasting. Monetary Policy Wing, Central Bank of Norway, 1-33.

Baharumshah, A. Z. (2001). The effect of exchange rate on bilateral trade balance: New evidence from Malaysia and Thailand. *Asian Economic Journal*, 15(3), 291-312.

Baharumshah, A. Z., Mohd, S.H. and Masih, A. (2009). The stability of money demand in China: Evidence from the ARDL model. *Economic Systems*, 33(3), 231-244.

Baharumshah, A. Z., Tze-Haw, C. and Fountas, S. (2008). Re-examining purchasing power parity for East-Asian currencies: 1976–2002. *Applied Financial Economics*, 18, 75-85.

Bahmani-Oskooee, M. (2001). Nominal and real effective exchange rates of Middle Eastern countries and their trade performance. *Journal of Applied Economics*, 33, 103-111.

Bahmani-Oskooee, M. and Alse, J. (1994). Short-run versus long-run effects of devaluation: Error correction modelling and cointegration. *Eastern Economic Journal*, 20(4), 453-464.
Bahmani-Oskooee, M. and Goswami, G.G. (2004). Exchange rate sensitivity of Japan's bilateral trade flows. *Japan and the World Economy*, 16(1), 1-15.
Bahmani-Oskooee, M., Hegerty, S.W. and Jiam X, (2012). Exchange-rate volatility and industry trade between Japan and China. *Global Economy Journal*, 12(3), 1-19.
Bahmani-Oskooee, M. and Nasir, A.B.M. (2004). ARDL approach to test the productivity bias hypothesis. *Review of Development Economics*, 8(3), 483-488.
Bahmani-Oskooee, M. and Rehman, H. (2005). Stability of the money demand function in Asian developing countries. *Applied Economics*, 37, 773-792.
Bahmani-Oskooee, M. and Sohrabian, A. (1992). Stock prices and the effective exchange rate of the dollar. *Applied Economics*, 24, 459-464.
Bahmani-Oskooee, M. and Wing Ng, R.C. (2002). Long-run demand for money in Hong Kong: An application of the ARDL model. *International Journal of Business and Economics*, 1(2), 147-155.
Bai, J. and Perron, P. (1998). Estimating and testing linear models with multiple structural changes. *Econometrica*, 66, 47-78.
____________ (2003). Critical values for multiple structural change tests. *Business and Economics*, 2, 147-155.
____________ (2003a). Computation and analysis of multiple structural change models. *Journal of Applied Econometrics*, 18, 1-22.
____________ (2003b). Critical values for multiple structural change tests. *Econometrics Journal*, 6, 72-78.
Baig, T. and Goldfajn, I. (1999). Financial market contagion in the Asian crisis. *IMF Staff Papers*, 46(2), 167-195.
Baillie, R.T. and Bollerslev, T. (1989). The message in daily exchange rates: A conditional variance tale. *Journal of Business and Economic Statistics*, 7(3), 297-305.
____________ (1991). Intra-day and inter-market volatility in foreign exchange rates. *Review of Economic Studies*, 58, 565–585.
____________ (1994). Cointegration, fractional cointegration and exchange rate dynamics. *Journal of Finance*, 49 (2), 737-745.
Baillie, R.T. and Osterberg, W.P. (1997.) Central Bank intervention and risk in the forward market. *Journal of International Economics*, 43, 483-497.
Balassa, B. (1964). The purchasing-power parity doctrine: A reappraisal. *Journal of Political Economy*, 72(6), 584-596.
Banerjee, A. and Urga, G. (2005). Modelling structural breaks, long memory and stock market volatility: An overview. *Journal of Econometrics*, 29, 1-34.
Banerjee, A., Lumsdaine, R.L. and Stock, J.H. (1992). Recursive and sequential tests of the unit-root and trend-break hypotheses: Theory and international evidence. *Journal of Business and Economic Statistics*, 10, 271-287.
Barber, W. and Tobin, J. (1997). *The Works of Irving Fisher*. Pickering and Chatto: London.
Barkoulas, J.T., Baum, C.B. and Caglayan, M. (1999). Long memory or structural breaks: Can either explain non-stationary real exchange rates under the current float? *Journal of International Financial Markets, Institutions and Money*, 9, 359-376.
Baron, D.P. (1976). Fluctuating exchange rates and the pricing of exports. *Economic Inquiry*, 14(3), 425-438.
Bates, J.M. and Granger, C.W.J. (1969). Combination of forecasts. *Operational Research Quarterly*, 20, 451-468.
Baum, C. F., Caglayan, M. and Ozkan, N. (2003). Nonlinear effects of exchange rate volatility on the volume and volatility of bilateral exports. *Journal of Applied Econometrics*, 19(1), 1-23.
Becker, R. and Clements, A.E. (2008). Are combination forecasts of S&P 500 volatility statistically superior. *International Journal of Forecasting*, 24(1), 122-133.
Beim, D.O. and Calomiris, C.W. (2001). *Emerging Financial Markets*. McGraw-Hill: New York.
Beine, M., Lahaye, J., Laurent, S., Christopher J. N. and Franz C. P. (2006). Central Bank intervention and exchange rate volatility, its continuous and jump components. *Working Paper*, 031B, Federal Reserve Bank of St. Louis.
Benavides, G. and Capistran, C. (2009). Forecasting exchange rate volatility: The superior performance of conditional combinations of time series and option implied forecasts. *Working Paper*, 01, Banco de Mexico.

Bera, A. K. and Higgings, M. L. (1993). ARCH models: Properties, estimation and testing. *Journal of Economic Surveys*, 7(4), 307-366.

Berenson, L. M. and Levine, M. D. (1992). *Basic Business Statistics*. Prentice-Hall: London.

Berg, A., Borenztein, E. and Mauro, P. (2003). Monetary regime options for Latin America. *Finance and Development*, 40, 24-27.

Berg, A., and Patillo, C. (1999). Are currency crises predictable? A test. *IMF Staff Papers*, 46(2), 107-138.

Berganza, J.C. and Broto, C. (2011). Flexible inflation targets, FOREX interventions and exchange rate volatility in emerging countries. Bank of Spain *Working Paper*, 1105, 1-37.

Berger, D. W., Chaboud, A.P., Chernenko, S.V., Howorka, E. and Wright, J.H. (2008). Order flow and exchange rate dynamics in electronic brokerage system data. *Journal of International Economics*, 75(1), 93-109.

Berndt, E.K., Hall, B.H. and Hall, R.E. (1974). Estimation and inference in nonlinear structural models. *Annals of Economic and Social Measurement*, 3(4), 103-116.

Bértola, L. and J.A. Ocampo (2012). *The Economic Development of Latin America since Independence*. Oxford University Press: Oxford.

Berument, M.H. and Dogan, N. (2012). Stock market return and volatility: Day-of-the-week effect. *Journal of Economics and Finance*, 36(2), 282-302.

Bini-Smaghi, L. (1991). Exchange rate variability and trade: Why is it so difficult to find any empirical relationship? *Applied Economics*, 23(5), 927-935.

Bird, G. and Rajan, R. (2002). The evolving Asian financial architecture. Centre for International Economic Studies, *Discussion Paper*, 0203, Adelaide University.

Birer, G., Holler, J. and Weichselbaumer, M. (2005). Forecasting the exchange rate: A forecasting application with the exchange rate between the Euro and the US dollar (1980-2003). Department of Economics, University of Vienna.

BIS (2013). Triennial Central Bank survey - Foreign exchange turnover in April 2013: Preliminary global results. Monetary and Economic Department, Bank of International Settlements.

Bischoff, C.W. (1989). The combination of macroeconomic forecasts. *Journal of Forecasting*, 8, 293-314.

Bissoondeeal, R.K. (2008). Post-Bretton Woods evidence on PPP under different exchange rate regimes. *Applied Financial Economics*, 18(18), 1481-1488.

Bissoondeeal, R.K., Binner, J.M. and Elger, T. (2009). Monetary models of exchange rates and sweep programs. *Applied Financial Economics*, 19(14), 1117-1129.

Bjørnland, H.D., Gerdrup, K., Jore, A.S., Smith, C. and Thorsrud, L.A. (2010). Does forecast combination improve Norges Bank inflation forecasts? *Working Paper*, 2, Centre for Applied Macroeconomic Research (CAMAR), Norwegian School of Management.

Boero, G., Smith, J. and Wallis, K.F. (2010). Modeling UK inflation uncertainty, 1958-2006. In *Volatility and Time Series Econometrics: Essays in Honor of Robert F. Engle*, (Ed.) Bollerslev, T., Russell, J.R. and Watson, M.W. Oxford University Press: Oxford.

Bollerslev, T. (1986). Generalised autoregressive conditional heteroscedasticity. *Journal of Econometrics*, 31, 307-327.

Bollerslev, T. (1990). Modeling the coherence in short-run nominal exchange rates, a multivariate generalized ARCH model. *Review of Economics and Statistics*, 72, 498-505.

Bollerslev, T., Chou, R.Y. and Kroner, K. F. (1992). ARCH modelling in finance. *Journal of Econometrics*, 52, 5-59.

Bollerslev, T. and Melvin, M. (1994). Bid-ask spreads and volatility in the foreign exchange market: An empirical analysis. *Journal of International Economics*, 36, 355-372.

Botha, I. and Pretorius, M. (2009). Forecasting the exchange rate in South Africa: A comparative analysis challenging the random walk model. *African Journal of Business Management*, 3(9) 486-494.

Boug, P. and Fagereng, A. (2010). Exchange rate volatility and export performance: A cointegrated VAR Approach. *Applied Economics*, 42(7), 851-864.

Bowd, R. and Chikwanha, A.B. (2010). Understanding Africa's contemporary conflicts: Origins, challenges and peace building. African Institute of Security Studies, ISS monograph for the Africa Human Security Initiative, 173, 1-278.

Box, G. E. P. and Tiao G. C. (1975). Intervention analysis with applications to economic and environmental problems. *Journal of the American Statistical Association*, 70 (349), 70-79.

Box, G. E. P. and Jenkins, G. (1976). *Time Series Analysis, Forecasting and Control*. McGraw Hill: New York

Boyd, D., Caporale, G.M and Smith, R. (2001). Real exchange rate effects on the balance of trade: Cointegration and the Marshall-Lerner condition. *International Journal of Finance and Economics*, 6, 187-200.
Brada, J.C. and Mendez, J. A. (1988). Exchange rate risk, exchange rate regime and the volume of international trade. *International Review of Social Sciences*, 41(2), 263-280.
Brailsford, T. J. and Faff, R. W. (1996). An evaluation of volatility forecasting techniques. *Journal of Banking and Finance*, 20(3), 419-438.
Brandt, H., Gsanger, H., Otzen, U. and Qualmann, R. (2000). Approaches to promote regional integration in the Southern African development community (SADC). German Institute for Development Policy: Bonn.
Broda, C. and Romalis, J. (2003). Identifying the relationship between trade and exchange rate volatility. Available at https//faculty.chicagobooth.edu/john.romalis/research/erv_trade.pdf
Brohman, J. (1996). New directions in tourism for third world development. *Annals of Tourism Research*, 23(1), 48-70.
Broll, U. (1994). Foreign production and forward markets. *Australian Economic Papers*, 33, 1-6.
Broll, U. and Eckwert, B. (1999). Exchange rate volatility and international trade. *Southern Economic Journal*, 66, 178-185.
Brooks, C. (2008). *Introductory Econometrics for Finance*. Cambridge University Press: Cambridge.
Brooks, C. and Persand, G. (2003). Volatility forecasting for risk management. *Journal of Forecasting*, 22, 1-22.
Brown, R.L., Durbin J. and Evans J.M. (1975). Techniques for testing the constancy of regression relationships over time. *Journal of the Royal Statistical Society*, Series B, 35, 149-192.
Bryman, A. and Bell, E. (2007). *Business Research Methods*. Oxford University Press: Oxford.
Bulmer-Thomas, V. (1998). The Central American common market: From closed to open regionalism. *World Development*, 26(2), 313-322.
Bunn, D. W. and Mustafaoglu, M. M. (1978). Forecasting political risk. *Management Science*, 11, 1557-1567.
Bunn, D. W. and Oliver, R.M. (1989). Combinations of forecasts: A model-building perspective. *Operation Research Letters*, 8, 179-184.
Calvo, G.A. and Reinhart, C.M. (2002). Fear of floating. *The Quarterly Journal of Economics*, 117(2), 379-408.
Cameron, S. (2005). *Econometrics*. McGraw Hill: Maidenhead.
Campbell, J.Y. (1987). Does saving anticipate declining labour income? An alternative test of the permanent income hypothesis. *Econometrica*, 55, 1249-1273.
Campbell, J.Y. and Shiller, R.J. (1987). Cointegration and tests of present value models. *Journal of Political Economy*, 95, 1062-1088.
Campbell, J.Y. and Hentschel, L. (1992). No news is good news: An asymmetric model of changing volatility in stock returns. *Journal of Financial Economics*, 31(3), 281-318.
Campbell, J.Y., Lo, A.W. and MacKinlay A. C. (1997). *The Econometrics of Financial Markets*. Princeton University Press: New Jersey.
Canales-Kriljenko, J. I. (2003). Foreign exchange intervention in developing and transition economies: Results of a survey. *IMF Working Paper*, WP/03/99, 1-58.
____________ (2004). Foreign exchange market organisation in selected developing and transition economies: Evidence from a survey. *IMF Working Paper*, WP/04/4, 1-46.
Cappiello, L. and Gianluigi, F. (2008). The Sustainability of China's Exchange Rate Policy and Capital Account Liberalisation. Occasional Paper, 82(3), European Central Bank: Frankfurt.
Caramazza, F. and Aziz, J. (1998). Fixed or flexible: Getting the exchange rate right in the 1990s. *IMF Economic Issues*, 13, 1-25.
Cashin, P. and McDermott, C.J. (2001). The long-run behavior of commodity prices: Small trends and big variability. *IMF Working Paper*, WP/01/68, 1-27.
Cashin, P., Cespedes, L.F. and Sahay, R. (2004). Commodity currencies and the real exchange rate. *Journal of Development Economics*, 75(1), 239-268.
Cassel, G. (1918). Abnormal deviations in international exchanges. *The Economic Journal*, 28, 413-415.
Cavoli, T. (2008). The exchange rate and optimal monetary policy rules in open and developing economies: some simple analytics. *Economic Modelling*, 25, 1011-1021.
Central Intelligence Agency (2012). The world FACTBOOK. CIA Library Publications, various issues, Washington D.C.

Chatrath, A., Ramchander, S. and Song, F. (1996). The role of futures trading activity in exchange rate volatility. *Journal of Futures Markets*, 16(5), 561-58.

Chan, F., Lim C. and McAleer, M. (2005). Modelling multivariate international tourism demand and volatility. *Tourism Management*, 26(3), 459-471.

Chang, C.C. (2001). Regime changes and econometric modeling of the demand for money in Korea. Department of Economics, University of Southampton.

Chang, J.F. (2009). Exchange rate forecasting with combined genetic algorithms. Department of International Business, National Kaohsiung University of Applied Sciences.

Chang, R., Kaltani L. and Loayza, N.V. (2009). Openness can be good for growth: The role of policy complementarities. *Journal of Development Economics*, 90, 33-49.

Chang, E.J. and Tabak, M. B. (2007). Are implied volatilities more informative? The Brazilian real exchange rate case. *Applied Financial Economics*, 17(7), 569-576.

Chaudhary, G. M., Zulfiqar, S. A. S. and Bagram, M. M. (2012). Do exchange rate volatility effects foreign direct investment? Evidence from selected Asian economies. *Journal of Basic and Applied Scientific Research*, 2(4), 3670-3681.

Chen, Y.C. (2004). Exchange rates and fundamentals: Evidence from commodity economies. Department of Economics, University of Washington.

Chen, Y.C. and Rogoff, K. (2003). Commodity currencies. *Journal of International Economics*, 60(1), 133-160.

Chong, C. W., Idrees, M. A. and Abdullah M. Y. (1999). Performance of GARCH model in forecasting stock market volatility. *Journal of forecasting*, 18(5), 333-343.

Chou, W. L. (2000). Exchange rate variability and China's exports. *Journal of Comparative Economics*, 28, 61-79.

Choudhry, T. (1997). Stochastic trends in stock prices: Evidence from Latin American markets. *Journal of Macroeconomics*, 19, 285-304.

__________ (2005). Exchange rate volatility and the United States exports: Evidence from Canada and Japan. *Journal of the Japanese International Economics*, 19, 51-71.

Chowdhury, A.R. (1993). Does exchange rate volatility depress trade flows? Evidence from error-correction models. *Review of Economics and Statistics*, 75, 700-706.

Chowdhury, A.R. and Wheeler, M. (2008). Does real exchange rate volatility affect foreign direct investment? Evidence from four developed economies. *International Trade Journal*, 22(2), 1-28.

Chowdhury, K. (2007). Are the real exchange rate indices of Australia non-stationary in the presence of a structural break? *International Review of Business Research Papers*, 3, 161-181.

__________ (2012). Modelling the dynamics, structural breaks and the determinants of the real exchange rate of Australia. *Journal of International Financial Markets, Institutions and Money*, 22, 343-358.

Christiano, L.J. (1992). Searching for a break in GDP. *Journal of Business and Economic Statistics*, 10, 237-249.

Christie, A.A. (1982). The Stochastic behaviour of common stock variances: Value, leverage and interest rate effects. *Journal of Financial Economics*, 10, 407-432.

CIA (2012) see *Central Intelligence Agency (2012)*

Claessens, S. (1991). Balance of payments crises in an optimal portfolio model. *European Economic Review*, 35, 81-101.

Clark, P.B. and MacDonald, R. (1999). Exchange rate and economic fundamentals. In *Equilibrium Exchange Rates* (Ed.) R. MacDonald and J.L. Stein. Kluwer Academic Publishers: Amsterdam.

Clemen, R.T. (1989). Combining forecasts: A review and annotated bibliography. *International Journal of Forecasting*, 5, 559-583.

Clemen, R.T., Murphy, A.H. and Winkler, R.L. (1995). Screening probability forecasts: Contrast between choosing and combining. *International Journal of Forecasting*, 11, 133-146.

Cline, W.R. and Delgado, E. (1978). Economic integration in Central America. The Brookings Institution, Washington D.C.

Coakley, J. and Fuertes, A.M. (2001). Nonparametric cointegration analysis of real exchange rates. *Applied Financial Economics*, 11(1), 1-8.

Cochran, S.J. and Defina, R.H. (1995). New evidence on predictability in world equity markets. *Journal of Business Finance and Accounting*, 22(6), 845-854.

Codruta, F.M. and Deszi, E. (2012). Exchange rates forecasting: Exponential smoothing techniques and ARIMA models. Faculty of Economics and Business Administration, University Cluj-Napoca.

Coleman, A.K. and Tettey, K.F.A. (2008). Effect of exchange-rate volatility on foreign direct investment in sub-Saharan Africa: The case of Ghana. *Journal of Risk Finance*, 9(1), 52-70.

Connolly, M. and Devereux, J. (1995). The equilibrium real exchange rate: Theory and evidence for Latin America. In *Fundamental Determinants of Exchange Rates* (Ed.) J. L. Stein, P. R. Allen and Associates. Oxford University Press, New York.

Connolly, R. and Limratanamongkol, P. (2000). Cointegration modeling of expected exchange rates. *Journal of Economics and Finance*, 36, 282-302.

Copeland, L. (2008). *Exchange Rates and International Finance*. Prentice Hall/Financial Times Press: Harlow.

Cordoba, N. (2012). Snapshot of MERCOSUR and the EU. Report on European Economy and International Economic Relations, University of Wuppertal.

Corsetti, G., Prsenti, P. and Roubini, N. (1999). What caused the Asian currency and financial crisis? *Japan and the World Economy*, 11, 305-373.

Corte, P.D., Sarno, L. and Tsiakas, I. (2007). An economic evaluation of empirical exchange rate models. Finance Group, Warwick Business School, University of Warwick.

Coshall, J.T. (2009). Combining volatility and smoothing forecasts of UK demand for international tourism. *Tourism Management*, 30, 495-511.

Coshall, J.T. and Charlesworth, R. (2011). A management orientated approach to combination forecasting of tourism demand. *Tourism Management*, 32, 759-769.

Cushman, D.O. (1983). The effects of real exchange rate risk on international trade. *Journal of International Economics*, 15, 45-63.

__________ (1986). Has exchange risk depressed international trade? The impact of third country exchange risk. *Journal of International Money and Finance*, 5, 361-379.

__________ (1988). U.S. bilateral trade flows and exchange risk during the floating period. *Journal of International Economics*, 25, 317-330.

Dara, L. (2008). Purchasing power parity and real exchange rate in Japan. *Munich Personal RePEc Archive*, 11173, 1-28.

Dara, L. and Samreth, S. (2008). The monetary model of exchange rate: Evidence from the Philippines using ARDL approach. *Munich Personal RePEc Archive*, 9822, 1-13.

Davradakis, E. (2004). Macroeconomic fundamentals and exchange rates: A non-parametric cointegration analysis. *Applied Financial Economics*, 15(7), 439-446.

De Grauwe, P. (1988). Exchange rate variability and the slowdown in growth of international trade. *IMF Staff Papers*, 35, 63-84.

__________ (1994). *The Economics of Monetary Integration*. Oxford University Press: Oxford.

De Grauwe, P. and Verfaille, G. (1988). Exchange rate variability, misalignment and the European monetary system. In *Misalignment of Exchange Rates: Effects on Trade and Industry*, (Ed.) University of Chicago Press: Chicago.

De Grauwe, P. and Markiewicz, A. (2012). Learning to forecast the exchange rate: Two competing approaches. *Journal of International Money and Finance*, 30, 1-35.

Dehn, J., Christopher, L. G. and Varangies, P. (2004). Commodity price volatility, draft chapter for: *Managing Volatility and Crises: A Practitioner's Guide*. (Ed.) Azainman, J. and Pinto, B. Cambridge University Press: Cambridge.

De Menezes, L.M. and Bunn, D.W. (1998). The persistence of specification problems in the distribution of combined forecast errors. *International Journal of Forecasting*, 14, 415-426.

De Menezes, L.M., Bunn, D.W. and Taylor, J.W. (2000). Review of guidelines for the use of combined forecasts. *European Journal of Operational Research*, 120, 190-204.

De Vita, G. and Abbot, A. (2004). Real exchange rate volatility and US exports: An ARDL bounds testing approach. *Economic Issues*, 9(1), 69-78.

Diamandis, P., Drakos, A. and Volis, A. (2007). The impact of stock incremental information on the volatility of the Athens stock exchange. *Applied Financial Economics*, 17, 413-424.

Dickey D.A. and Fuller W.A. (1979). Distributions of the estimators for autoregressive time series with a unit root. *Journal of American Statistical Association*, 74, 427-431.

Diebold, F.X. (1989). Forecast combination and encompassing: Reconciling two divergent literatures. *International Journal of Forecasting*, 5(4), 589-592.

Diebold, F.X., Gardeazabal, J. and Yilmaz, K. (1994). On cointegration and exchange rate dynamics. *Journal of Finance*, 49(2), 727-735.

Diebold, F.X. and Lopez, J.A. (1996). Forecast evaluation and combination. Department of Economics Papers, University of Pennsylvania.

Diebold, F.X. and Pauly, P. (1987). Structural change and the combination of forecasts. *Journal of Forecasting*, 6, 21-40.

Diebold, F.X. and Diebold, F.X. (1990). The use of prior information in forecast combination. *International Journal of Forecasting*, 6(4), 503-508.

Dimson, E. and Marsh, P. (1990). Volatility forecasting without data-snooping. *Journal of Banking and Finance*, 44, 399-421.

Dollar, D. (1992). Outward-oriented developing economies really do grow more rapidly: Evidence from 95 LDCs, 1976-1985. *Economic Development and Cultural Change*, 40(3), 523-544.

Dollar, D. and Kraay, A. (2004). Trade, growth, and poverty. *The Economic Journal*, 114, 22-49.

Dominguez, K. M. (1998). Central Bank intervention and exchange rate volatility. *Journal of International Money and Finance*, 17, 161-190.

Dornbusch, R. (1982). Equilibrium and disequilibrium exchange rates. *Journal of Economic and Social Sciences*, 102(6), 573-599.

Dornbusch, R. (1983). Flexible exchange rates and interdependence. *IMF Staff Papers*, 30(1), 3-38.

Dornbusch, R. and Fisher, S. (1980). Exchange rates and the current account. *American Economic Review*, 70, 960-971.

Dowrick, S. and Golley, J. (2004). Trade openness and growth: Who benefits? *Oxford Review of Economic Policy*, 20(1), 38-56.

Dritsakis, N. (2011). Demand for money in hungary: An ARDL Approach. Economics and Social Sciences Department, University of Macedonia.

Duasa, J. (2007). Determinants of Malaysian trade balance: An ARDL bound testing approach. *Journal of Economic Cooperation*, 28(3), 21-40.

______ (2009). Asymmetric cointegration relationship between real exchange rate and trade variables: The case of Malaysia. *Munich Personal RePEc Archive*, 14535, 1-14.

Duan, J. C. (1993). The GARCH option pricing model. *Mathematical Finance*, 5(1), 13-32.

Dunis, C., Timmermann, A. and Moody, J. (2001). *Developments in Forecast Combination and Portfolio Choice*. Wiley: New York.

Dutt, S. D. and Ghosh, D. (2000). An empirical note on the monetary exchange rate model. *Applied Economics Letters*, 7(10), 669-671.

ECA (2008a). *Assessing Regional Integration in Africa III, Towards Monetary and Financial Integration in Africa*. United Nations Economic Commission for Africa: Addis Ababa.

ECLAC (2007). The United Nations statistics and economic projections division of the economic commission for Latin America and the Caribbean, Projections 2006-2007. ECLAC: Santiago de Chile.

ECLAC (2011). The United Nations statistics and economic projections division of the economic commission for Latin America and the Caribbean, Projections 2010-2011. ECLAC: Santiago de Chile.

Edison, H. and Pauls, B.D. (1993). A re-assessment of the relationship between real exchange rates and real interest rates. *Journal of Monetary Economics*, 31(2), 165-187.

Edwards, S. (1987). Real exchange rate variability: An empirical analysis of the developing countries case. *International Economic Journal*, 1(1), 91-106

________ (1988a). The real and monetary determinants of real exchange rate behavior: Theory and evidence from developing countries. *Journal of Development Economics*, 29, 311-341

_________ (1988b). Exchange rate misalignment in developing countries. John Hopkins University Press: Baltimore.

_________ (1989). The debt crisis and economic adjustment in Latin America. *Latin American Research Review*, 24(3), 172-186.

_________ (1993). Openness, trade liberalisation, and growth in developing countries. *Journal of Economic Literature*, 31(3), 1358-1393.

_________ (1998). Openness, productivity and growth: What do we really know? *The Economic Journal*, 108, 383-398.

Edwards, S. and Susmel, R. (2001). Volatility dependence and contagion in emerging equity markets. *Journal of Development Economics*, 66, 505-532.

Edwards, S. and Wijnbergen, S. V. (1987). Tariffs, the real exchange rate and the terms of trade: On two popular propositions in international economics. *Oxford Economic Papers*, 39, 458-464.

Égert, B. and Morales-Zumaquero, A. (2008). Exchange rate regimes, foreign exchange volatility, and export performance in central and Eastern Europe: Just another blur project? *Review of Development Economics*, 12(3), 577-593.

Eguizabal, C. (2010). The United States and Central America since 2000. A chapter for *Contemporary U.S.* In *Latin American Relations: Cooperation or conflict in the 21st Century* (Ed.) Dominguez, J.I. and De Castro, R.F. Routledge: Oxon.

Eichengreen, B. (1998). International economic policy in the wake of the Asian crisis. Centre for international and development economics research, Working Paper Series, Institute for Business and Economic Research, UC Berkeley.

Eichengreen, B., Ito, T., Kawai, M. and Portes, R. (1998). Recent currency crisis in Asia. *Journal of the Japanese and International Economies*, 12, 535-542.

Eichengreen, B. (1999). Kicking the habit: Moving from pegged rates to greater exchange rate flexibility. *Economic Journal*, 109, 1-14.

Eizaguirre, J.C., Biscarri, J.G. and Gracia Hidalgo, F.P. (2009). Financial liberalisation, stock market volatility and outliers in emerging economies. *Applied Financial Economics*, 19, 809-823.

Elbadawi, I. A. (1994). Estimating long-run equilibrium real exchange rates. In J. Williamson (Ed.), *Estimating Equilibrium Exchange Rates* (Institute for International Economics, Washington DC), 93-131.

Employers' Confederation of Thailand (2012). Thailand country report. The 37th ACE CEOs and BODs meeting, Singapore, May 14th.

Engle, R. F. (1982). Autoregressive conditional heteroscedasticity with estimates of the variance of United Kingdom inflation. *Econometrica*, 50(4), 987-1007.

Engle, R. F. and Granger C.W.J. (1987). Cointegration and error correction: Representation, estimation, and testing. *Econometrica*, 55(2), 251-276.

Engle, R. F. and Yoo, B.S. (1987). Forecasting and testing in cointegrated systems. *Journal of Econometrics*, 35, 143-159.

Engle, R. F. and Ng, V. K. (1993). Measuring and testing the impact of news on volatility. *Journal of Finance*, 48 (5), 1749-1778.

Engel, C. and West, K. (2005). Exchange rates and fundamentals. *Journal of Political Economy*, 113, 485-518.

Enisan, A. and Olufisayo, A. (2009). Stock market development and economic growth: Evidence from seven sub-Sahara African countries. *Journal of Economics and Business*, 61, 162-171.

Erdinc, H. and Milla, J. (2009). Analysis of cointegration in capital markets of France, Germany and United Kingdom. *Economics and Business Journal: Inquiries and Perspectives*, 2(1), 109-123.

Ethier, W. (1973). International trade and the forward exchange market. *American Economic Review*, 63, 494-503.

European Central Bank (2010). ECB statistics: An Overview. ECB: Frankfurt.

Evans D.D. and Lyons, R.K. (2002). Order flow and exchange rate dynamics. *Journal of Political Economy*, 110(1), 170-180.

Evans, T. and McMillan, D.G. (2007). Volatility forecasts: The role of asymmetric and long-memory dynamics and regional evidence. *Applied Financial Economics*, 17, 1421-1430.

Ewing, B.T., Thompson, M.A., and Yanochik, M.A. (2007). Using volume to forecast stock market volatility around the time of the 1929 crash. *Applied Financial Economics*, 17, 1123-1128.

Fama, E. (1965). The Behaviour of stock market prices. *Journal of Business*, 38(1), 34-105.

Fang, Y. (2003). Forecasting combination and encompassing tests. *International Journal of Forecasting*, 19(1), 87-94.

Fang, Y. and Xu, D. (2003). The predictability of asset returns: an approach combining technical analysis and time series forecasts. *International Journal of Forecasting*, 19, 369-385.

Fajnzylber, P. and Lopez, J.H. (2008). Remittances and development: Lessons from Latin America. the World Bank, Washington, D.C.

Feridun, M. (2005). Can we explain the long-term real equilibrium exchange rate through purchasing power parity? An empirical investigation (1965-1995). *Economisky Casopis*, 53(3), 273-282.

Fernandez-Rodriguez, F. and Sosvilla-Rivero, S. (1997). Combining information in exchange rate forecasting: evidence from the EMS. *Applied Economics Letters* 4(7), 441-444.

Fernandez-Rodriguez, F. and Sosvilla-Rivero, S. (2003). Modeling the linkages between US and Latin American stock markets. *Applied Economics*, 35, 1423-1434.

Financial Times (2011). Success has its downside. FT Publications: London.

Fiordaliso, A. (1999). A nonlinear forecasts combination method based on Takagi-Sugeno fuzzy systems. *International Journal of Forecasting*, 14, 367-379.

Fischer, I. and Harvey, N. (1999). Combining forecasts: What information do judges need to outperform the simple average? *International Journal of Forecasting*, 15, 227-246.

Fleming, J. (1998). The quality of market volatility forecasts implied by S&P 100 index option prices. *Journal of Empirical Finance*, 5, 317-345.

Flood, R.P. and Rose, A. K. (1995). Fixing exchange rates: A virtual quest for fundamentals. *Journal of Monetary Economics*, 36, 3-37.

Flood, R.P. and Rose, A. K. (1999). Understanding exchange rate volatility without the contrivance of macroeconomics. *The Economic Journal*, 109(459), 66-72.

Forbes, K. and Rigobon, R. (2002). No contagion, only interdependence: Measuring stock market co-movements. *Journal of Finance*, 57(5), 2223-2261.

Franchi, M. (2010). A Representation theory for polynomial co-fractionality in vector autoregressive models. *Econometric Theory*, 26(40), 1201-1217.

Frankel, J. A.(1983). Monetary and portfolio-balance models of exchange rate determination. In *Economic Interdependence and Flexible Exchange Rates*. (Ed.) J. Bhandari and B. H. Putnam. MIT Press: Cambridge.

_________ (2002). *Forward to the Economics of Exchange Rates*. By Sarno.L and Taylor, M.P. Cambridge University Press: Cambridge.

_________ (2007). On the rand: Determinants of the South African exchange rate. *South African Journal of Economics*, 75(3), 425-441.

Frankel, J. A. and Froot, K. (1987). Using survey data to test standard propositions regarding exchange rate expectations. *American Economic Review*, 77, 133-153.

Frankel, J. A. and Romer, D. (1999). Does trade cause growth? *American Economic Review*, 89(3), 379-399.

Frankel, J. A. and Wei, S. J. (1993). Trade blocks and currency blocks. *NBER Working Papers*, 4345, Cambridge.

Franses, P. H. and Van Dijk, D. (1996). Forecasting stock market volatility using non-linear GARCH models. *Journal of Forecasting*, 15, 229-235.

Franses, P. H. and Van Dijk, D. (2000). *Nonlinear Time Series Models in Empirical Finance*. Cambridge University Press: Cambridge.

Fratzcher, M. (2003). On currency crises and contagion. *International Journal of Finance and Economics*, 8, 109-129.

French, K.R., Schwert, G.W. and Stambaugh, R.F. (1987). Expected stock returns and volatility. *Journal of Financial Economics*, 19, 3-29.

Frenkel, R. and Rapetti, M. (2011). External fragility or deindustrialisation: What is the main threat to Latin American countries in the 2010? *ECLAC Economic Development Division Working Papers*, 1-23.

Freund, C. and Bolaky, B. (2008). Trade, regulations, and income. *Journal of Development Economics*, 87, 309-321.

Friedman, M. and Schwartz, A.J. (1963). *A Monetary History of the United States, 1867-1960*. Princeton University Press: Princeton.

Fritz, R.G., Brandon, C. and Xander, J. (1984). Combining time-series and econometric forecasts of tourism activity. *Annals of Tourism Research*, 11, 219-229.

Frömmel, M. (2010). Volatility regimes in Central and Eastern European countries' exchange rates. *Czech Journal of Economics and Finance*, 60(1), 2-21.

Frömmel, M. and Menkhoff L. (2003). Increasing exchange rate volatility during the recent float. *Applied Financial Economics*, 13, 877-883.

Frömmel, M., McDonald, R. and Menkhoff, L. (2005). Markov switching regimes in a monetary exchange rate model. *Economic Modelling*, 22, 485–502.

Froot, K.A. and Rogoff, K. (1995). Perspectives on PPP and long-run real exchange rate. In *Handbook of International Economics*, (Ed.) G. Gossman and K. Rogoff, 3, 1647-1688.

Fu, R. and Pagani, M. (2012). On the cointegration of international stock indices. *Journal of Economics and Finance*, 36, 463-480.

Fullerton, Jr. T.M. (1989). A composite approach to forecasting state government revenues: Case study of the Idaho sales tax. *International Journal of Forecasting*, 5, 373-380.

Fukuta, Y. and Saito, M. (2002). Forward discount puzzle and liquidity effects: Some evidence from exchange rates among the United States, Canada, and Japan. *Journal of Money, Credit and Banking*, 34, 1014-1033.

Galati, G. and Ho, C. (2003). Macroeconomic news and the euro/dollar exchange rate. *Economic Notes*, 32(3), 371-398.

Gallo, G.M. and Otranto, E. (2007). Volatility transmission across markets: A Multi-chain Markov switching model. *Applied Financial Economics*, 17(8), 659-670.

Gallo, G.M. and Pacini B. (1998). Early news is good news: The effects of market opening on market volatility. *Studies in Nonlinear Dynamics and Econometrics*, 2, 115-131.

Garcia, C.J. and Gonzalez, W.D. (2013). Exchange rate intervention in small open economies: The role of risk premium and commodity price shocks. *International Review of Economics and Finance*, 25, 424-447.

Gardner, Jr. E.S. and McKenzie, E. (1985). Forecasting trends in time series. *Management Science*, 31, 1237-1246.

Ghassem, A. (2004). *Managing Global Financial and Foreign Exchange Rate Risk*. Wiley: Hoboken.

Ghatak, S. and Siddiki, J. (2001). The use of ARDL approach in estimating virtual exchange rates in India. *Journal of Applied Statistics*, 28(5), 573-583.

Gilbert, C. L. (1989). The impact of exchange rates and developing country debt on commodity prices. *The Economic Journal*, 99, 773-784.

Giovannini, A. (1988). Exchange rates and traded goods prices. *Journal of International Economics*, 24, 45-68.

Giovannini, A. and Jorion, P. (1987). Interest rates and risk premium in the stock market and in the foreign exchange market. *Journal of International Money and Finance*, 6, 107-124.

Glosten, L. R., Jagannathan R. and Runkle D. (1993). On the relation between the expected value and the volatility of the normal excess return stocks. *Journal of Finance*, 48, 1779-1801.

Gokcan, S. (2000). Forecasting volatility of emerging stock markets: Linear versus non-linear GARCH models. *Journal of Forecasting*, 19(6), 499-504.

Goodhart, C. A. E. and Figliuoli L. (1991). Every minute counts in financial markets. *Journal of International Money and Finance*, 10, 23-52.

Goodhart C. A. E., Hall S. G., Henry S. G. B. and Pesaran B. (1993). News effects in high frequency model of the sterling-dollar exchange rate. *Journal of Applied Econometrics*, 8, 1-13.

Goodwin, P. (2000). Correct or combine? Mechanically integrating judgmental forecasts with statistical methods. *International Journal of Forecasting*, 16, 261-275.

Gotur, P. (1985). Effects of exchange rate volatility on trade. *IMF Staff Papers*, 32, 475-512.

Granger, C. W. J. (1981). Some properties of time series data and their use in econometric model specification. *Journal of Econometrics*, 16, 121-130.

__________ (1983). Forecasting white noise. In *Applied Time Series Analysis of Economic Data*. (Ed.) Zellner, A., 308-314.

__________ (1984). Improved methods of combining forecasts. *Journal of Forecasting*, 3, 197-204.

Granger, C. W. J. and Poon, S.H. (2003). Forecasting volatility in financial markets: A review. *Journal of Economic Literature*, 41, 478-539.

Granger, C. W. J. and Ramanathan, R. (1984). Improved methods of combining forecasts. *Journal of Forecasting*, 3, 197-204.

Greene, W.H. (2003). *Econometric Analysis*. Upper Saddle River: New Jersey.

Greenwood, J. (1984). Non-traded goods, the trade balance and the balance of payments. *Canadian Journal of Economics*, 17, 806-823.

Greer, M. (2005). Combination forecasting for directional accuracy: An application to survey interest rate forecasts. *Journal of Applied Statistics* 32(6), 607-615.

Grier, K. B. and Perry M. J. (1996). Inflation, inflation uncertainty, and relative price dispersion: Evidence from bivariate GARCH-M models. *Journal of Monetary Economics*, 38, 391-405.

Grier, K. B. and Perry M. J. (1998). On inflation and inflation uncertainty in the G7 countries. *Journal of International Money and Finance*, 38, 391-405.

Groen, J. (2002). Cointegration and the monetary exchange rate model revisited. *Oxford Bulletin of Economics and Statistics*, 64(4), 361-380.

Guerrero, R. B. (2009). Regional integration: The ASEAN vision in 2020. Bank for International Settlements Seminar Papers, 32, 52-58.

__________ (1994). Managerial judgment and forecast combination. *Marketing Letters*, 5(1), 2-17.

Guidolin, M. and Timmermann, A. (2009). Forecasts of US short-term interest rates: A flexible forecast combination approach. *Journal of Econometrics*, 150(2), 297-311.

Hafer, R.W. and Jansen, D.W. (1991). The demand for money in the United States: Evidence from cointegration test. *Journal of Money, Credit and Banking*, 23(2), 155-168.
Hairault, J., Patureau, L., Sopraseuth, T. (2004). Overshooting and the exchange rate disconnect puzzle: A reappraisal. *Journal of International Money and Finance*, 23, 615-643.
Halicioglu, F. and Ugur, M. (2005). On stability of the demand for money in a developing OECD country: The case of Turkey. *Global Business and Economics Review*, 7(2-3), 203-213.
Hall, A.D., Anderson, H.M. and Granger, C.W.J. (1992). A cointegration analysis of treasury bill yields. *Review of Economics and Statistics*, 48, 213-228.
Hall, S.G. and Mitchell, J. (2007). Combining density forecasts. *International Journal of Forecasting*, 23, 1-13.
Hallwood, C.P. and MacDonald, R. (2000). *International Money and Finance*. Blackwell: Oxford.
Hamilton, J. D. (1990). Analysis of time series subject to changes in regime. *Journal of Econometrics*, 45, 39-70.
Harvard Institute for International Development (1998). The Central American competitiveness report. Harvard Centre of International Studies: Cambridge.
Hasan, I. and Francis B. B. (1998). Macroeconomic factors and the asymmetric predictability of conditional variances. *European Financial Management*, 4, 207-230.
Hassan, G. and Al Refai, H.M. (2012). Can macroeconomic factors explain equity returns in the long-run? The case of Jordan. *Applied Financial Economics*, 22, 1029-1041.
Hassan, K.M., Choudhury, A.R. and Waheeduzzaman, M. (1995). On black market exchange rate and demand for money in developing countries: The case of Nigeria. *Atlantic Economic Journal*, 23(1), 35-44.
Hassapis, C. (1995). Exchange risk in the EMS: Some evidence based on the GARCH model. *Bulletin of Economic Research*, 47, 295-303.
Hau, H. (2002). Real exchange rate volatility and economic openness: Theory and evidence. *Journal of Money, Credit and Banking*, 34(3), 611-630.
Hayo, B. and Ali, M. K. (2005). The impact of news, oil prices, and global market developments on Russian financial markets. *Economics of Transition*, 13(2), 373-393.
Hendry, D.F. and Juselius, K. (1999). Explaining cointegration analysis: Part I. *The Energy Journal International Association for Energy Economics*, 21(1), 1-42.
Hibon, M. and Evgeniou, T. (2005). To combine or not to combine: Selecting among forecasts and their combinations. *International Journal of Forecasting*, 21, 15-24.
Himarios, D. (1989). Devaluations improve the trade balance? The evidence revisited. *Economic Inquiry*, 27(1), 143-168.
Holden, K. and Peel, D.A. (1986). An empirical investigation of combinations of economic forecasts. *Journal of Forecasting*, 5, 229-242.
Homaifar, G. A. (2004). Managing global financial and foreign exchange rate risk. Wiley: Hoboken.
Hooper, P. and Kohlhagen, S. (1978). The effect of exchange rate uncertainty on the prices and volume of international trade. *Journal of International Economics*, 8, 483-511.
Hoque, M.M. and Yusop, Z. (2010). Impacts of trade liberalisation on aggregate import in Bangladesh: An ARDL bounds test approach. *Journal of Asian Economics*, 21, 37-52.
Hornbeck, J.F. (2012). The Dominican Republic-Central America-United States free trade agreement: Development in trade and investment. Congressional Research Service, CRS Report for Congress.
Howells, P. and Bain, K. (2007). *Financial Markets and Institutions*. Prentice Hall: Harlow.
Huchet-Bourdon, M. and Korinek, J. (2012). Trade effects of exchange rates and their volatility: Chile and New Zealand. *OECD Trade Policy Papers*, 136, 1-48.
Hurley, D.T. and Santos, R.A. (2003). Analysis of linkages and volatility of ASEAN currencies. *Journal of Asian Business*, 19, 1-26.
Husted, S. and MacDonald, R. (1999). The Asian currency crash: Were badly driven fundamentals to blame? *Journal of Asian Economics*, 10, 537-550.
Hwang, J.K. (2002). The demand for money in Korea: Evidence from the cointegration test. *International Advances in Economic Research*, 8(3), 188-195.
IMF (2003) see *International Monetary Fund (2003)*
IMF (2003) see *International Monetary Fund (2005)*
IMF (2011) see *International Monetary Fund (2011)*
IMF (2013) see *International Monetary Fund (2013)*

Ince, H. and Trafalis, T. B. (2006). A hybrid model for exchange rate prediction. *Decision Support Systems*, 42(2), 1054-1062.

Inter-American Development Bank (2000). Report on Central America: Central American integration system. Department of Integration and Regional Programs: The Institute for Integration in Latin American and the Caribbean BID-INTAL, 1, Buenos Aires.

International Trade Centre (2012). Peru: Company perspectives. An ITC Series on Non-Tariff Measures, ITC, 1-113.

International Monetary Fund (2003). Exchange arrangements and foreign exchange markets: Development and issues. IMF Publication, Washington, D.C.

__________ (2005). Does inflation targeting work in emerging markets? In World Economic Outlook, September, 161-186.

__________ (2011). Annual report on exchange arrangements and exchange restrictions. IMF Publication, Washington, D.C.

__________ (2013). Heavily indebted poor countries (HIPC) initiative and multilateral debt relief initiative (MDRI) – statistical update. IMF Publication, Washington, D.C.

__________ (2013). International financial statistics. IMF Database CD-ROM, Washington, D.C.

Ivanov, S. (2010). Quantitative analysis of the price discovery in the NAFTA stock markets. *Global Journal of Finance and Banking Issues*, 4(4), 1-14.

Jacome, L.I, Sedik, T.S. and Towsend, S. (2012). Can emerging market central banks bail out banks? A cautionary tale from Latin America. *Emerging Market Review*, 13, 424-448.

Jalil, A. and Feridun, M. (2011). The impact of growth, energy and financial development on the environment in China: A cointegration analysis. *Energy Economics*, 33, 284-291.

Jalil, A. and Feridun, M. and Ma, Y. (2010). Finance-growth nexus in China revisited: New evidence from principal components and ARDL bounds tests. *International Review of Economics and Finance*, 19, 189-195.

Jamil, M., Streissler, E.W. and Kunst, R.M. (2012). Exchange rate volatility and its impact on industrial production, before and after the introduction of common currency in Europe. *International Journal of Economics and Financial Issues*, 2(2), 85-109.

Jaramillo, M. and Servan, S. (2012). Modeling exchange rate dynamics in Peru: A cointegration approach using the UIP and PPP. *Superintendencia de Banca, Seguros y Administratdoras Privadas de Fondos de Pensiones*, 1-33.

Jeffrey, S. and Kotschwar, B. (2002). Readiness indicators for Central America, 2002 update. Institute for International Economics, Washington.

Jimoh, A. (2004). The monetary approach to exchange rate determination: Evidence from Nigeria. *Journal of Economic Cooperation*, 25(2), 109-130.

Jochum, C. and Kodres, L. (1998). Does the introduction of futures on emerging market currencies destabilize the underlying currencies? *IMF Staff Papers*, 45(3), 486-521.

Johansen, S. (1988). Statistical analysis of cointegrating vectors. *Journal of Economic Dynamics and Control*, 12(2-3), 25-31.

__________ (1991). Estimation and hypothesis testing of cointegration vectors in Gaussian vector autoregressive models. *Econometrica*, 59(6), 1551–1580.

Johansen, S. and Juselius, K. (1990). Maximum likelihood estimation and inferences on cointegration with applications to the demand for money. *Oxford Bulletin of Economics and Statistics*, 52(2), 169-210.

Johnston, J. and Di Nardo, J. (1997). *Econometric Methods*. McGraw Hill: New York.

Johnston, R. B. and Swinburne, M. (1999). Exchange rate arrangements and currency convertibility: Developments and issues. *IMF Publications*, Washington, D.C.

Jorion, P. (1995). Predicting volatility in the foreign exchange market. *Journal of Finance*, 50, 507-528.

Josheski, D. and Lazarov, D. (2012). Exchange rate volatility and trade: A Meta-Regression Analysis. *International Journal of Business and Economics*, 1, 24-49.

Kamaly, A. and Tooma, E.A. (2009). Calendar anomalies and stock market volatility in selected Arab stock exchanges. *Applied Financial Economics*, 19(11), 881-892.

Kaminsky, G., Lizondo, S. and Reinhart, C. M. (1998). Leading indicators of currency crises. *IMF Staff Papers*, 45, 1-48.

Kamstra, M. and Kennedy, P. (1998). Combining qualitative forecasts using logit. *International Journal of Forecasting*, 14, 83-93.

Kapetanios, G. Labhard, V. and Price, S. (2008). Forecast combination and the Bank of England's suite of statistical forecasting models. *Economic Modelling*, 25(4), 772-792.

Keynes, J. M. (1924). *A Tract on Monetary Reform*. MacMillan: London.

Kim S. and Rui M. (1999). Price, volume and volatility spill-over among New York, Tokyo and London stock markets. *International Journal of business*, 4, 41-61.

Keho, Y. (2009). Inflation and financial development: Cointegration and causality analysis for the UEMOA countries. *International Research Journal of Finance and Economics*, 27, 117-123.

Kenen, P. T. and Rodrik, D. (1986). Measuring and analysing the effects of short-term volatility in real exchange rates. *The Review of Economics and Statistics*, 68, 311-315.

Kilian, L. and Taylor, M.P. (2003). Why is it so difficult to beat the random walk forecast of exchange rates? *Journal of International Economics*, 60(1), 85-107.

Kim, D. and Kon, S.J. (1994). Alternative models for the conditional heteroskedasticity of stock returns. *Journal of Business*, 67, 563-598.

King, R.G., Plosser, C.I., Stock, J.H. and Watson, M.W. (1991). Stochastic trends and economic fluctuations. *American Economic Review*, 81, 819-840.

Kiyota, K. and Urata, S. (2004). Exchange rate, exchange rate volatility and foreign direct investment. *World Economics*, 27(10), 1501-1536.

Klein, M.W. and Shambaugh, J.C. (2010). *Exchange Rate Regime in the Modern Era*. MIT Press Books: Cambridge.

Klodt, H. and Lehment, H. (2009). *The Crisis and Beyond*. Kiel Institute for the World Economy: Kiel.

Kollias, C., Mylonidis, N. and Paleologou, S. (2008). The Feldstein-Horioka puzzle across EU members: Evidence from the ARDL bounds approach and panel data. *International Review of Economics and Finance*, 17, 380-387.

Konstantakopoulou, I. and Tsionas, E. (2001). The business cycle in Eurozone economies (1960 to 2009). *Applied Financial Economics*, 21, 1495-1513.

Kontonikas, A. (2010). A new test of the inflation–real marginal cost relationship: ARDL bounds approach. *Economics Letters*, 108, 122-125.

Koray, F. and Lastrapes, W. D. (1989). Real exchange rate volatility and U.S. bilateral trade: A VAR approach. *Review of Economics and Statistics*, 71, 708-712.

Koutmos, G. and Booth, G. (1995). Asymmetric volatility transmission in international stock markets. *Journal of International Money and Finance*, 14(6), 747-762.

Krause, A. (2002). Developments in forecasts combination and portfolio choice. *International Journal of Forecasting*, 18(3), 562-563.

Kroner, K. F. and Lastrapes, W.D. (1993). The impact of exchange rate volatility on international trade: Reduced form estimates using the GARCH-in-mean model. *Journal of International Money and Finance*, 12, 298-331.

Kroner, K. F. and Sultan J. (1991). Exchange rate volatility and time varying hedge ratios. *Pacific-Basin Capital Markets Research*, 2, 397-412.

Krugman, P. (1991). *Currencies and Crises*. MIT Press: Cambridge.

__________ Target zones and exchange rate dynamics. *The Quarterly Journal of Economics*, 106, 669-682.

Kumar, V., Nagpal, A. and Venkatesan, R. (2002). Forecasting category sales and market share for wireless telephone subscribers: A combined approach. *International Journal of Forecasting*, 18, 583-603.

Laeven, L. and Valencia, F. (2012). Systemic banking crisis database: An update. *IMF Working Papers*, WP/12/163, 1-32.

Landon, S. and Smith, C. (2003). The risk premium, exchange rate expectations and the forward exchange rate: estimates for the Yen-Dollar rate. *Review of International Economics*, 11, 144–158.

Larrick, R. and Sol, J. (2006). Intuitions about combining opinions: Mis-appreciation of the averaging principle. *Management Science*, 52(1), 111-127.

Laurenceson, J. and Chai, C.H. (2003). *Financial Reform and Economic Development in China*. Advances in Chinese Economic Studies Series. Edward Elgar Publishing: Cheltenham.

Lawrence, R.C. (1998). Combining probabilistic and subjective assessments of error to provide realistic appraisals of demographic forecast uncertainty: Alho's approach. *International Journal of Forecasting*, 14, 523-526.

Lee, H.Y., Ricci, L.A. and Rigobon, R. (2004). Once again, is openness good for growth? *NBER Working Papers*, 10749, 1-28.

Lee, J. and Strazicich, M.C. (2003). Minimum LM unit root test with two structural breaks. *Review of Economics and Statistics* 85(4), 1082-1089.

Lemke, C. and Gabrys, B. (2010). Meta-learning for time series forecasting and forecast combination. *Neurocomputing*, 73(10-12), 2006-2016.
Lettau, M. and Ludvigson, S. (2001). Consumption, aggregate wealth and expected stock returns. *Journal of Finance*, 56, 815-850.
Levich, R. M. (2001). *International Financial Markets*. 2nd edition. McGraw-Hill: New York.
Lewis, C.D. (1982). *Industrial and Business Forecasting Methods: A Practical Guide to Exponential Smoothing and Curve Fitting*. Butterworth Scientific: London.
Li, H. (2007). BEKK international linkages of the Chinese stock exchanges: A multivariate GARCH analysis. *Applied Financial Economics*, 17, 285-297.
Li, X. (2004). Trade liberalisation and real exchange rate movement. *IMF Staff Papers*, 51(3), 553-584.
Liau, Y.S. and Yan, J.W. (2007). The mean/volatility asymmetry in Asian stock markets. *Applied Financial Economics*, 18, 411-419.
Liew, V.K.S., Chong, T.T.L. and Lim, K.P. (2003). The inadequacy of linear autoregressive model for real exchange rates: Empirical evidences from Asian economies. *Applied Economics*, 35, 1387-1392.
Lim, G.C. (1993). The demand for the components of broad money: Error correction and generalized asset adjustment system. *Applied Economics*, 25(8), 995-1004.
Lim, J.S. and O'Connor, M. (1995). Judgmental adjustment of initial forecasts: Its effectiveness and biases. *Journal Behavioural Decision Making*, 8(3), 149-168.
Lin, C.H. (2011). The co-movement between exchange rates and stock prices in the Asian emerging markets. *International Review of Economics and Finance*, 22, 161-172.
Liow, K.H. (2006). Dynamic relationship between stock and property markets. *Applied Financial Economics*, 16, 371-376.
Liu, S. (2007). Currency derivatives and exchange rate forecastability. *Financial Analysts Journal*, 63(4), 72-78.
Ljung, G. M. and Box, G. E. P. (1978). On a measure of lack of fit in time series models. *Biometrika*, 65, 297-303.
Longmore, R. and Robinson, W. (2005). Modeling and forecasting exchange rate dynamics in Jamaica: An application of asymmetric volatility models. *Money Affairs*, 18(1), 23-56.
Lopez, J.A. (1999). Exchange rate cointegration across central bank regime shifts. Economic Research Department, Federal Reserve Bank of San Francisco.
Lorenzo, F. and Vaillant, M. (2004). MERCOSUR under the creation of the free trade area of the Americas. Woodrow Wilson Center of Scholars, Latin American Program, Red Mercosur, Washington.
Louis-Philippe, R. and Sergio, R. (2006). *Monetary and Exchange Rate Systems: A Global View of Financial Crises*. Edward Elgar: Cheltenham.
Lubik, T.A. and Russ, K.N. (2012). Exchange rate volatility in a simple model of firm entry and FDI. *Economic Quarterly*, 98(1), 51-76.
Lyons, R.K. (2001). New perspective on FX markets: Order flow-analysis. *International Finance*, 4(2), 303-320.
Mabro, R. (1984). On oil price concepts. *Oxford Institute for Energy Studies*, 3, 1-78.
MacDonald, R. (1990). Empirical studies of exchange rate determination. In *Current Issues in Monetary Economics*. (Ed.) Lewellyn, D., Milner, C. Macmillan: London.
_________ (2007). *Exchange Rate Economics: Theories and Evidence*. Routledge: London.
MacDonald, R. and Taylor, M.P. (1994). The monetary model of the exchange rate: Long-run relationships, short-run dynamics and how to beat a random walk. *Journal of International Money and Finance*, 13(3), 276-290.
MacDonald, R. and Marsh, I.W. (1994). Combining exchange rate forecasts: What is the optimal consensus measure? *Journal of Forecasting*, 13, 313-332.
Mackinnon, J. E. (1991). Critical values for cointegration tests, in long-run economic relationships. (Ed.) R.F. Engle and C. W. J. Granger. Oxford University Press: Oxford.
Mahdavi, S. and Sohrabian, A. (1993). The exchange value of the dollar and the US trade balance: An empirical investigation based on cointegration and Granger causality tests. *Quarterly Review of Economics and Finance*, 33, 343-358.
Mahmoud, E. (1989). Combining forecasts: Some managerial issues. *International Journal of Forecasting*, 5(4), 599-600.
Maines, L.A. (1996). An experimental examination of subjective forecast combination. *International Journal of Forecasting*, 12, 223-233.

Mair, S. and Christian, P.B. (2001). Regional integration and cooperation in sub-Saharan Africa: Case study of EAC, ECOWAS and SADC. Research report by the Federal Ministry for Economic Cooperation and Development: Bonn.
Makridakis, S. (1989). Why combining works? *International Journal of Forecasting*, 5(4), 601-603.
Makridakis, S., Andersen, A., Carbone, R., Fildes, R., Hibon, M., Lewandowski, R., Newton, J., Parzen, E. and Winkler, R. (1982). The accuracy of extrapolation (time series) methods: Results of a forecasting competition. *Journal of Forecasting*, 1, 111-153.
Makridakis, S., Chatfield, C., Hibon, M., Lawrence, M., Tills, T., Ord, K. and Simmons, L.F. (1993). The M2-competition: A real-time judgmentally based forecasting study. *International Journal of Forecasting*, 9, 5-22.
Makridakis, S. and Hibon, M. (2000). The M3-competition: Results, conclusions and implications. *International Journal of Forecasting*, 16, 451-476.
Makridakis, S. and Winkler, R. (1983). The combination of forecasts. *Journal of the Royal Statistical Society*, 146(2), 150-157.
Malamud, A. (2005). MERCOSUR turns 15: Between rising rhetoric and declining achievement. *Cambridge Review of International Affairs*, 18(3), 1-16.
Maniatis, P. (2012). Forecasting the exchange rate between Euro and USD: Probabilistic approach versus ARIMA and exponential smoothing techniques. *The Journal of Applied Business Research*, 28(2), 171-192.
Mark, N.C. and Sul, D. (2001). Nominal exchange rates and monetary fundamentals: Evidence from a small post-Bretton Woods panel. *Journal of International Economics*, 53(1), 29-52.
Markiewicz, A. (2012). Model uncertainty and exchange rate volatility. *International Economic Review*, 53(3), 815-844.
Mascarenhas, B. and Sand, O.C. (1989). Combination of forecasts in the international context: Predicting debt rescheduling. *Journal of International Business Studies*, 20(3), 539-552.
Maswood, S.J. (2002). *Japan in Crisis*. Palgrave Macmillan: Basingstoke.
Maté, C.G. (2011). A Multivariate analysis approach to forecasts combination: Application to foreign exchange markets. *Revista Colombiana de Estadistica*, 34(2), 347-375.
Mboweni, T. T. (2000). Recent developments in South Africa's financial markets. Bank of International Settlement Review, 40, 1-5.
McCarthy, F.D. and Dhareshwar, A. (1992). Economic shocks and the global environment. *World Bank Policy Research Papers*, WPS 870, 1-55.
McInish, T. (2000). *Capital Markets: A Global Perspective*. Blackwell Publishers: Oxford.
McKenzie, M.D. (1999). The impact of exchange rate volatility on international trade flows. *Journal of Economic Surveys*, 13, 71-106.
McKinnon, R. and Schnabl, G. (2004). The return of soft dollar pegging to East Asia: Mitigating conflicted virtue. *International Finance*, 7(2), 169-201.
_________ (2004). The East Asian dollar standard, fear of floating and original sin. *Review of Development Economics*, 8(3), 331-360.
Meese, R. A. and Rogoff, R. (1983). Empirical exchange rate models of the seventies. *Journal of International Economics*, 14, 3-24.
Melvin, M. (2004). *International Money and Finance*. Addison-Wesley: London.
Melvin, M., Menkhoff, L. and Schmeling, M. (2009). Exchange rate management in emerging markets: Intervention via an electronic limit order book. *Journal of International Economics*, 79, 54-63.
Metzger, M. (2008). Regional cooperation and integration in sub-Saharan Africa. United Nations Conference on Trade and Development, *Discussion Papers*, 189, 1-33.
Miller, S. (1991). Monetary dynamics: An application of cointegration and error-correction modeling. *Money Credit Bank*, 23(2), 139-154.
Mills, T. and Stephenson, M.J. (1985). Forecasting contemporaneous aggregates and the combination of forecasts: The case of the UK monetary aggregates. *Journal of Forecasting*, 4, 273-281.
Mirdala, R. (2012). Sources of exchange rate volatility in the European transition economies (effects of economic crisis revealed). *Munich Personal RePEc Archive*, 7(3), 270-282.
Mishkin, F.S. (1996). The channels of monetary transmission: Lessons for monetary policy. *NBER* Working Paper, 5464, 1-27.
_________ (1999). Lessons from the Asian crisis. *Journal of International Money and Finance*, 18, 709-723.
_________ (2004). Can Central Bank transparency go too far? *NBER* Working Paper, 10829, 1-31.

Miyakoshi, T. (2000). The monetary approach to the exchange rate: Empirical observations from Korea. *Applied Economics Letters* 7(12), 791-794.

Moghadam, R. (2011). Enhancing international monetary stability - A role for the SDR? The Strategy, Policy and Review Department, International Monetary Fund.

Molana, H. and Osei-Assibey, K. (2010). Inflation uncertainty, exchange rate depreciation and volatility: Evidence from Ghana, Mozambique and Tanzania. *Dundee Discussion Papers in Economics*, University of Dundee, 246, 1-7.

Morana, C. and Beltratti, A. (2000). Structural change and long range dependence in volatility of exchange rates: Either, neither or both? *Journal of Empirical Finance*, 11, 629-658.

Morley, B. (2007). The monetary model of the exchange rate and equities: An ARDL bounds testing approach. *Applied Financial Economics*, 17, 391-397.

Morley, S. and Piñeiro, V. (2007). The impact of CAFTA on employment, production and poverty in Honduras. Paper prepared for the Economic Commission for Latin America and the Caribbean, International Food Policy Research Institute, Washington, D.C.

Mundell, R.A. (1961). A theory of optimum currency areas. *The American Economic Review*, 51(4), 657-665.

Muniandy, S.V. and Uning, R. (2006). Characterisation of exchange rate regimes based on scaling and correlation properties of volatility for ASEAN-5 countries. *Physica: Statistical Mechanics and its Applications*, 371(2), 585-598.

Mussa, M. (1976). The exchange rate, the balance of payments and monetary and fiscal policy under a regime of controlled floating. *Scandinavian Journal of Economics*, 78(2), 229-248.

________ (1983). External and internal adjustment costs and the theory of aggregate and firm investment. *Economica*, 47, 163-178.

Naoui, K., Khemiri, S. and Liouane, N. (2010). Crises and financial contagion: The subprime crisis. *Journal of Business Studies Quarterly*, 2(1), 15-28.

Narayan, P.K., (2005). The saving and investment nexus for China: Evidence from cointegration tests *Applied Economics*, 37(17), 1979-1990.

Neely, C. J. (2009). Forecasting foreign exchange volatility: why is implied volatility biased and inefficient? And does it matter? *Journal of International Financial Markets*, Institutions and Money, 19(1), 188-205.

Neely, C. J. and Sarno. L, (2002). How well do monetary fundamentals forecast exchange rates? Federal Reserve Bank of St. Louis, 9, 51-74.

Nelson, D.B. (1990). ARCH models as diffusion approximations. *Journal of Econometrics*, 45, 7-38.

__________ (1991). Conditional heteroskedasticity in asset returns: A new approach. *Econometrica*, 59, 347-370.

Newbold, P. and Granger, C. W. J. (1974). Experience with forecasting univariate time series and the combination of forecasts. *Journal of the Royal Statistical Society*, 137(2), 131-165.

Ngandy, S. (2005). Mineral prices and the exchange rate: What does the literature say. Employment Growth and Development Initiative, Pretoria.

Ngouana, C.L. (2012). Exchange rate volatility under peg: Do trade patterns matter? *IMF Working paper*, 12/73, Washington, D.C.

Nieh, C. C. (2002). The effect of the Asian financial crisis on the relationships among open macroeconomic factors for Asian countries. *Applied Economics*, 34, 491-502.

Nieh, C. C. and Wang, Y.S. (2005). ARDL approach to the exchange rate overshooting in Taiwan. *Review of Quantitative Finance and Accounting*, 25(1), 55-71.

Nieh, C. C., Lin, J.B. and Wang, Y.S. (2008). Exchange rate uncertainty and corporate values: Evidence from Taiwan. *Applied Financial Economics*, 18(14), 1181-1192.

Nikkinen, J. and Vähämaa, S. (2009). Central Bank interventions and implied exchange rate correlations. *Journal of Empirical Finance*, 16(5), 862-873.

Nouri, I. (2011). Exchange rate forecasting: A combination approach. *American Journal of Scientific Research*, 22, 110-118.

Nunnenkamp, P. (1985). *The International Debt Crisis of the Third World: Causes and Consequences for the World Economy*. Harvester Wheatsheaf: Brighton.

Obstfeld, M. and Rogoff, K. (1995). Mirage of fixed rates. *Journal of Economic Perspectives*, 9, 73-96.

OECD (2012) see *Organisation of Economic Cooperation and Development (2012)*

Ocampo, J. A. and Parra, M. A. (2010). The terms of trade for commodities since the mid-nineteenth century. *Revista de Historia Económica - Journal of Iberian and Latin American Economic History*, 28(1), 11-37.

Ogun, O., Egwaikhide, F.O. and Ogunleye, E.K. (2012). Real exchange rate and foreign direct investment in sub-Saharan Africa: Some empirical results. *Economia Mexicana*, 21(1), 175-202.

Ogunleye, E.K. (2009). Exchange rate volatility and FDI in sub-Saharan Africa: Evidence from Nigeria and South Africa. In Adenikiju, A, A. Busari and S.Olofin, (Ed.). *Applied Econometrics and Macroeconometric Modelling In Nigeria*. Ibadan University Press: Ibadan.

Oluwole, O. and Olugbenga, A. O. (2007). M2 targeting, money demand and real GDP growth in Nigeria: Do rules apply? *Journal of Business and Public Affairs*, 1(2), 1-20.

OPEC (2012) see *Organisation of the Petroleum Exporting Countries (2012)*

Organisation of Economic Cooperation and Development (2012). Development and cooperation report 2012: Lessons linking sustainability and development. OECD Publishing.

Organisation of the Petroleum Exporting Countries (2012). Annual report 2012. Organisation of the Petroleum Exporting Countries, Vienna.

Otuori, O. H. (2013). Influence of exchange rate determinants on the performance of commercial banks in Kenya. *European Journal of Management Sciences and Economics*, 1(2), 86-98.

Panopoulou, E. and Pantelidis, T. (2009). Integration at a cost evidence from volatility impulse response functions. *Applied Financial Economics*, 19, 917-933.

Pattanachak, K. and Lee, J.M. (2010). Sources of output volatility from financial crisis in emerging markets. *Applied Financial Economics*, 20(3), 183-199.

Payaslioglu, C. (2008). Revisiting East Asian exchange rates: The same spirit under different sky. *Applied Financial Economics*, 18(15), 1263-1276.

Peijie, W. (2005). *The Economics of Foreign Exchange and Global Finance*. Springer: Berlin.

Pentecost, E. J. (1993). *Exchange Rate Dynamics: A Modern Analysis of Exchange Rate Theory and Evidence*. Edward Elgar: Aldershot.

Perron, P. (1989). The Great crash, the oil shock and the unit root hypothesis. *Econometrica*, 57, 1361-1402.

_______ (1994). Trend, unit root and structural change in macroeconomic time series. In *Cointegration for the Applied Economist*. Rao, B.B. (Ed.). Macmillan: Basingstoke.

_______ (1997). Further evidence on breaking trend functions in macroeconomic variables. *Journal of Econometrics*, 80 (2), 355-385.

Pesaran, M.H. and Pesaran, B. (1997). *Working with Microfit 4.0: Interactive Econometric Analysis*. Oxford University Press: Oxford.

Pesaran, M.H. and Shin, Y. (1995). Long-run structural modeling. University of Cambridge.

Pesaran, M.H. and Shin, Y. (1999). *An Autoregressive Distributed Lag Modeling Approach to Cointegration Analysis*. Cambridge University Press: Cambridge.

Pesaran, M.H., Shin, Y. and Smith, R. J. (2001). Bounds testing approaches to the analysis of level relationships. *Journal of Applied Econometrics*, 16, 289-326.

Peters, E.E. (1996). *Chaos and Order in the Capital Markets: A New View of Cycles, Prices, and Market Volatility*. Wiley: New York.

Peters, W.C. (2010). *The Quest for an African Economic Community, Regional Integration and its Role in Achieving African Unity - the case of SADC*. Peter Lang: Hamburg.

Phylaktis, K. (1991). The black market for dollars in Chile. *Journal of Development Economics*, 37 (1-2), 155-172.

Phylaktis, K. (1992). Purchasing power parity and cointegration: The Greek evidence from the 1920s. *Journal of International Money and Finance*, 11(5), 502-513.

Phylaktis, K. and Kassimatis, Y. (1997). Black and official exchange rate volatility and foreign exchange controls. *Applied Financial Economics*, 7(1), 15-24.

Pilbeam, K. (2005). *Finance and Financial Markets*. Palgrave Macmillan: Basingstoke.

Pincheira, P. (2013). Interventions and inflation expectations in an inflation targeting economy. BIS Working Papers No. 247, 1-27.

Pontines, V. and Rajan, R.S. (2011). Foreign exchange market intervention and reserve accumulation in emerging Asia: Is there evidence of fear of appreciation? *Economics Letters*, 111, 252-255.

Poon, S.H. and Granger, C.W.J. (2003). Forecasting volatility in financial markets: A review. *Journal of Economic Literature*, 41(2), 478-539.

Poon, W.C. (2010). Augmented MCI: An indicator of monetary policy stance for ASEAN-5? *Monash Economics Working Papers*, 25-10, Monash University.

Popper, H. and Montgomery, J.D. (2001) Information sharing and Central Bank intervention in the foreign exchange market. *Journal of International Economics*, 55(2), 295-316.

Poterba, J. M. and Summers, L. H. (1988). Mean reversion in stock prices: Evidence and implications. *Journal of Financial Economics*, 22, 27-59.

Pradhan, B. and Subaramanian, A. (2003). On the stability of the demand for money in a developing economy: Some empirical issues. *Journal of Development Economics*, 72, 335-351.

Quantitative Micro Software (2004). *EViews 5 Users' Guide*. Quantitative Micro Software LLC: Irvine.

Rahman, M. and Mustafa, M. (1996). The Dancing of the real exchange rate of US Dollar and the US real trade balance. *Applied Economics Letters*, 3(12), 807-808.

Rahman, M., Mustafa, M. and Burckel, D.V. (1997). Dynamics of the Yen Dollar real exchange rates and the US-Japan real trade balance. *Applied Economics*, 29, 661-664.

Rana, P. B. (1981). Exchange rate risk under generalized floating. *Journal of International Economics*, 11, 459-467.

Rapach, D. E. and Wohar, M.E. (2002).Testing the monetary model of exchange rate determination: New evidence from a century of data. *Journal of International Economics*, 58(2), 359-385.

Rapach, D. E. and Strauss, J.K. (2008). Forecasting US employment growth using forecast combining methods. *Journal of Forecasting*, 27, 75-93.

Rapach, D. E., Strauss, J.K and Zhou, G. (2010). Out-of-sample equity premium prediction: Combination forecasts and links to the real economy. *Review of Financial Studies*, 23(2), 821-862.

Rapach, D. E. and Wohar, M. E. (2002). Testing the monetary model of exchange rate determination: New evidence from a century of data. *Journal of International Economics*, 59(1), 1-12.

Reinhart, C.M. and Rogoff, K.S. (2004). The monetary history of exchange rate arrangements: An interpretation. *Quarterly Journal of Economics*, 107, 797-817.

Rincon, C.H. (1998). Testing the short-and-long-run exchange rate effects on trade balance: The case of Colombia. Unpublished PhD thesis, University of Illinois at Urbana-Champaign.

Rochon, L. and Rossi, S. (2006). *Monetary and Exchange Rate Systems: A Global View of Financial Crises*. Edward Elgar: Cheltenham.

Rodriguez, P. L., Morales, J.R. and Monaldi, F.J. (2012). Direct distribution of oil revenues in Venezuela: A viable alternative? Centre for Global Development, *Working Paper*, Washington, D.C.

Rogoff, K. (2002). Dornbusch's overshooting model after twenty-five years. *IMF Staff Papers*, 49, 1-35.

Rogoff, K., Hussain, A., Mody, R., Brooks, N. and Oomes, N. (2003). Evolution and performance of exchange rate regimes. *IMF working paper*, 03/243, 1-83.

Rosenberg, M. (2003). *Exchange-Rate Determination: Models and Strategies for Exchange-Rate Forecasting*. McGraw-Hill Library of Investment and Finance: New York.

Ruiz, I. (2009). Common volatility across Latin American foreign exchange markets. *Applied Financial Economics*, 19(15), 1197-1211.

Rushdi, M., Kim, J. and Silvapulle, P. (2012). ARDL bounds tests and robust inference for the long- run relationship between real stock returns and inflation in Australia. *Economic Modelling*, 29, 535-543.

Sabaté, M., Gadea, M.D. and Serrano, J.M. (2003). PPP and structural breaks. The peseta-Sterling rate, 50 years of a floating regime. *Journal of International Money and Finance*, 22, 613-627.

Saborio, S. and Michalopoulos, C. (1992). Central America at a crossroads. *International Economics Department Working papers*, 922, The World Bank.

Sachs, J. D. and Warner, A. M. (1995). Natural resource abundance and economic growth. *NBER Working Papers*, 5398, 1-47.

Saeed, A., Awan, R.U., Sial, M.H. and Falak, S. (2012). An econometric analysis of determinants of exchange rate in Pakistan. *International Journal of Business and Social Science*, 3(6), 184-196.

Sahoo, S. (2012). Volatility transmission in the exchange rate of the Indian rupee. *Reserve Bank of India Publications Working Paper*, 8, 1-23.

Samreth, S. (2008). Estimating money demand function in Cambodia: ARDL approach. *Munich Personal RePEc Archive*, 16274, 1-16.

Samuelson, P. A. (1964). Theoretical notes on trade problems. *Review of Economics and Statistics*, 46(2), 145-154.

Sanders, N. and Ritzman, L. (1995). Bringing judgment into combination forecasts. *Journal of Operations Management*, 13(4), 311-321.

Sarno, L. (2003). Nonlinear exchange rate models: A selective overview. *IMF Working Paper*, 03-111, 1-38.

Sarno, L. and Taylor, M. P. (2001). Official intervention in the foreign exchange market: Is it effective, and if so, how does it work? *Journal of Economic Literature*, 34, 839-868.

Sarno, L. (2002). *The Economics of Exchange Rates*. Cambridge University Press: Cambridge.

Sbeiti, W. and Al Shammari, T. (2010). Integration of stock markets in the GCC countries: An application of the ARDL bounds testing model. *European Journal of Economics Finance and Administrative Sciences*, 20, 35-43.

Schwarz, G. (1978). Estimating the dimension of a model. *The Annals of Statistics*, 6, 461-464.

__________ (1990). Stock market volatility. *Financial Analysts Journal*, May-June, 23-34.

__________ (1990b). Stock volatility and the crash of '87'. *Review of Financial Studies*, 3, 77-102.

Seerattan, D. and Spagnolo, N. (2009). Central Bank intervention and foreign exchange markets. *Applied Financial Economics*, 19(17), 1417-1432.

Sekantsi, L. (2011). The impact of real exchange rate volatility on South African exports to the United States: A bounds testing approach. *Review of Economic and Business Studies*, 4(2), 119-139.

Sercu, P. and Uppal, R. (1995). *International Financial Markets and the Firm: Current Issues in Finance*. South-Western College Publishing: Boston.

Sercu, P. (2000). *Exchange Rate Volatility, Trade, and Capital Flow under Alternative Exchange Rate Regimes*. Cambridge University Press: Cambridge.

Sercu, P. and Vanhulle, C. (1992). Exchange rate volatility, international trade and the value of exporting firms. *Journal of Banking and Finance*, 16, 155-182.

Servén, L. (2002). Real exchange rate uncertainty and private investment in developing countries. *Policy Research Working Paper*, 2823, World Bank, Washington DC.

Shah, M.K.A., Hyder, Z. and Pervaiz, M. K. (2009). Central Bank intervention and exchange rate volatility in Pakistan: An analysis using GARCH-X model. *Applied Financial Economics*, 19(18), 1497-1508.

Shahrestani, H. and Sharifi-Rehani, H. (2008). Demand for money in Iran: An ARDL approach. *Munich Personal RePEc Archive*, 11451, 1-10.

Shahriari, M. (2011). A combined forecasting approach to exchange rate fluctuations. *International Research Journal of Finance and Economics*, 79, 112-119.

Shapiro, A. C. (2010). *Multinational Financial Management*. 9th edition. Wiley: New Jersey.

Shehu, A.A. and Youtang, Z. (2012). Exchange rate volatility, trade flows and economic growth in a small open economy. *International Review of Business Research Papers*, 8(2), 118-131.

Shen, S., Li, G. and Song, H. (2011). Combination forecasts of international tourism demand. *Annals of Tourism Research*, 38(1), 72-89.

Shrestha, M.B. and Chowdhury, K. (2007). Testing financial liberalisation hypothesis with ARDL modeling approach. *Applied Financial Economics*, 17(18), 1529-1540.

Siddiki, J. (2000). Demand for money in Bangladesh: A cointegration analysis. *Applied Economics*, 32(15), 1977-1984.

______ (2000). Black market exchange rates in India: An empirical analysis. *Empirical Economics*, 25(2), 297-313.

Simons, H. (2004). Taking the commodity out of currencies. *Futures*, August, 42-45.

Simwaka, K. and Mkandawire, L. (2008). The efficacy of foreign exchange market intervention in Malawi. *Munich Personal RePEc Archive*, 15946, 1-38.

Sjölander, P. (2008). A new test for simultaneous estimation of unit roots and GARCH risk in the presence of stationary conditional heteroscedasticity disturbances. *Applied Financial Economics*, 18(7), 527-558.

Smith, D.R. (2008). Testing for structural breaks in GARCH models. *Applied Financial Economics*, 18(10), 845-862.

Smith, J. and Wallis, K.F. (2009). A simple explanation of the forecast combination puzzle. *Oxford Bulletin of Economics and Statistics*, 71(3), 331-355.

Staines, N. (2012). Interview with Rumo. Interview with the IMF Resident Representative in Angola, Luanda. (see IMF link: http://www.imf.org/external/country/ago/index.htm)

Stancik, J. (2007). Determinants of exchange rate volatility: The case of the new EU members. *Journal of Economics and Finance*, 57(9-10), 56-72.

Stanga, E., Anghel, F. and Avrigeanu, A. (2010). The long-short term strategy based on cointegration concept. *Romanian Economic and Business Review*, 5(1), 96-105.

Steiner, B. (2002). *Foreign Exchange and Money Markets: Theory, Practice and Risk Management*. Butterworth-Heinemann: Oxford.

Stensnes, K. (2006). Trade openness and economic: Do institutions matter? Norwegian Institute of International Affairs, 1-72.

Stobart, H. (2011). Media piracy in emerging economies, Chapter 7: Bolivia. Social Science Research Council, 327-338, New York.

Stock, J.H. and Watson, M.W. (2004). Combination forecasts of output growth in a seven-country data set. *Journal of Forecasting*, 23, 405-430.

Strauss, J. (1996). The cointegrating relationship between productivity, real exchange rates and purchasing power parity. *Journal of Macroeconomics*, 18, 299-313.

Suardi, S. (2008). Central Bank intervention, threshold effects and asymmetric volatility: Evidence from the Japanese yen-US dollar foreign exchange market. *Economic Modeling*, 25(4), 628-642.

Sukar, A.H. and Hassan, S. (2001). US exports and time-varying volatility of real exchange rate. *Global Finance Journal*, 12, 109-119.

Syrichas, G. (2010). Fixed Exchange Rate Regimes in Mediterranean Countries and the Experience of Cyprus. Central Bank of Cyprus Working Papers, 8, 1-38.

Tang, T.C. (2007). Money demand function for Southeast Asian countries: An empirical view from expenditure components. School of Business Information Technology, Monash University.

Tapia, M. and Tokman, A. (2004). Effects of foreign exchange intervention under public information: The Chilean case. *Economia*, 4(2), 215-256.

Taylor J.W. (2008). Exponentially weighted information criteria for selecting among forecasting models. *International Journal of Forecasting*, 24, 513–524.

_________ (2008). Volatility forecasting with smooth transition exponential smoothing. *International Journal of Forecasting*, 20, 273-286.

Taylor J.W. and Bunn, D.W. (1999). Investigating improvements in the accuracy of prediction intervals for combinations of forecasts: A simulation study. *International Journal of Forecasting*, 15, 325-339.

Taylor, M. P. (2004). Is official exchange rate intervention effective? *Economica*, 71, 1–11.

Taylor J.W. and Peel, D. A. (2000). Nonlinear adjustment, long-run equilibrium and exchange rate fundamentals. *Journal of International Money and Finance*, 19, 33–53.

Taylor J.W., Peel, D. A. and Sarno, L. (2001). Nonlinear mean reversion in real exchange rates: towards a solution to the purchasing power puzzles. *International Economics Review*, 42, 1015-1042.

Taylor J.W. and Sarno, L. (2002). *The Economics of Exchange Rates*. Cambridge University Press: Cambridge.

Tehranchian, A.M. and Behravesh, M. (2011). Testing currency substitution in Iran: An application of auto regressive with distributed lag model. *American Journal of Scientific Research*, 39, 47-54.

Terregrossa, S.J. (1999). Combining analysts' forecasts with causal model forecasts of earnings growth. *Applied Financial Economics*, 9(2), 143-153.

______ (2005). On the efficacy of constraints on the linear combination forecast model. *Applied Economics Letters*, 12, 19-28.

Terui, N. and van Dijk, H.K. (2002). Combined forecasts from linear and nonlinear time series models. *International Journal of Forecasting*, 18, 421-438.

Tetzlaff, R. and Jacobeit, C. (2005). *The post-colonial Africa: Politics - Economy – Society*. Lehrbuch, Grundwissen Politik, Wiesbaden.

The Economist (2009). A golden chance: A special report on Indonesia. September 12th, London.

______ (2009). Ecuador, Argentina and the IMF: The price of pride. September 12th, London.

______ (2009). Asian currencies: Hot air. October 3rd, London.

______ (2009). South-East Asian summitry: Distant dreams. October 31st, London.

______ (2009). Colombia's paramilitaries: Militias march again. October 31st, London.

______ (2009). A special report on business and finance in Brazil. November 14th, London.

______ (2009). Banyan: Barack Obama's Asian adventure. November 14th, London.

______ (2010). The World in 2010: After Lula. Special issue, London.

______ (2010). Costa Rica's new president: Tax increases, trade deals and antidisestablishmentarianism. May 8th, London.

______ (2010). A special report on banking in emerging markets. May 15th, London.

______ (2010). Asian currencies: Currencies around Asia are more flexible than you think. June 5th, London.

______ (2010). A Special Report on South Africa. June 5th, London.

______ (2010). Business is transforming Africa for the better. June 12th, London.
______ (2010). Crime and politics in Guatemala: Kamikaze mission. June 19th, London.
______ (2010). Brazil's presidential campaign: In Lula's footsteps. July 3rd, London.
______ (2010). Terrorism in Indonesia. August 14th, London.
______ (2010). The United States and Latin America: Latin America's new promise – and the need for a new attitude north of the Rio Grande. September 11th, London.
______ (2010). A special report on Latin America. September 11th, London.
______ (2010). Venezuela's economy: Disappearing dollars. September 18th, London.
______ (2010). The sorry state of Swaziland. September 18th, London.
______ (2010). Brazil's mining giant: Valuable Vale. September 25th, London.
______ (2010). Security in Colombia: The beginning of the end. October 2nd, London.
______ (2010). Indonesian banks: Profits puzzle. October 16th, London.
______ (2010). Chile's copper industry: Reviving Codelco. October 23rd, London.
______ (2010). The global monetary system. November 6th, London.
______ (2010). Illegal mining in South America: Turning the army to fight wildcat miners. November 20th, London.
______ (2010). Brazil's next government: Many questions, a few answers. November 27th, London.
______ (2010). The Latino-barometer poll: The democratic routine. December 4th, London.
______ (2010). El Salvador's president: So far, so good. December 18th, London.
______ (2011). Latin America's economies: Waging the currency war. January 15th, London.
______ (2011). Integrating Southeast Asia: China coming down the tracks. January 22nd, London.
______ (2011). Security in Colombia: Guerilla miners. January 29th, London.
______ (2011). Venezuela's economy: Oil leak. February 26th, London.
______ (2011). Central America's woes: The drug war hits Central America. April 16th, London.
______ (2011). South Africa: A ruling party at odds with itself. April 23rd, London.
______ (2011). The Chinese in Africa. April 23rd, London.

The Royal Swedish Academy of Sciences (2003). Time-Series Econometrics: Cointegration and Autoregressive Conditional Heteroskedasticity. Information Department, Stockholm.

Tian, G. G. and Ma, S. (2009). The effects of currency appreciation on share market return: ARDL approach. *Asian Finance Association*, Conference Paper Brisbane UQ Business School (UQBS), 1-26.

______ (2010). The relationship between stock returns and the foreign exchange rate: The ARDL approach. *Journal of the Asia Pacific Economy*, 15(4), 490-508.

Tibiletti, L. (1994). A non-linear combination of experts' forecasts: A Bayesian approach. *Journal of Forecasting*, 13, 21-27.

Timmermann, A. (2004). Forecast combinations. University of California San Diego Research Paper.

Tse, Y. and Booth, G. (1996). Common volatility and volatility spill-over between US and Eurodollar interest rates: Evidence from the future markets. *Journal of Economics and Business*, 48, 299-312.

Tumbarello, P. (2007). Are regional trade agreements in Asia stumbling or building blocks? Implications for the Mekong-3 countries. *IMF Working Paper*, WP/07/53, Washington, D.C.

Ulu, Y. (2007). Sampling properties of criteria for evaluating GARCH volatility forecasts. *Applied Financial Economics*, 17(8), 671-681.

Umar, A. (2010). GARCH and ARDL model of exchange rate: Evidence from Nigeria's retail Dutch auction system. *International Research Journal of Finance and Economics*, 49, 7-14.

Valdez, S. (2007). *An Introduction to Global Financial Markets*. Palgrave Macmillan: Basingstoke.

Valdez, S. and Molyneux, P. (2013). *An Introduction to Global Financial Markets*. 7th Edition, Palgrave Macmillan: Basingstoke.

Villarreal, M.A. (2012). The US-Colombia free trade agreement: Background and issues. CRS Report for Congress Prepared for Members and Committees of Congress, RL, 33470, 1-29.

Vogelsang, T. and Perron, P. (1998). Additional test for a unit root allowing for a break in the trend function at an unknown time. *International Economic Review*, 39, 1073-1100.

Vogelvang, B. (2005). *Econometrics: Theory and Applications with EViews*. Pearson Education: Harlow.

Wallis, K.F. (2011). Combining forecasts - forty years later. *Applied Financial Economics*, 21, 33-41.

Wang, P. (2005). *The Economics of Foreign Exchange and Global Finance*. Springer: Berlin.

Wellons, P. A. (1987). *Passing the Buck: Banks, Government and Third World Debt (1987)*. 5th Edition. Harvard Business School Press: Boston.
West, K. D. (2004). A standard monetary model and the variability of the Deutschemark-Dollar exchange rate. Department of Economics, University of Wisconsin-Madison.
White, H. (1980). A heteroscedasticity-consistent covariance matrix estimator and a direct test for heteroscedasticity. *Econometrica*, 48, 817-838.
Williamson, J. (1994). Estimates of FEERs. In J. Williamson (Ed.), *Estimating Equilibrium Exchange Rate*. Institute of International Economics: Washington.
Winkler, R.L. (1989). Combining forecasts; a philosophical basis and some current issues. *International Journal of Forecasting*, 5(4), 605-609.
Wolf, A. (1995). Import and hedging uncertainty in international trade. *Journal of Futures Markets*, 15(2), 101-110.
Wong, D.K.T. and Li, K.W. (2010). Comparing the performance of relative stock return differential and real exchange rate in two financial crises. *Applied Financial Economics*, 20(1), 137-150.
World Bank (1992). *World Development Report*. Oxford University Press: Washington.
______ (2002). *Globalization, Growth and Poverty*. Oxford University Press: New York
______ (2011). *World Development Report*. Oxford University Press: Washington.
______ (2010-2011). *World Economic Forum's Global Competitiveness Report*. Oxford University Press: Washington.
______ (2011-2012). *World Economic Forum's Global Competitiveness Report*. Oxford University Press: Washington.
Wu, T. (2012). Order flows in the South: Anatomy of the Brazilian FX market. *North American Journal of Economics and Finance*, 23, 310-324.
Yin, W. and Li, J. (2014). Macroeconomic fundamentals and the exchange rate dynamics: A no-arbitrage macro-finance approach. *Journal of International Money and Finance*, 41, 46-64.
Zakaria, M. and Ghauri, A.B. (2011). Trade openness and real exchange rate: Some evidence from Pakistan. *The Romanian Economic Journal*, 14(39), 201-229.
Zivot, E. and Andrews, D.W.K. (1992). Further evidence on the Great Crash, the oil price shock and the unit root hypothesis. *Journal of Business and Economic Statistics*, 10, 251-270.
Zou, H. and Yang, Y. (2004). Combining time series models for forecasting. *International Journal of Forecasting*, 20, 69-84.
http://www.imf.org/external/index.htm, accessed on May 4th, 2010
http://www.mas.gov.sg/news_room/statements/1998/Coping_With_the_Asian_Financial_Crisis__The_Singapore_Experience__30_Sep_1998.html, accessed on April 30th, 2010,
http://www.mas.gov.sg/resource/publications/staff_papers/MASOP019-ed.pdf, accessed on May 3rdth, 2010
http://www.mas.gov.sg/resource/publications/staff_papers/MASOP019-ed.pdf, accessed on May 4th, 2010
http://lcweb2.loc.gov/frd/cs/honduras/hn_appnb.html, accessed in May, 2011
www.switzerlandisyours.com, [http://switzerland.isyours.com/e/faq/swiss-franc.html], accessed on May 4th, 2010
http://www.imf.org/external/pubs/ft/fandd/basics/markets.htm, accessed in January 2013
http://www.bbc.co.uk/news/business-17595960, accessed in January 2011
http://business.inquirer.net/61905/single-asean-currency-idea-losing-steam, accessed in January 2011
http://www.aseansec.org/ accessed in January 2013
http://news.bbc.co.uk/2/hi/asia-pacific/country_profiles/4114415.stm accessed in January 2013
http://www.aseansec.org/about_ASEAN.htm accessed in June 2010
http://www.aseansec.org/about_ASEAN.html accessed in June 2010
http://www.aseansec.org/18619.htm accessed in June 2010
http://news.bbc.co.uk/2/hi/asia-pacific/country_profiles/4114415.stm accessed in June 2012
http://www.iadb.org/en/inter-american-development-bank,2837.html accessed in April 2012
http://www.cfr.org/trade/mercosur-south-americas-fractious-trade-bloc/p12762, accessed in March 2012
http://www.mercosur.int/t_generic.jsp?contentid=3862&site=1&channel=secretaria&seccion=2, accessed in July 2010
http://www.coha.org/, accessed in May 2012
http://www.comunidadandina.org/endex.htm, accessed in July 2010

http://en.mercopress.com/2012/07/03/astori-describes-mercosur-latest-decisions-as-aggression-and-major-institutional-blows, accessed in January 2012
http://www.brazilconfidential.com/, accessed in July 2012
http://www.sice.oas.org/trade/MRCSR/treatyasun_e.asp, accessed in May 2011
http://www.economist.com/node/21558609, accessed in July 2012
http://online.wsj.com/article/SB10000872396390444330904577539081063421986.html, accessed in July 2012
http://www.mercosur.int/t_generic.jsp?contentid=3862&site=1&channel=secretaria&seccion=2, accessed in July 2010
https://www.cia.gov/library/publications/the-world-factbook/accessed in July 2010
http://www.investopedia.com/terms/s/spotexchangerate.asp accessed in July 2012
http://www.investopedia.com/terms/h/heteroskedastic.asp accessed on May 1st, 2010
http://www.investopedia.com/terms/l/leptokurtic.asp accessed on May 1st, 2010
http://www.imf.org/external/country/ago/index.htm accessed on May 1st, 2012

Appendix 1 Exchange rate plots over time

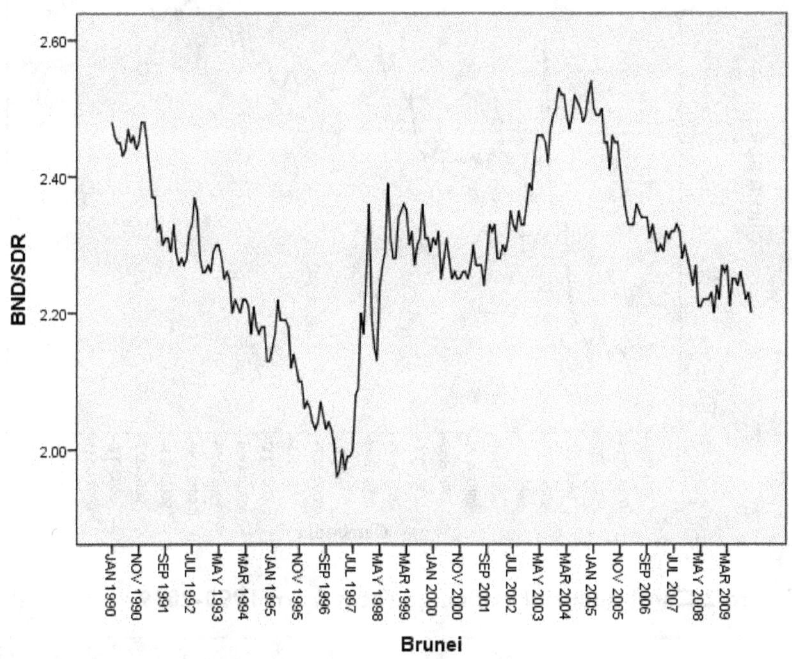

Figure 1 Brunei dollar exchange rates from 1990-2009

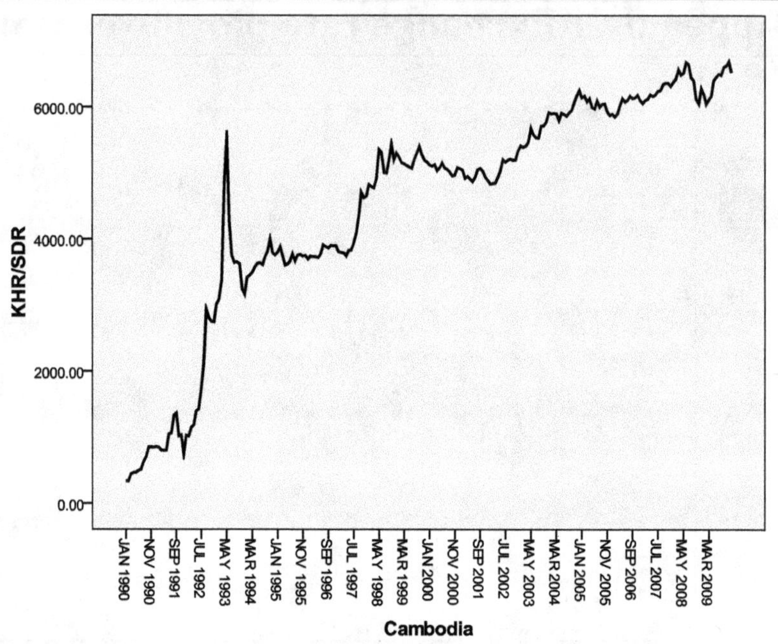

Figure 2 Cambodia riel exchange rates from 1990-2009

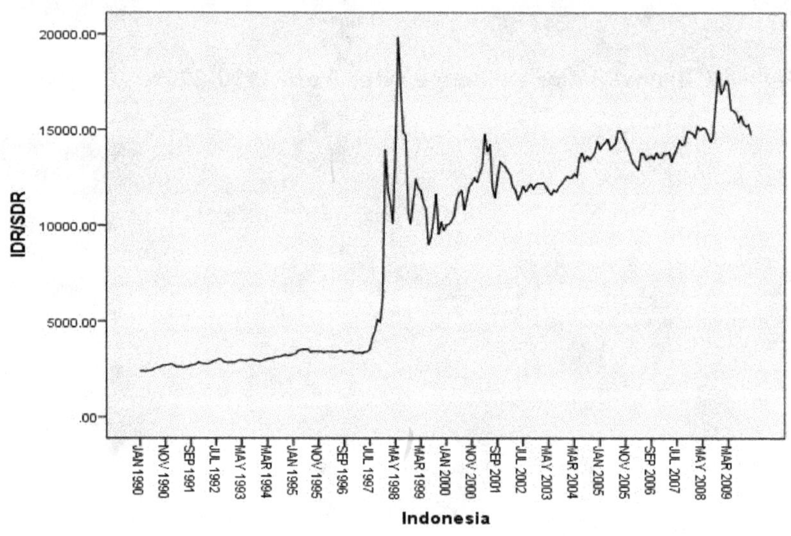

Figure 3 Indonesian rupiah exchange rates from 1990-2009

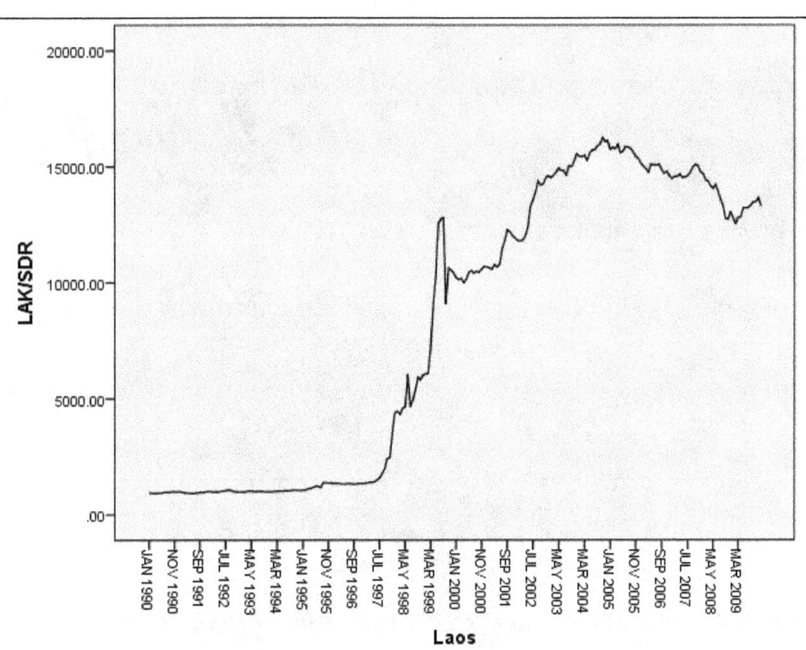

Figure 4 Laos's kip exchange rates from 1990-2009

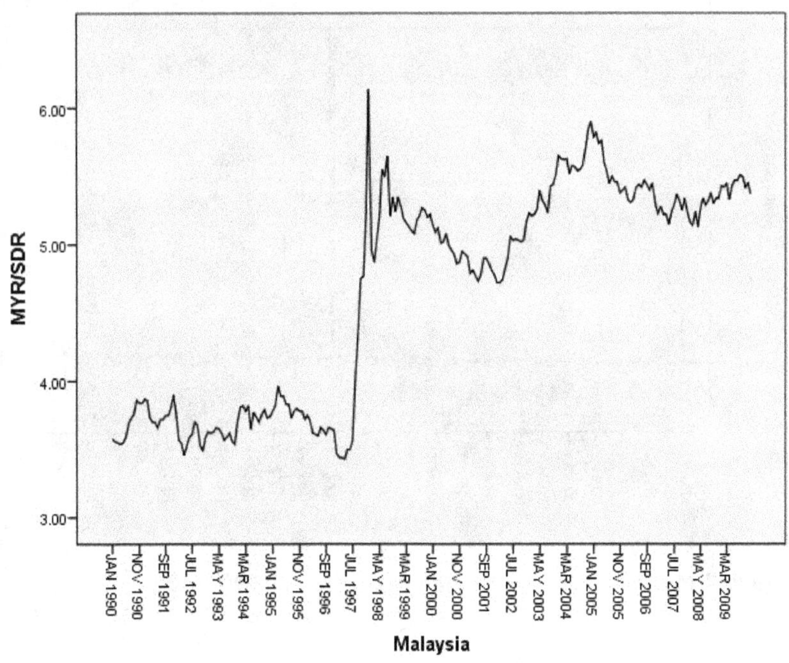

Figure 5 Malaysian ringgit exchange rate from 1990-2009

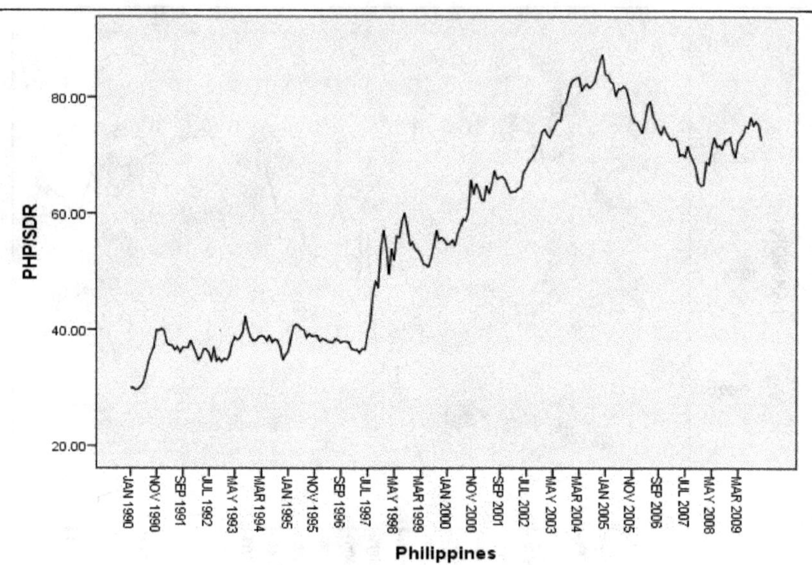

Figure 6 Philippines peso exchange rates from 1990-2009

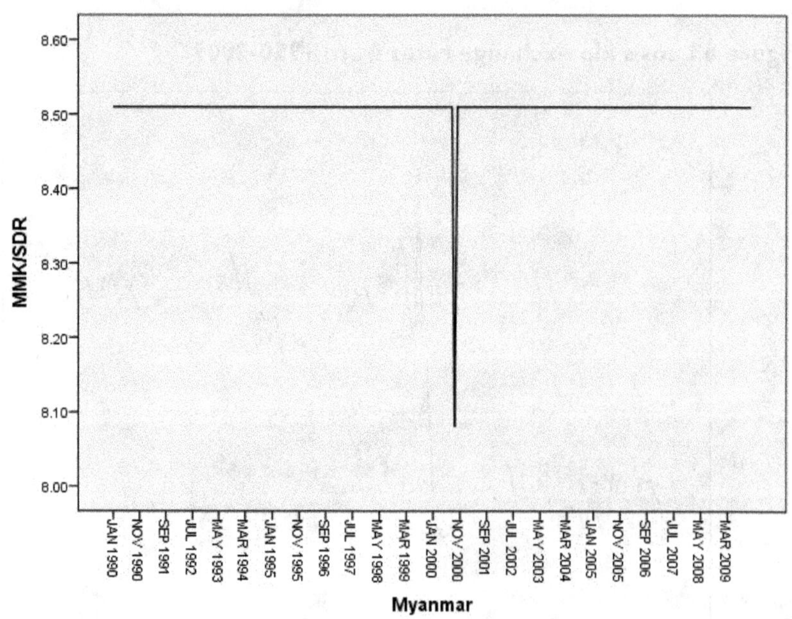

Figure 7 Myanmar kip exchange rates from 1990-2009

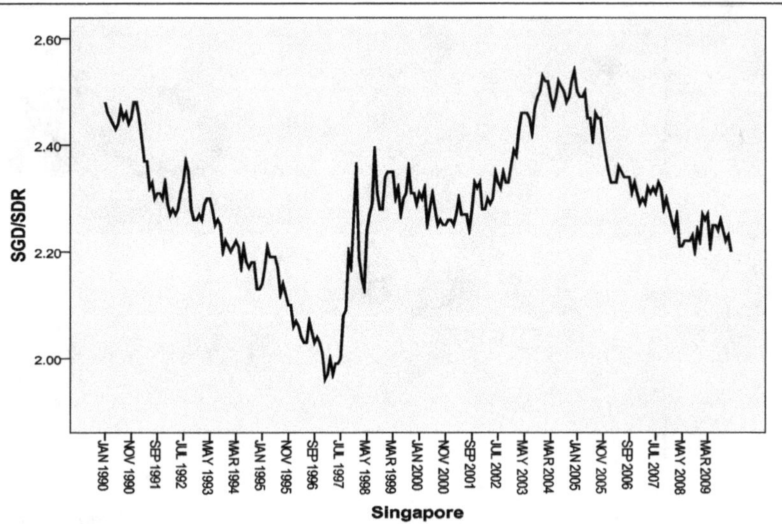

Figure 8 Singapore dollar exchange rates from 1990-2009

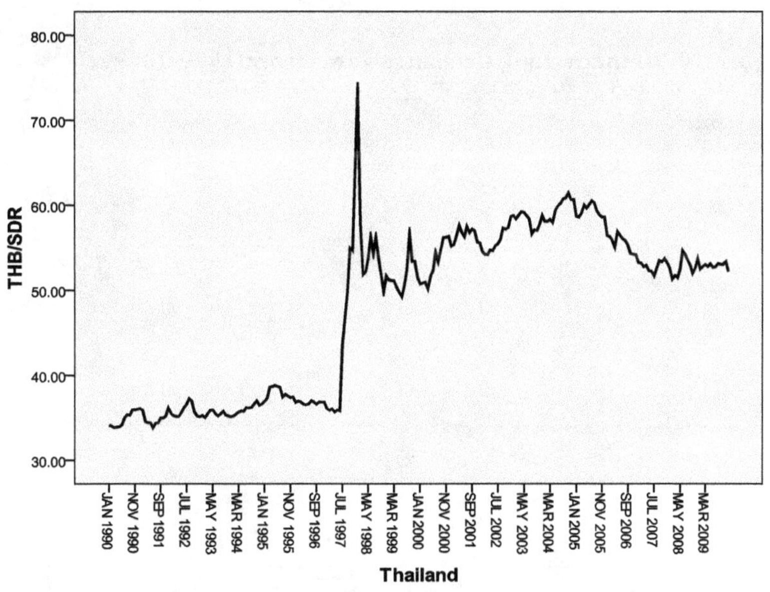

Figure 9 Thailand baht exchange rates 1999-2009

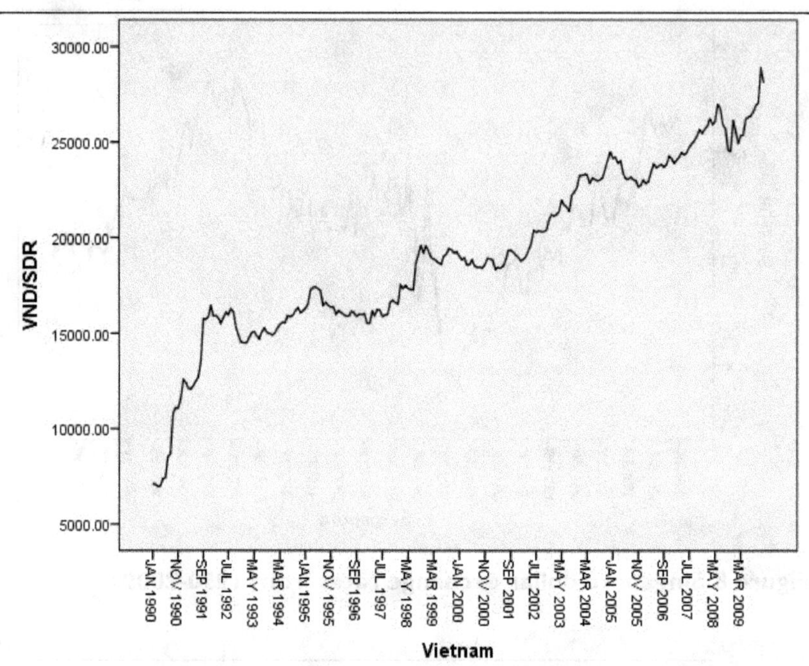

Figure 10 Vietnam dong exchange rates from 1990-2009

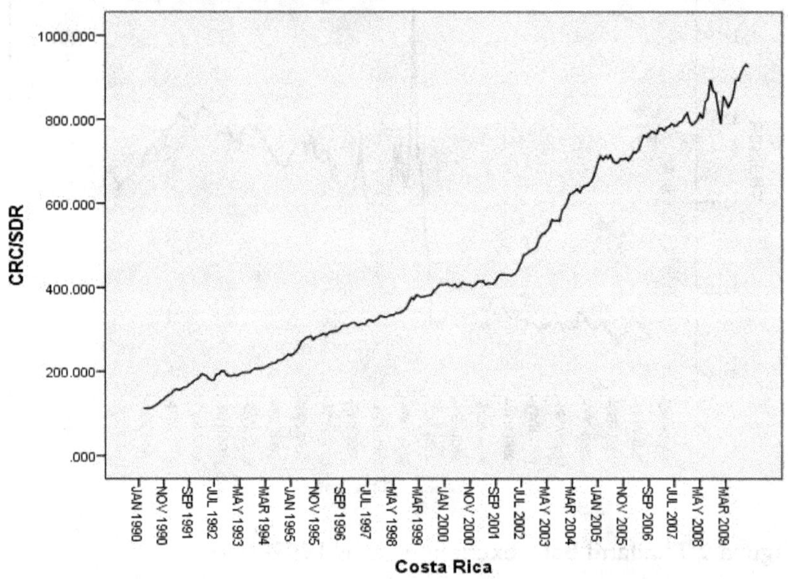

Figure 11 Costa Rica colon exchange rates from 1990-2009

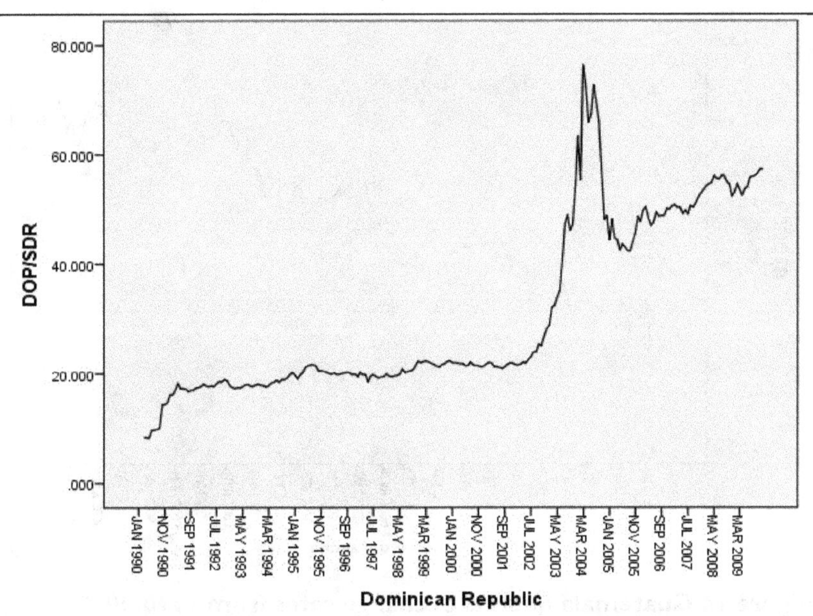

Figure 12 Dominican Republic peso exchange rates from 1990-2009

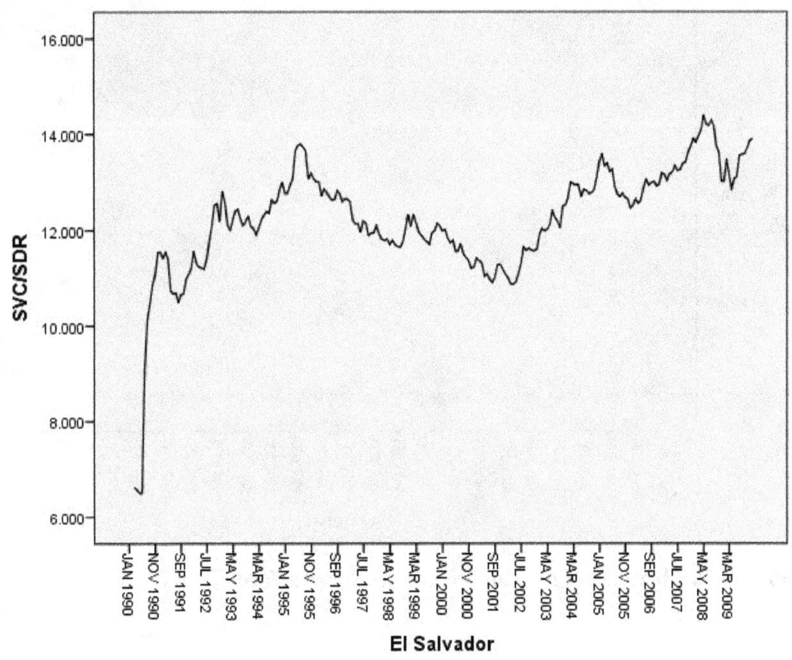

Figure 13 El Salvador colon exchange rates from 1990-2009

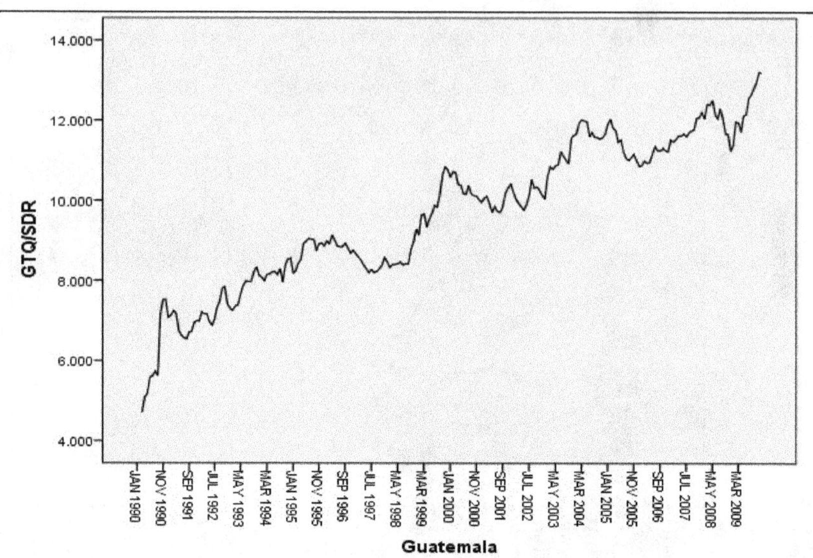

Figure 14 Guatemala quetzal exchange rates from 1990-2009

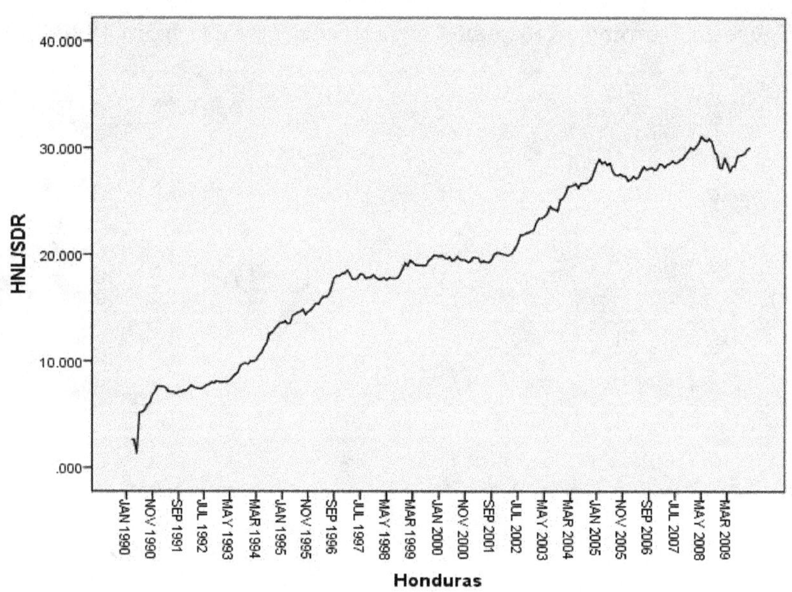

Figure 15 Honduras lempira exchange rate from 1990-2009

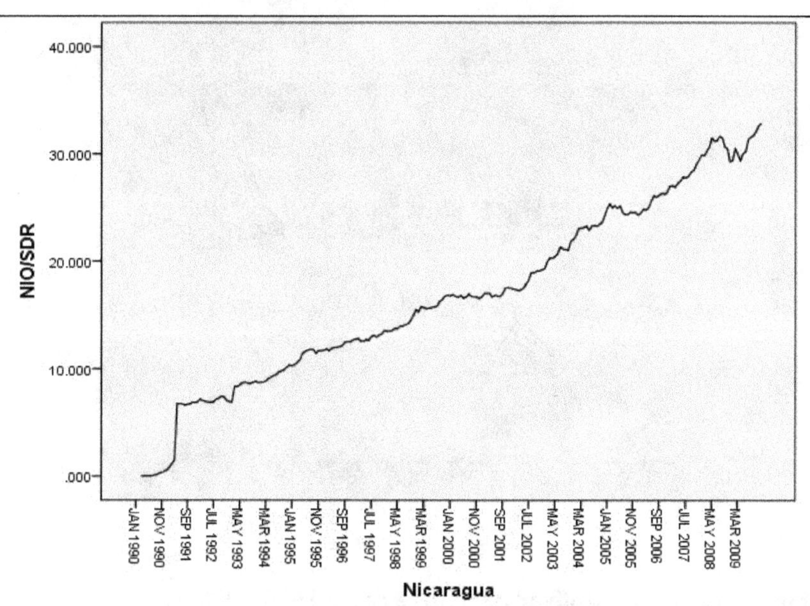

Figure 16 Nicaragua Cordoba exchange rates from 1990-2009

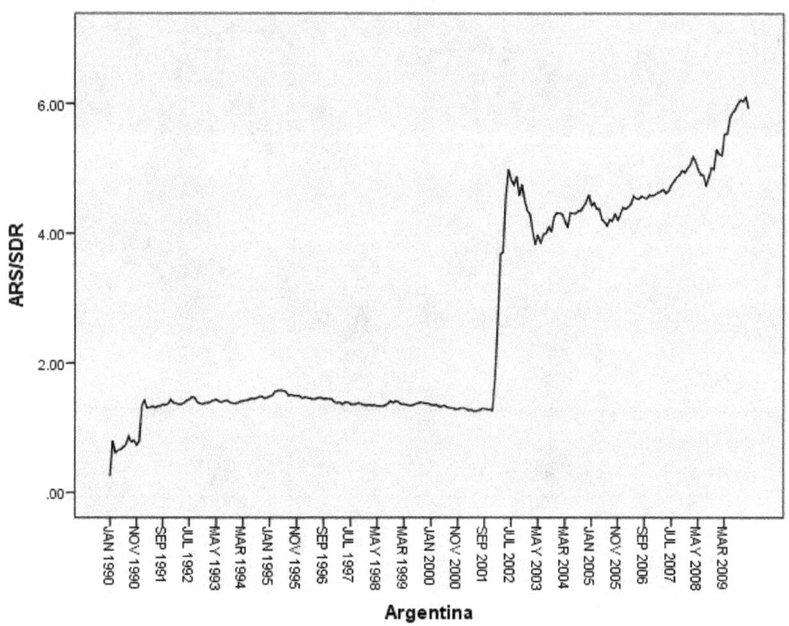

Figure 17 Argentina peso exchange rates from 1990-2009

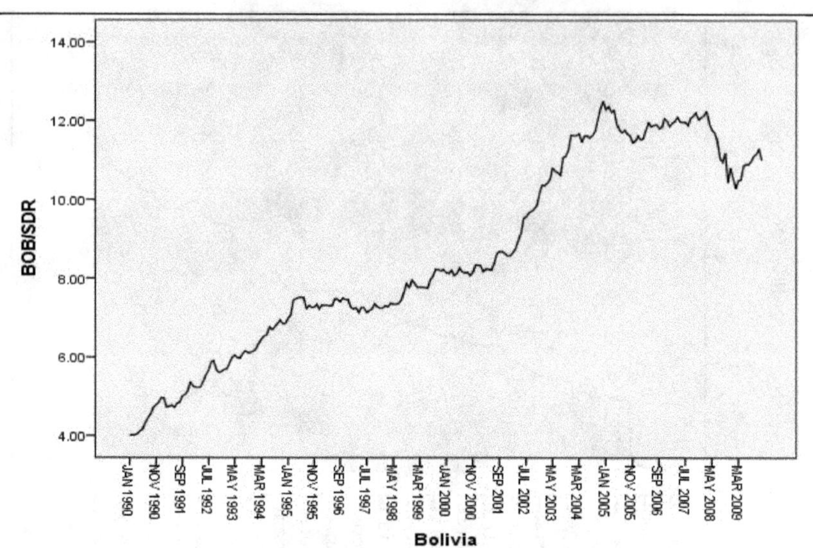

Figure 18 Bolivia Bolivar exchange rates 1990-2009

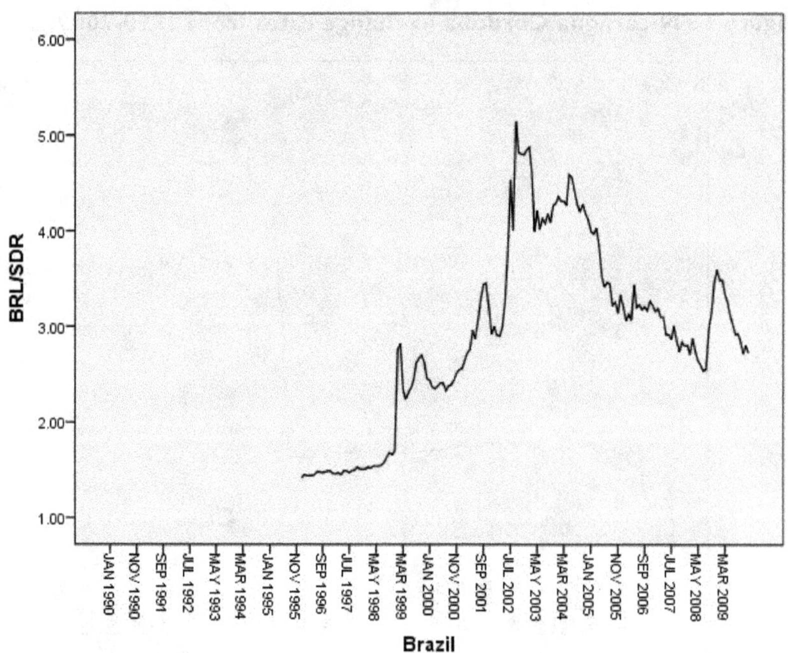

Figure 19 Brazilian real exchange rates from 1990-2009

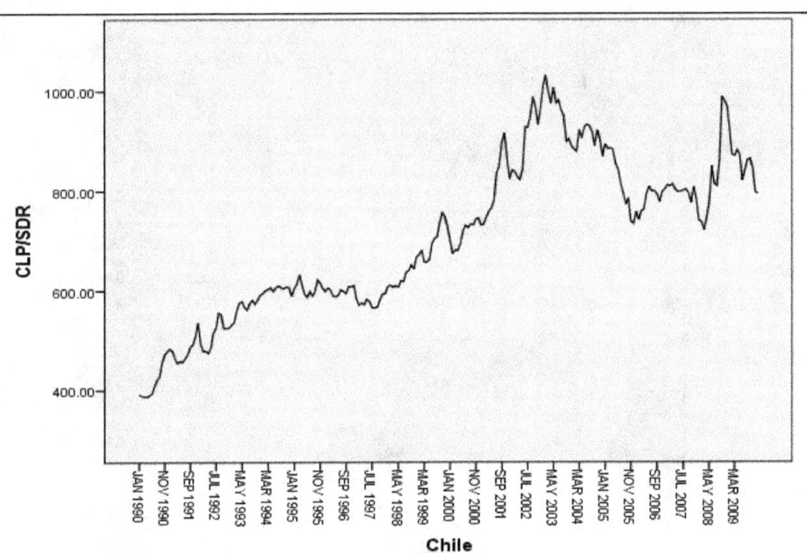

Figure 20 Chilean peso exchange rates from 1990-2009

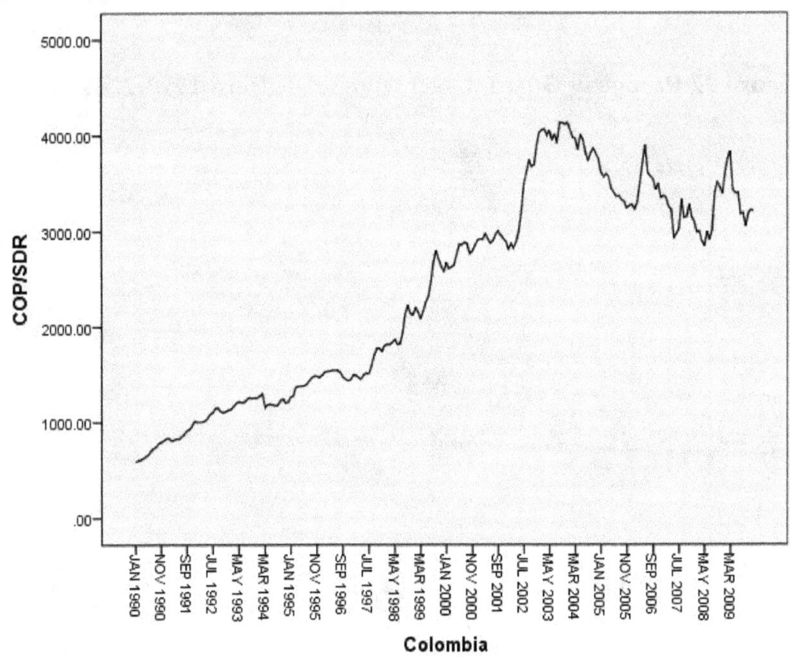

Figure 181 Colombian peso exchange rates from 1990-2009

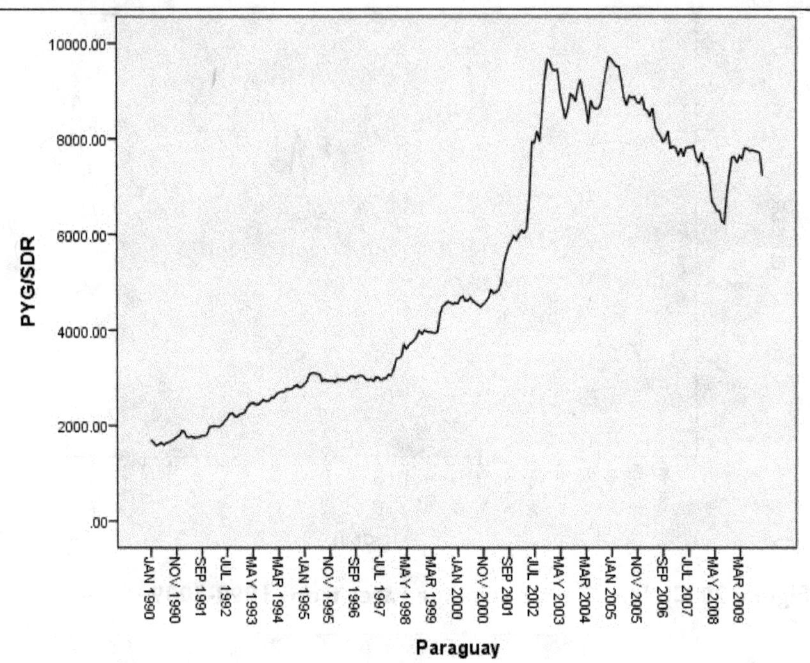

Figure 22 Paraguay Guaraní exchange rates from 1990-2009

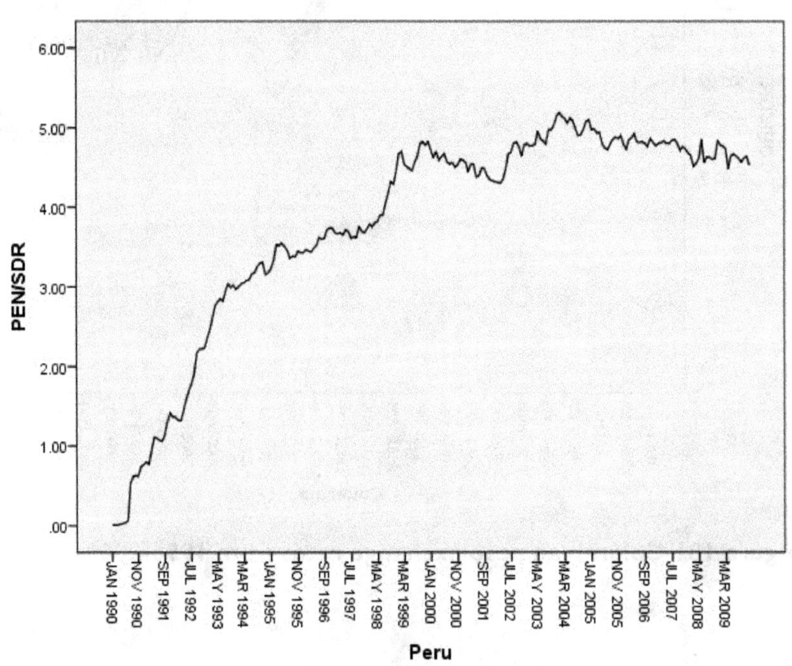

Figure 23 Peruvian new sol exchange rates 1990-2009

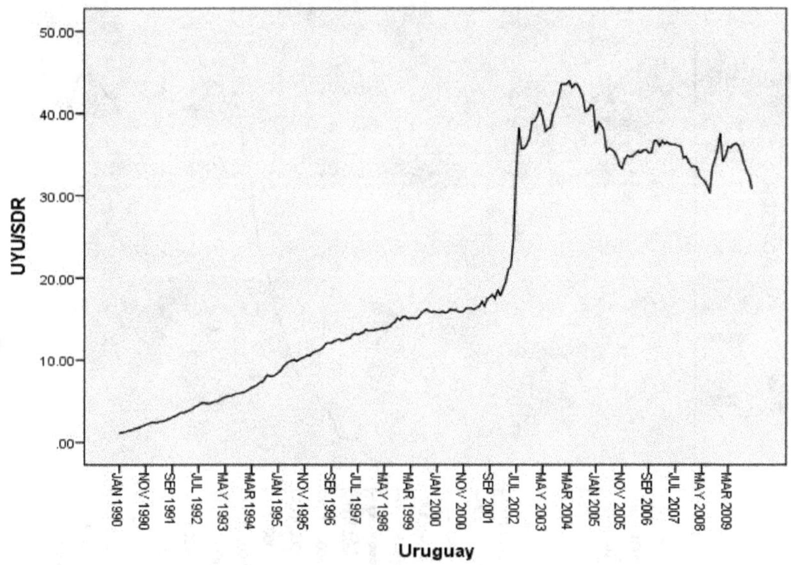

Figure 24 Uruguayan exchange rates from 1990-200

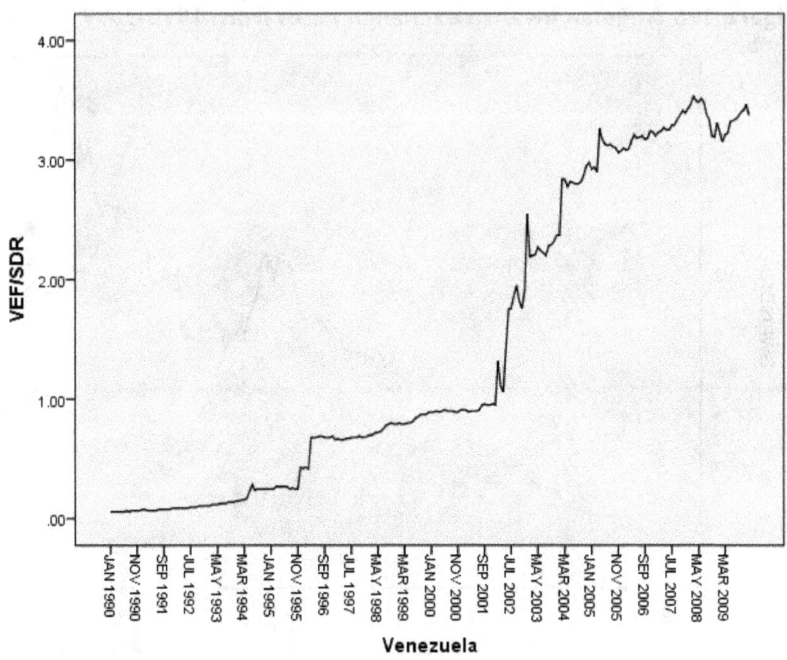

Figure 25 Venezuela exchange rates from 1990-2009

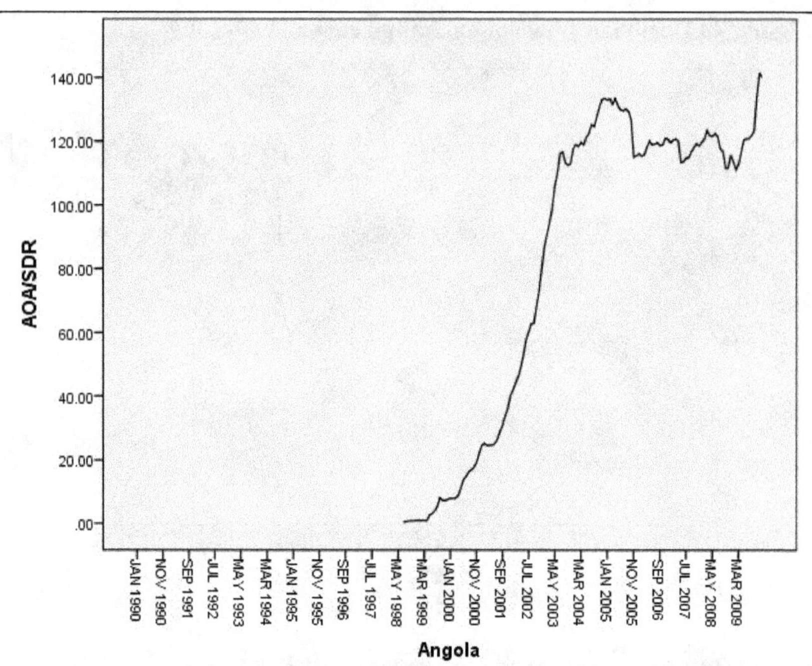

Figure 196 Angolan kwanza exchange rates from 1990-2009

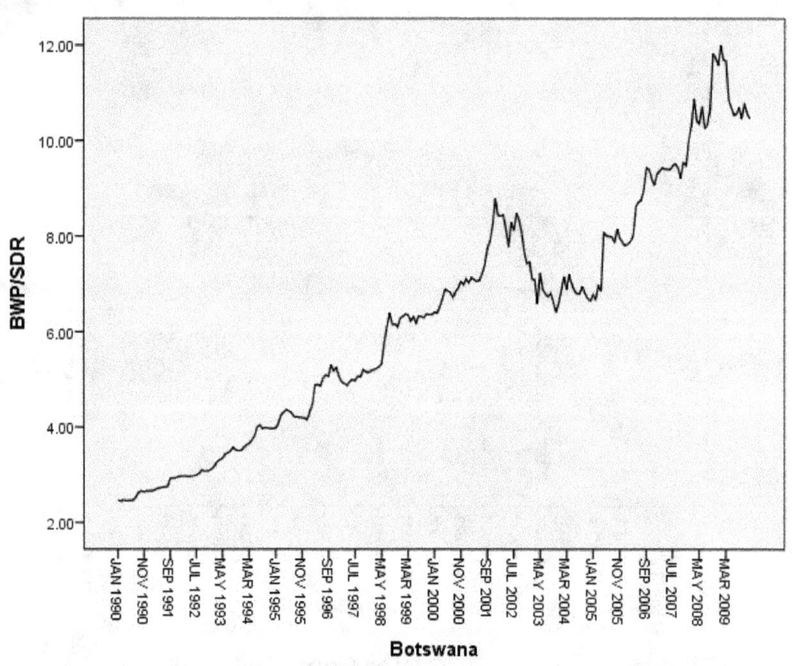

Figure 20 Botswana pula exchange rates from 1990-2009

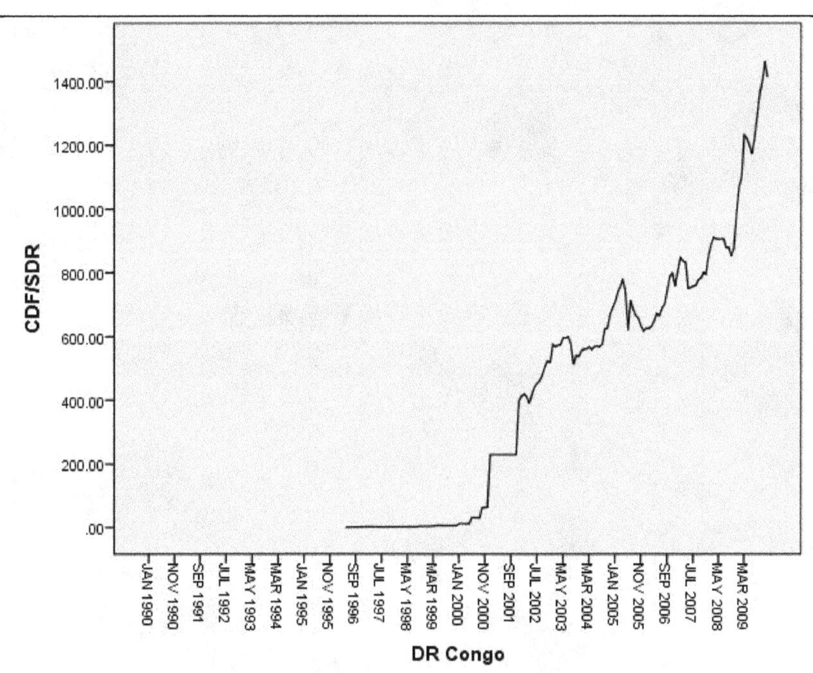

Figure 28 DR Congo exchange rates from 1990-2009

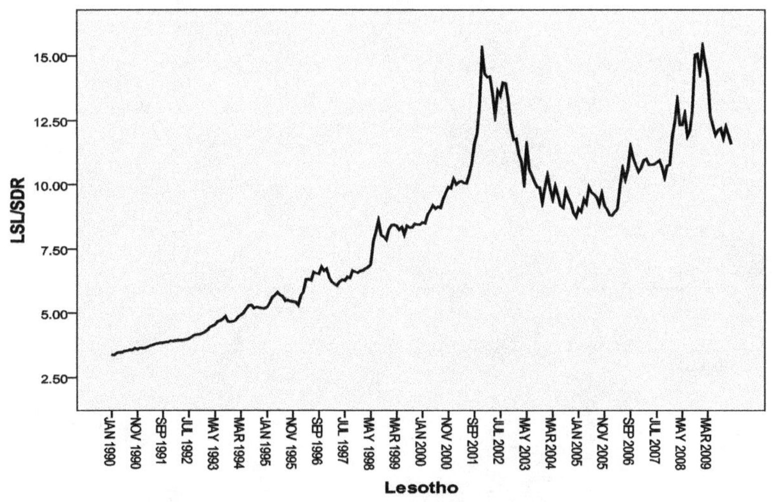

Figure 2921 Lesotho loti exchange rates from 1990-2009

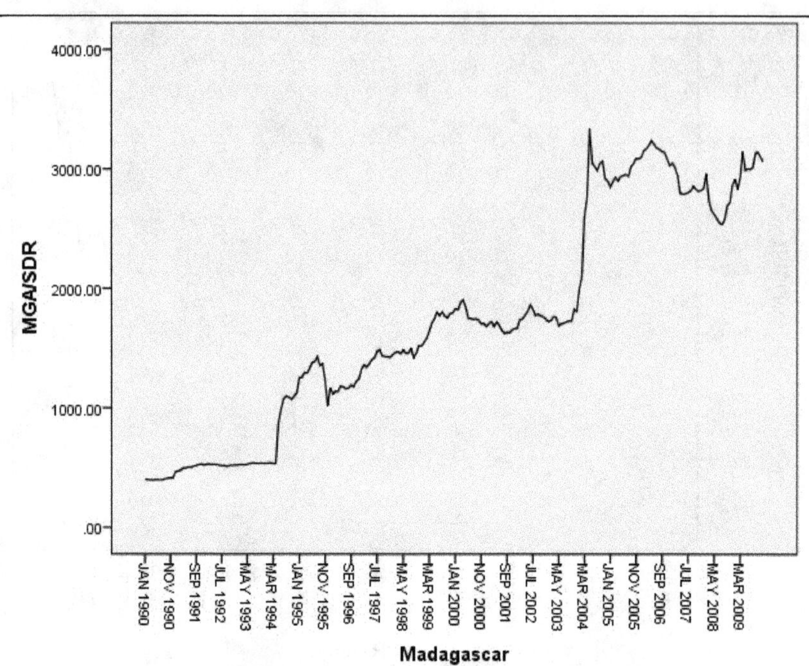

Figure 30 Madagascar ariary exchange rates from 1990-2009

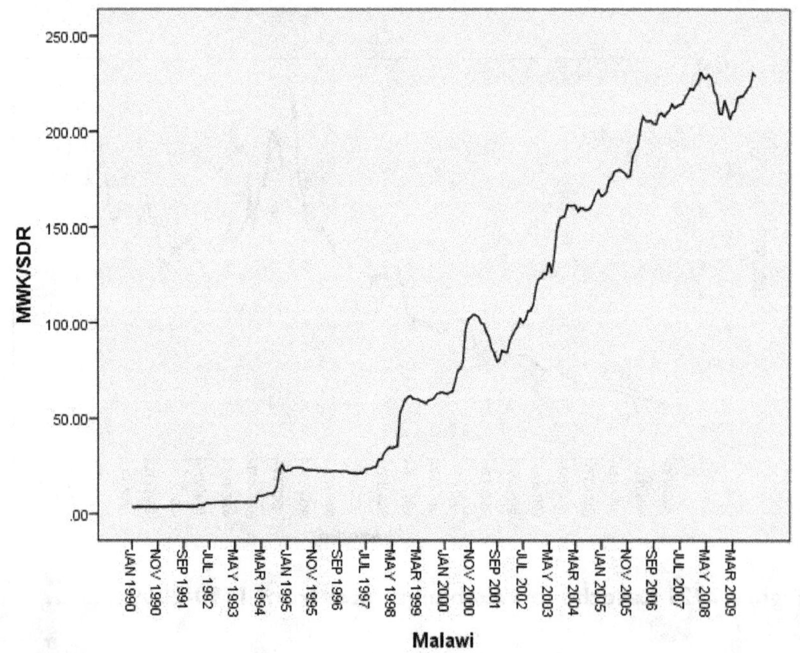

Figure 31 Malawi kwacha exchange rates from 1990-2009

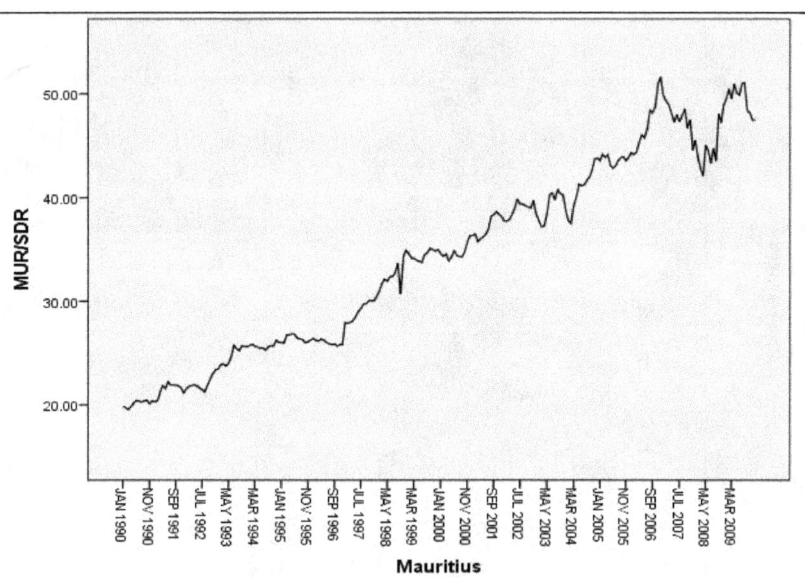

Figure 32 Mauritius rupee exchange rates from 1990-2009

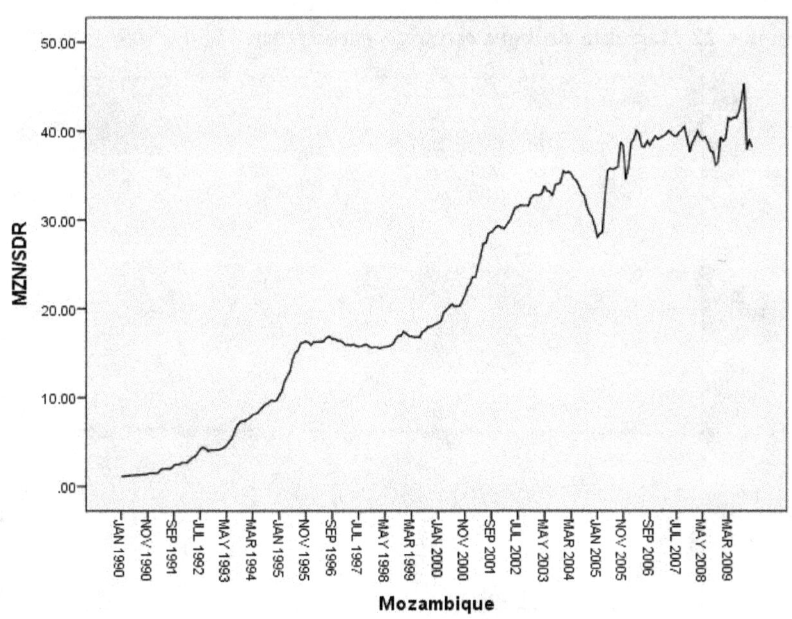

Figure 33 Mozambique metical exchange rates from 1990-2009

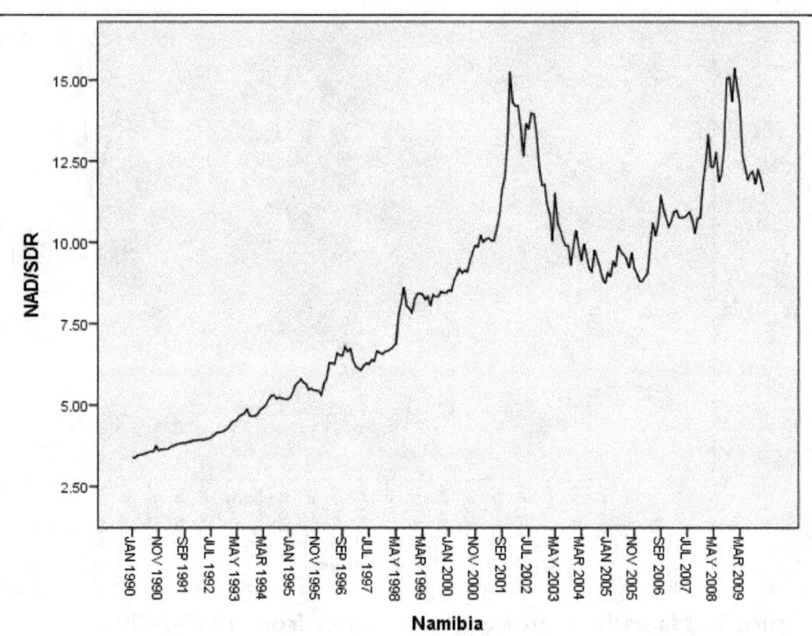

Figure 22 Namibia dollar exchange rates from 1990-2009

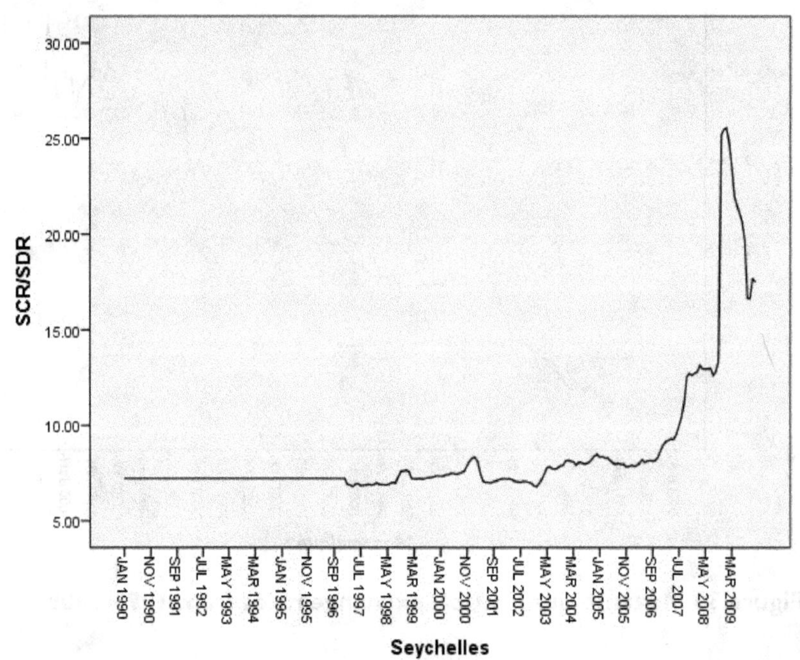

Figure 235 Seychelles rupee exchange rates from 1990-2009

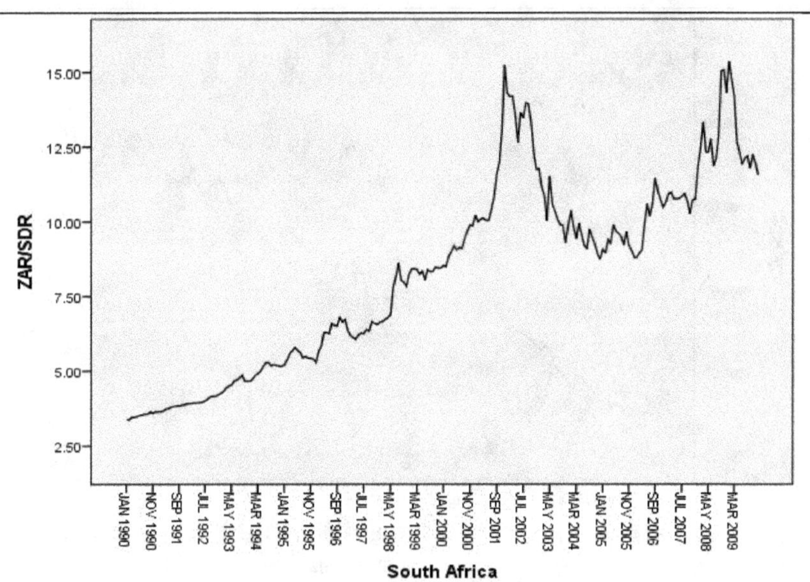

Figure 36 South African rand exchange rates from 1990-2009

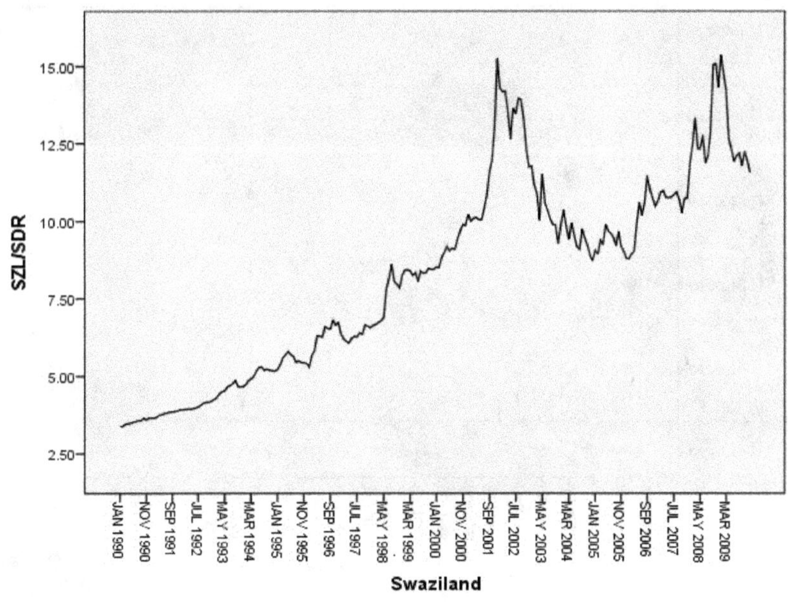

Figure 37 Swaziland lilangeni exchange rates from 1990-2009

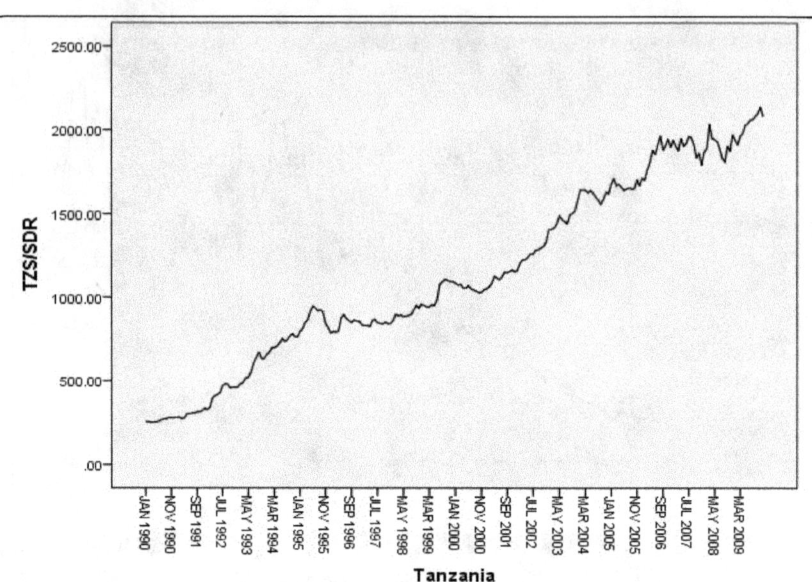

Figure 38 Tanzanian shilling exchange rates from 1990-2009

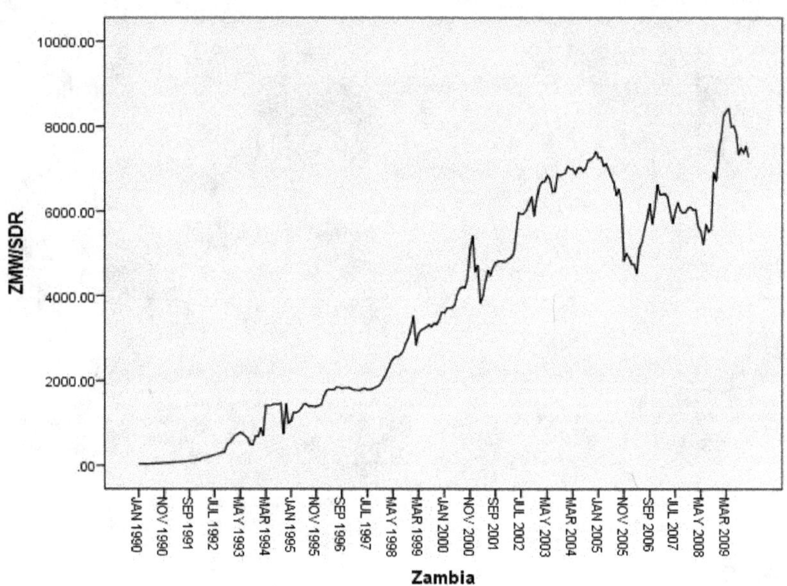

Figure 39 Zambian kwacha exchange rates from 1990-2009

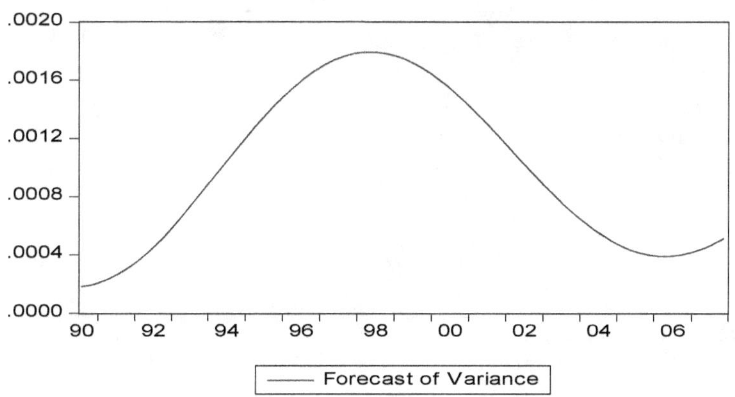

Figure 24 Brunei Dollar exchange rates variance plot overtime

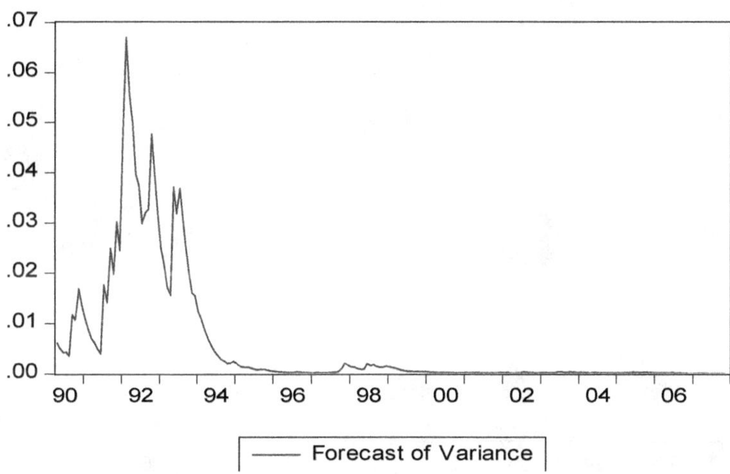

Figure 25 Cambodia Riel exchange rate variance plot overtime

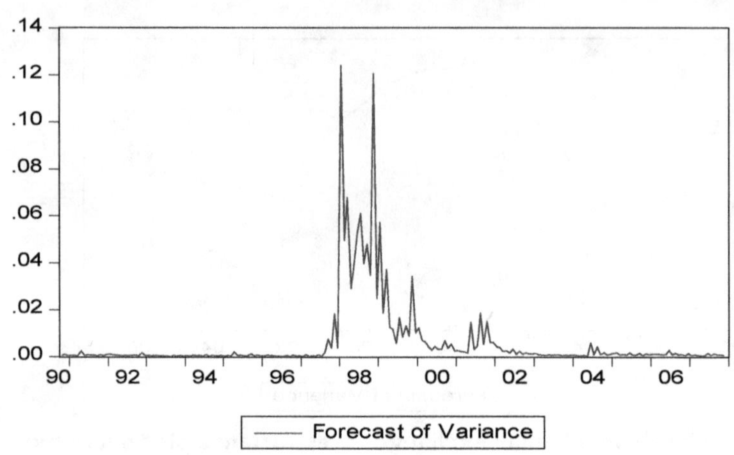

Figure 26 Indonesia Rupiah exchange rate variance plot overtime

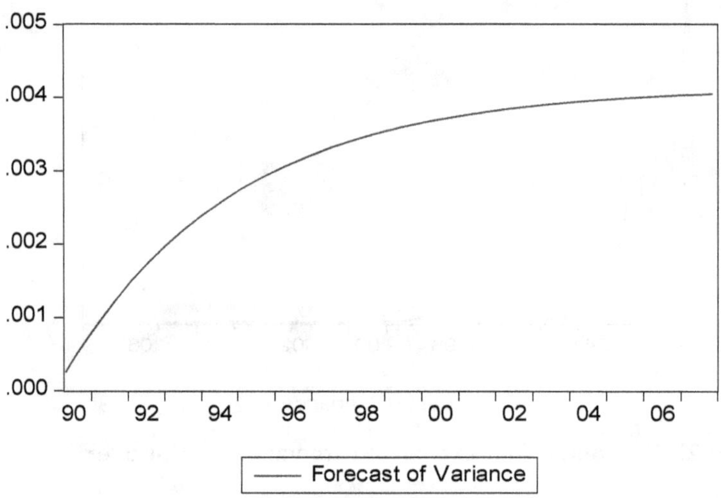

Figure 27 Laos Kip exchange rate variance plot overtime

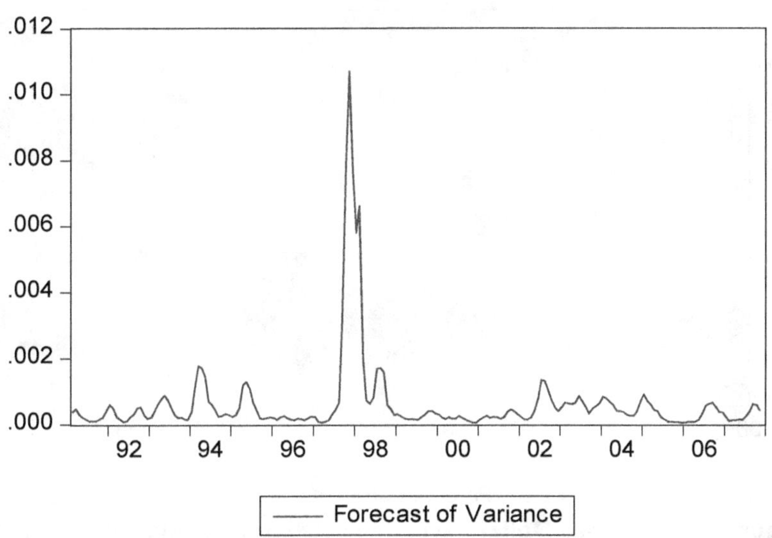

Figure 28 Malaysia Ringgit exchange rate variance plot overtime

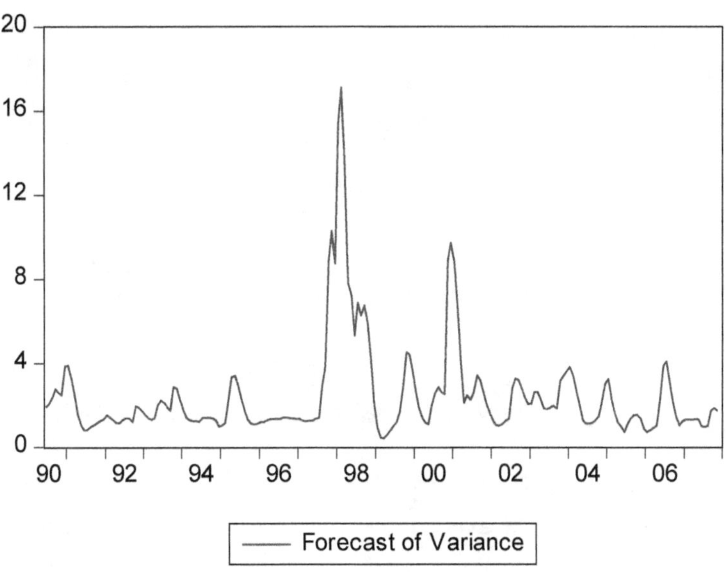

Figure 29 Philippines Peso exchange rate variance plot overtime

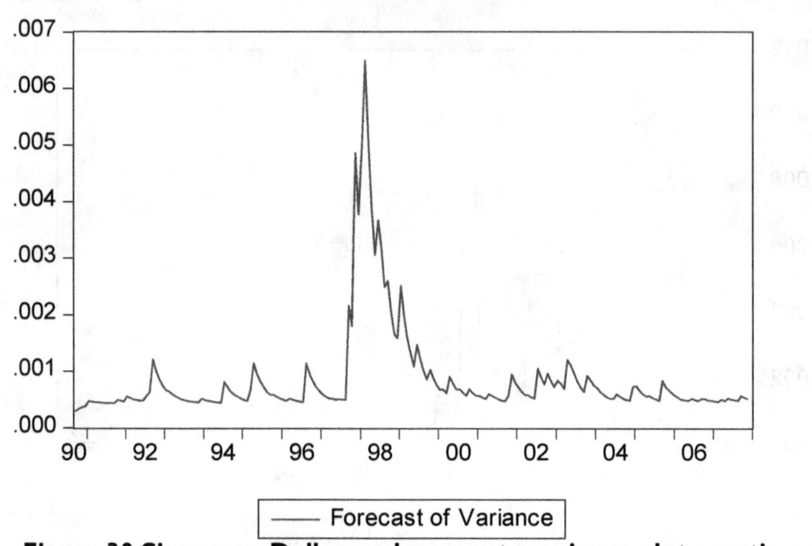

Figure 30 Singapore Dollar exchange rate variance plot overtime

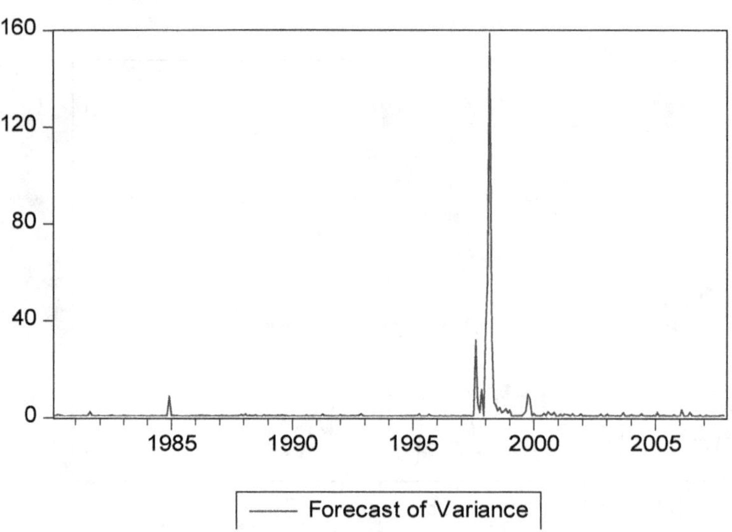

Figure 31 Thai Baht exchange rate variance plot overtime

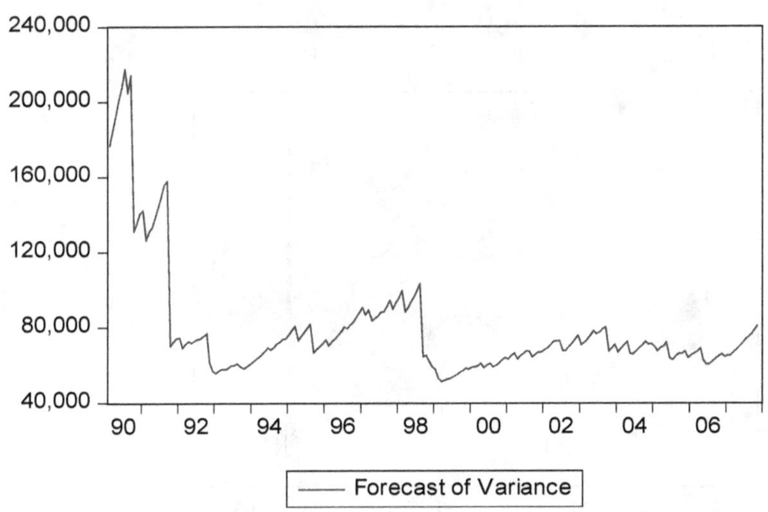

Figure 32 Vietnam Dong exchange rate variance plot overtime

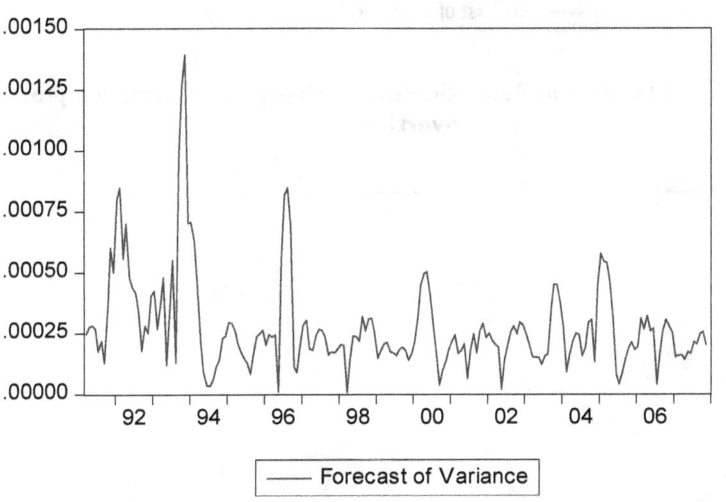

Figure 33 Costa Rica Colon exchange rate variance plot overtime

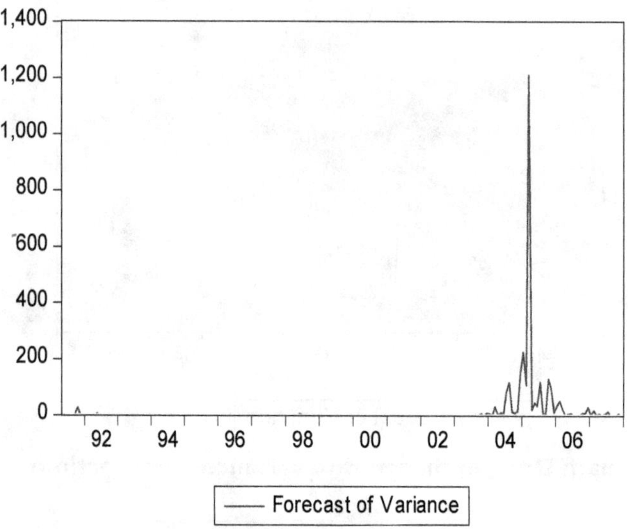

Figure 34 Dominican Republic Peso exchange rate variance plot overtime

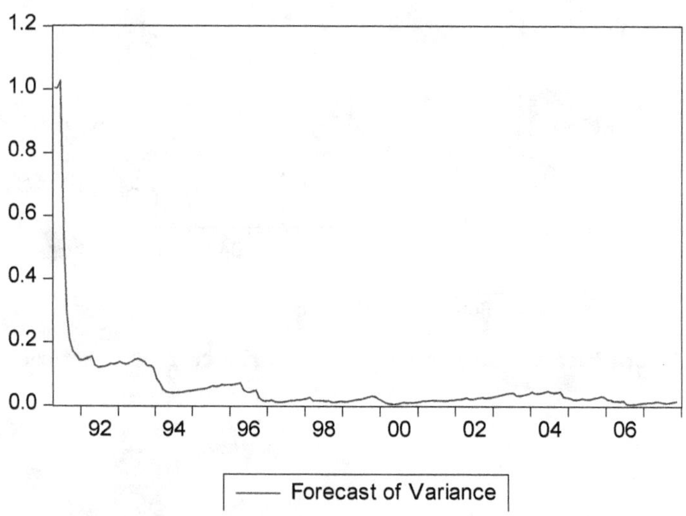

Figure 35 El Salvador Colon exchange rate variance plot overtime

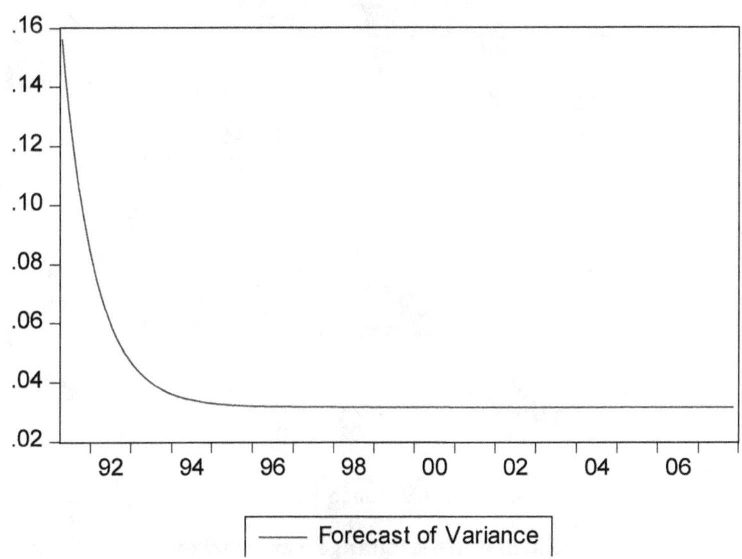

Figure 36 Guatemala Quetzal exchange rate variance plot overtime

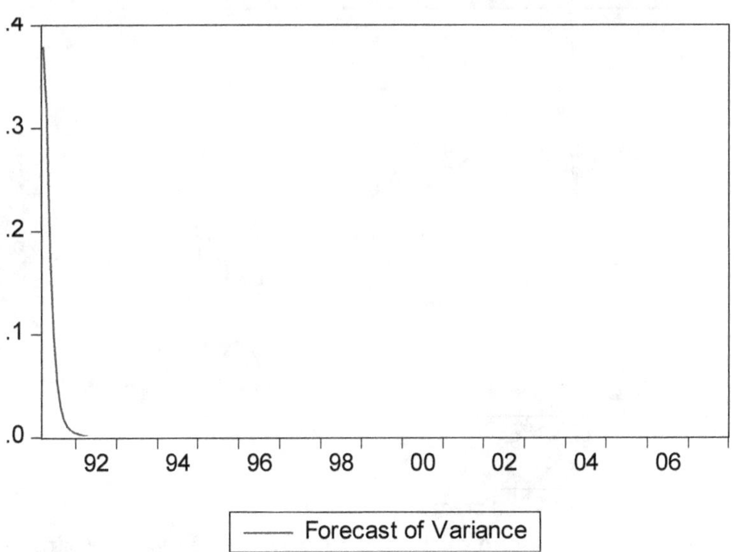

Figure 37 Honduras Lempira exchange rate variance plot overtime

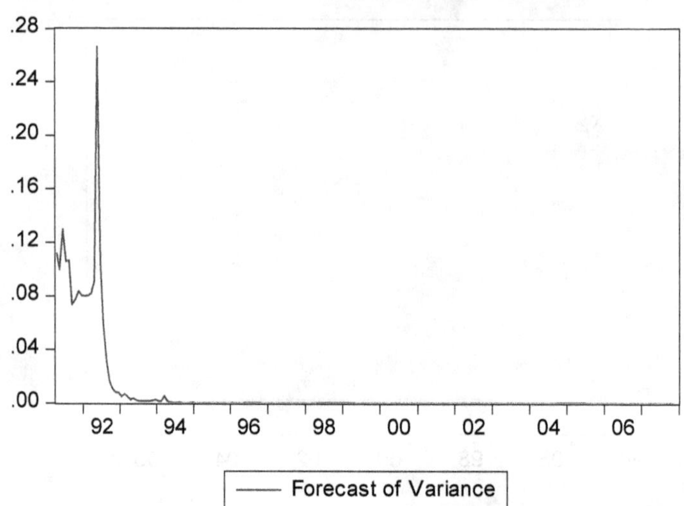

Figure 38 Niacaragua Cordoba exchange rate variance plot over-time

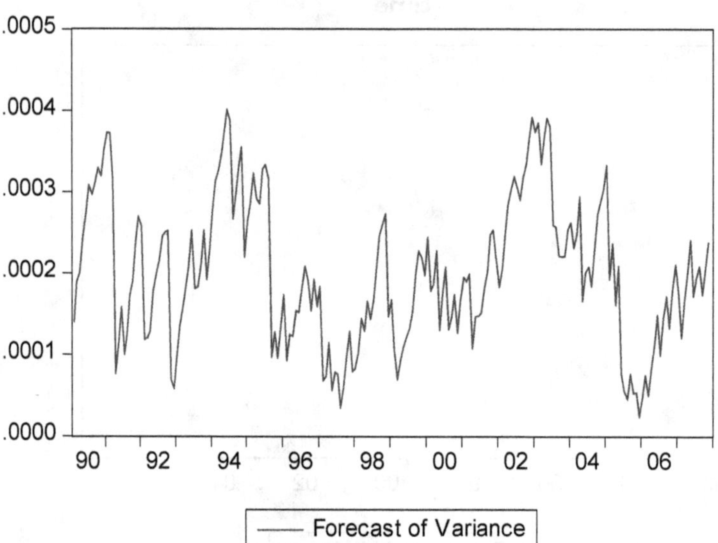

Figure 39 Bolivia Boliviano exchange rate variance plot overtime

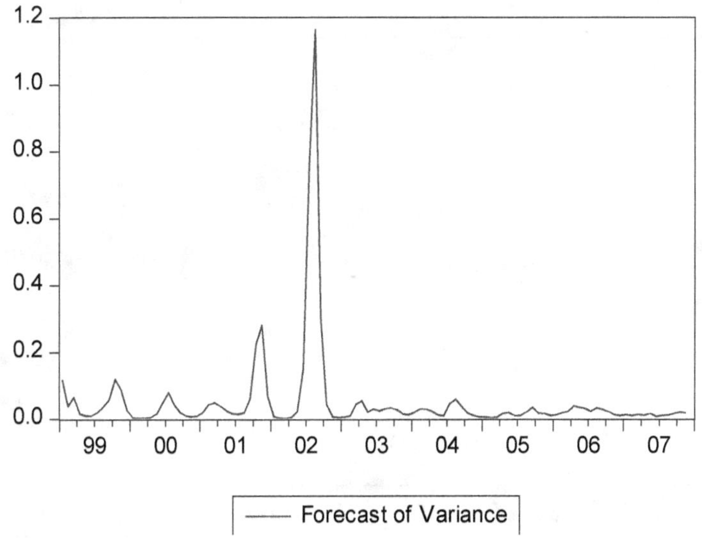

Figure 40 Brazil Real exchange rate variance plot overtime

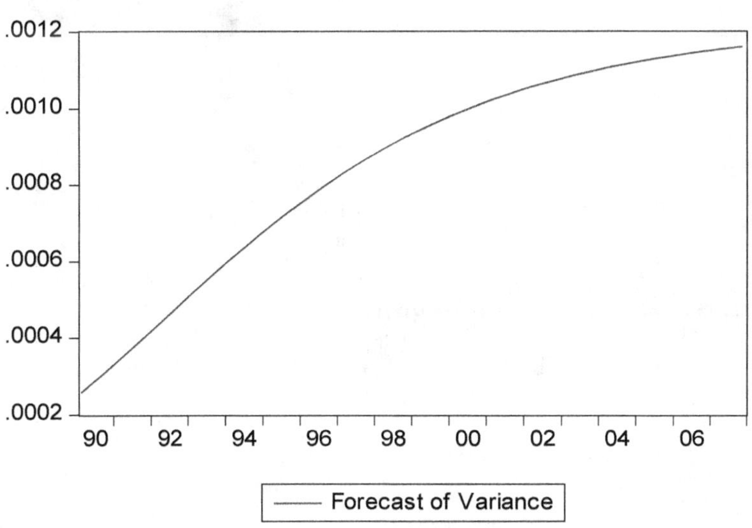

Figure 41 Chile Peso exchange rate variance plot overtime

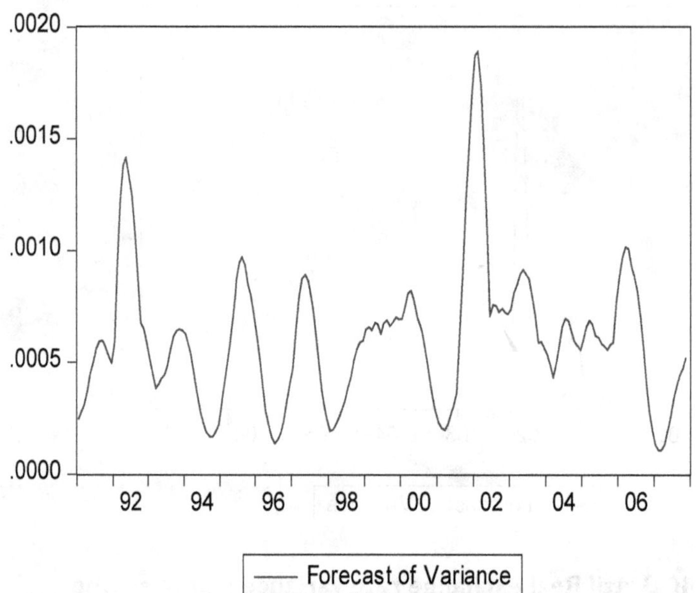

Figure 42 Colombia Peso exchange rate variance plot overtime

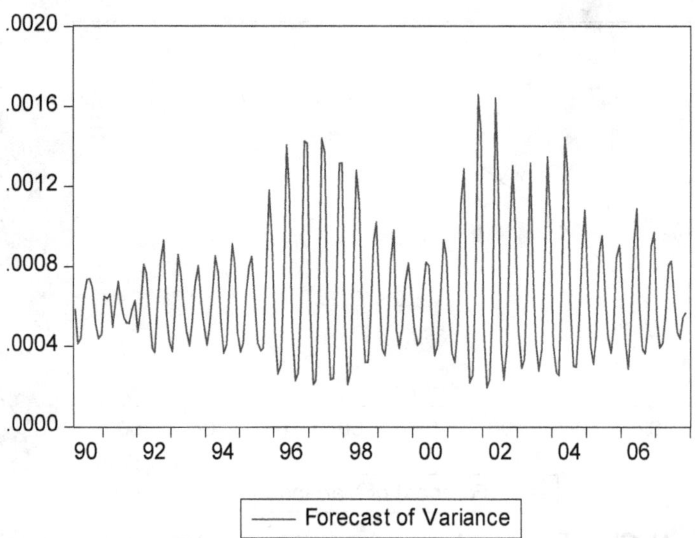

Figure 43 Paraguay Guarani exchange rate variance plot overtime

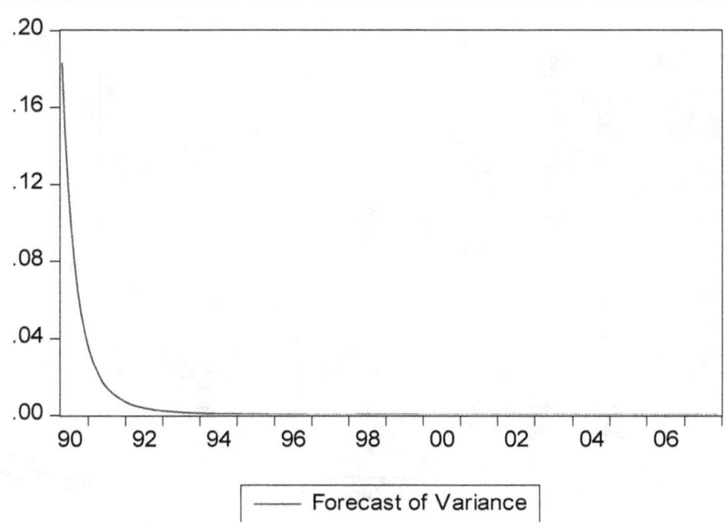

Figure 44 Peru New Sol exchange rate variance plot over time

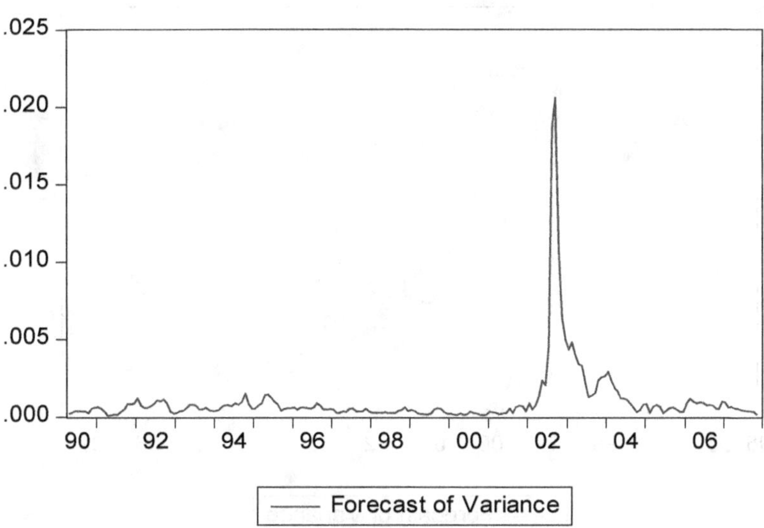

Figure 45 Uruguay Peso exchange rate variance plot over time

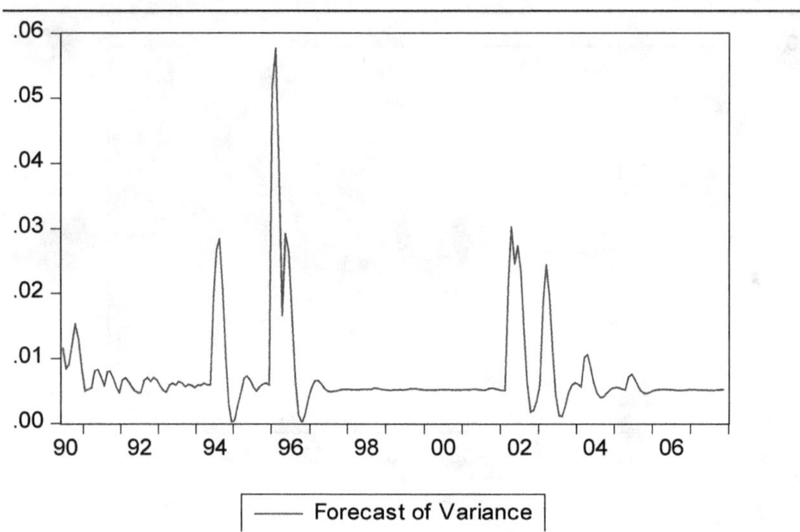

Figure 46 Venezuela Bolivar exchange rate variance plot overtime

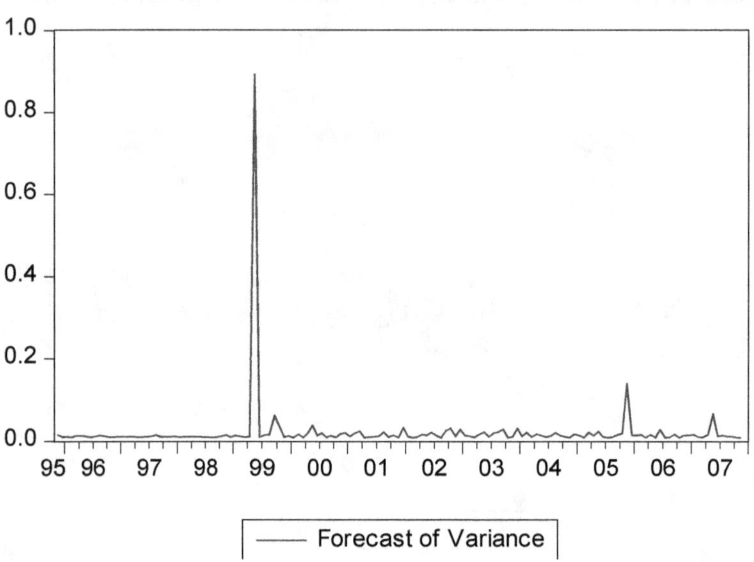

Figure 47 Angola Kwanza exchange rate variance plot overtime

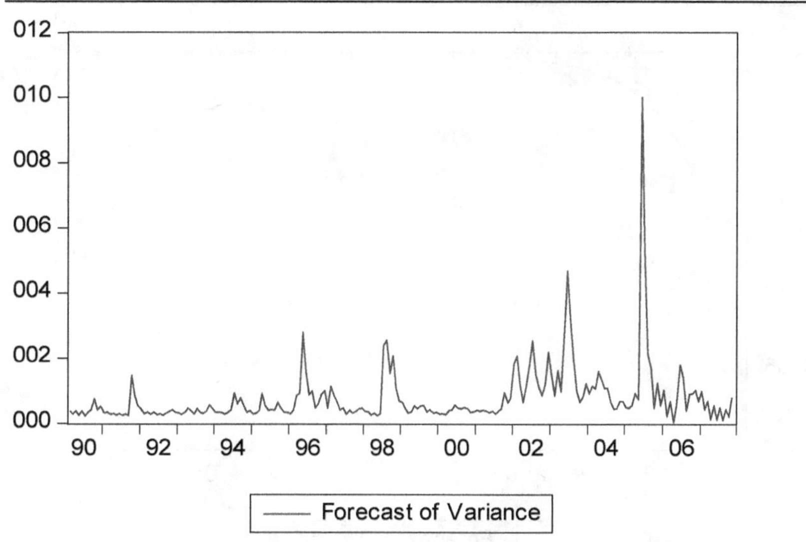

Figure 48 Botswana Pula exchange rate plot overtime

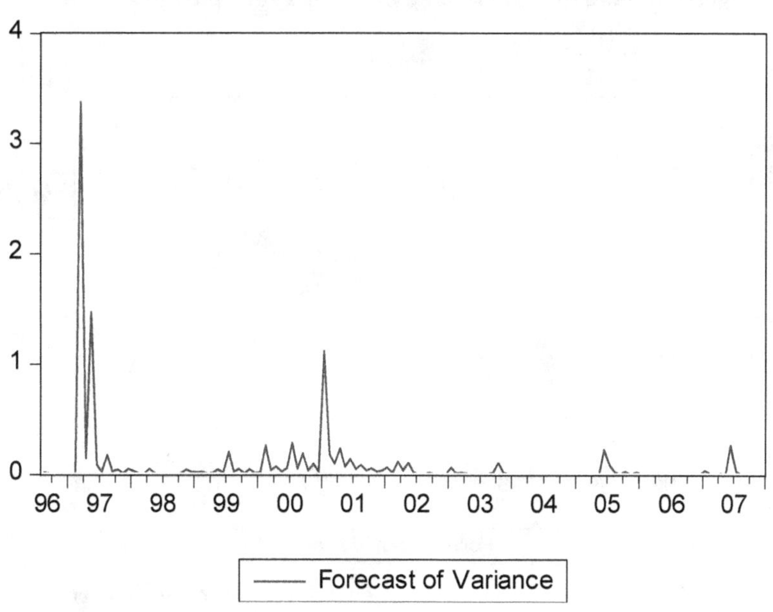

Figure 49 DRC Franc exchange rate variance plot overtime

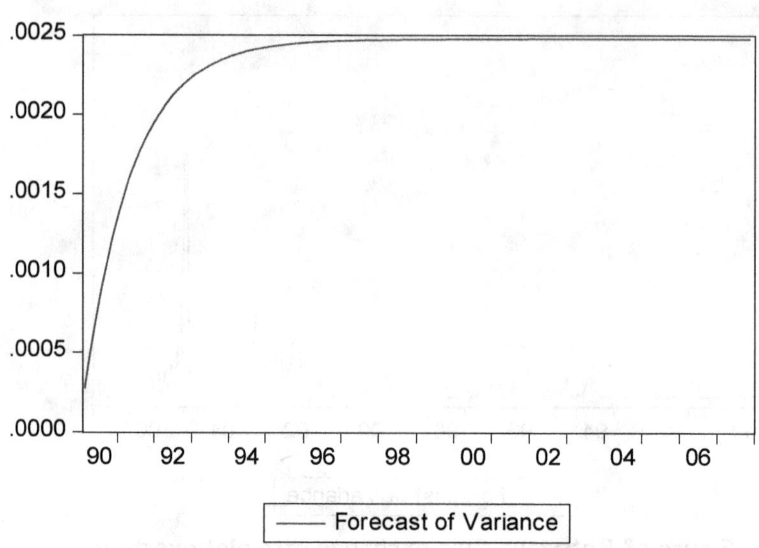

Figure 50 Madagascar Ariary exchange rate plot overtime

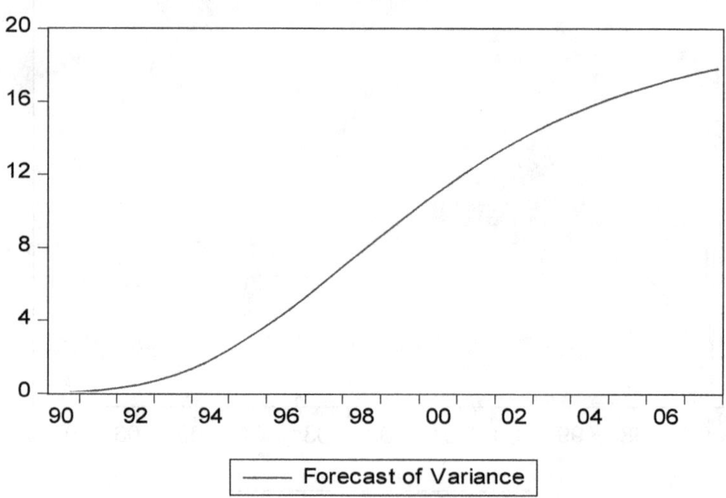

Figure 51 Malawi Kwacha exchange rate variance plot overtime

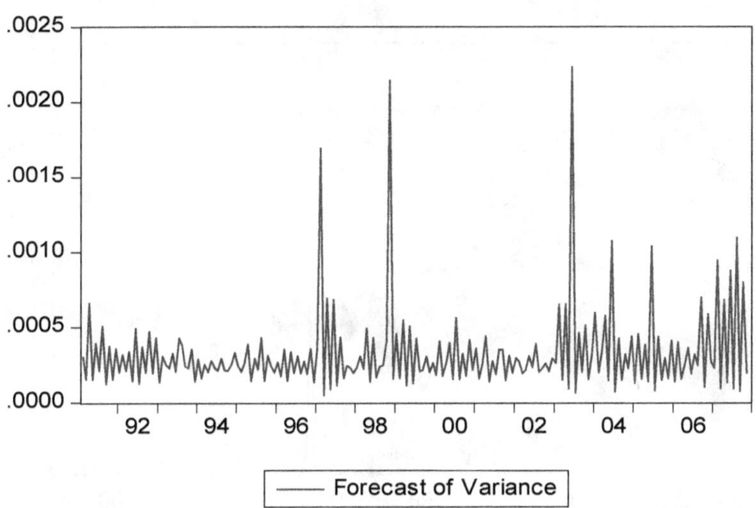

Figure 52 Mauritius Rupee exchange rate variance plot overtime

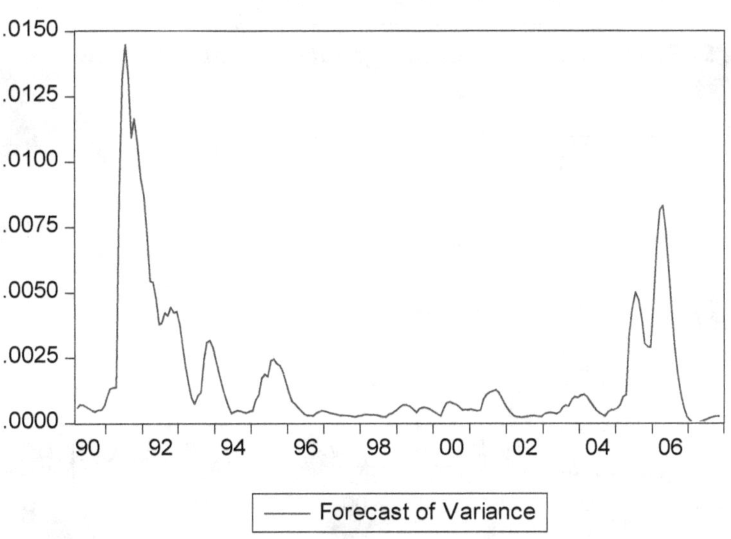

Figure 53 Mozambique Metical exchange rate variance plot overtime

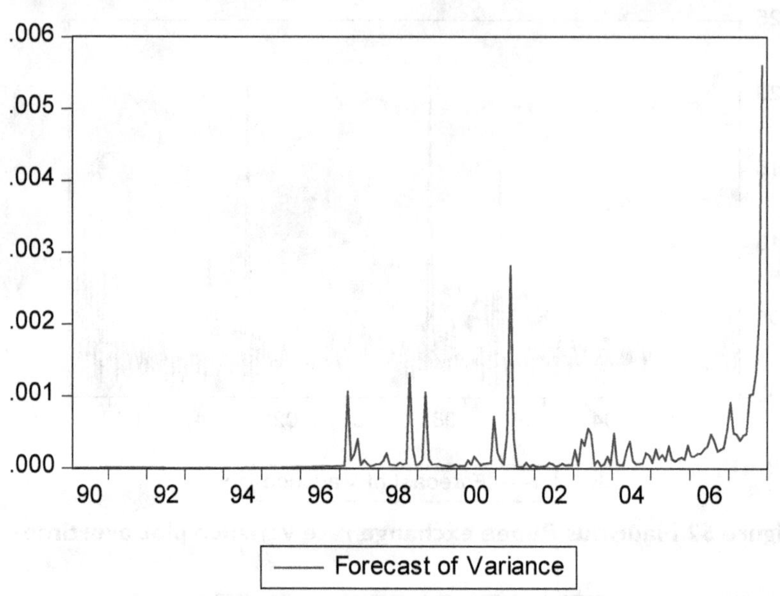

Figure 54 Seychelles Rupee exchange rate variance plot overtime

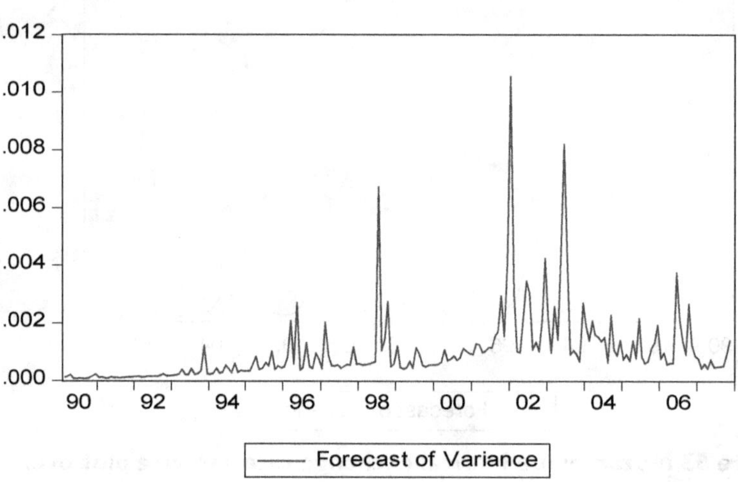

Figure 55 South African Rand exchange rate variance plot overtime

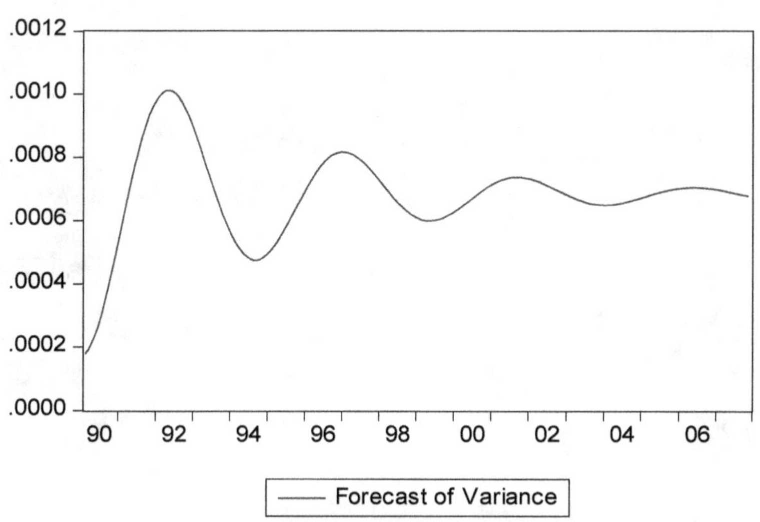

Figure 56 Tanzania Shilling exchange rate variance plot overtime

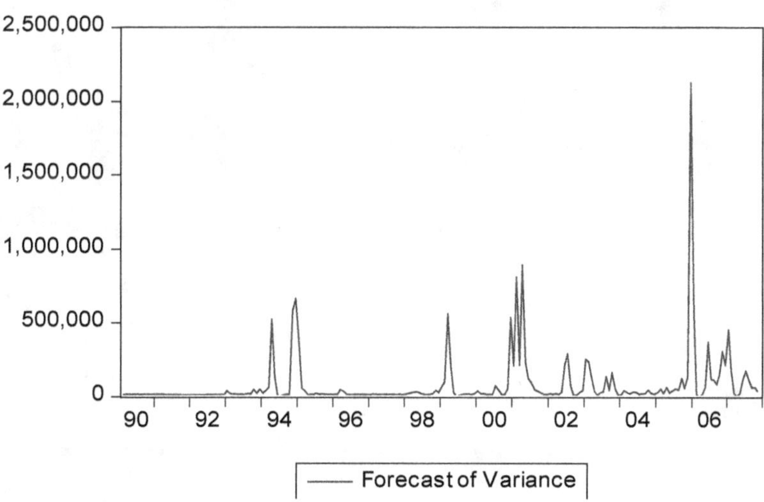

Figure 57 Zambian kwacha exchange rate variance plot overtime

www.ingramcontent.com/pod-product-compliance
Lightning Source LLC
Chambersburg PA
CBHW061209220326
41599CB00025B/4584